THE FAITH OF ISRAEL

THE FAITH OF
ISRAEL

ASPECTS OF
OLD TESTAMENT THOUGHT

*The James Sprunt Lectures
delivered at Union Theological Seminary,
Richmond, Virginia, 1955*

H. H. ROWLEY

SCM PRESS LTD

LONDON

334 00448 9

First published 1956
by SCM Press Ltd
56 Bloomsbury Street London, WC1
First cheap edition 1961
Second impression 1965
Third impression 1968
Fourth impression 1970
Fifth impression 1973
Sixth impression 1974
Seventh impression 1977

Printed in Great Britain by
Fletcher & Son Ltd, Norwich

CONTENTS

FOREWORD

PROFESSOR Rowley was an amazingly versatile and voluminous writer. Many of his books and articles were intended primarily for fellow scholars and were furnished with all the apparatus of learning, so much so that they will prove to be a mine of bibliographical information for many long years to come. But he was too great a man not to be aware of the need for making the results of biblical scholarship available to the many who are not scholars but are deeply interested in the Bible. This led him to write a number of books of a more popular nature which have reached and been welcomed by a wide circle of readers. The volume, *The Faith of Israel*, which is now being reissued, represents somewhat of a compromise between the two aims of speaking to other scholars—the characteristic documentation in the notes suggests that he had them partly in view—and of reaching interested non-specialists. Indeed this book may be confidently placed in that small group of books by biblical scholars of the first rank who have the enviable gift of combining depth with simplicity and can therefore be trusted to act as guides in the fields of thought in which they themselves move as masters. Moreover it is an admirable students' book.

It would be generally agreed that Professor Rowley was a middle-of-the-road interpreter of the Old Testament. Not for him the extremes of opinion associated with certain of his contemporaries. His most characteristic quality was a balance of judgement which enabled him to keep his head amid the proliferation of theories and the clash of argument. His range of knowledge was astonishing. Still more astonishing was the fact that he never failed to see the wood in spite of the trees. He was the most methodical of scholars, relentless in the pursuit of fact and meticulous to the last detail. He could look at the making of books from the point of view of the printer and publisher—a rare accomplishment in an author—and was a superb editor.

What his countless friends in this and other lands would like best to remember about Professor Rowley is the wonderful generosity with which he put his immense knowledge and expertise at the disposal of others. He could be exacting at times and he had no use for shoddy work, but he made bigger demands on himself than on anyone else. Though he lived among books and preferred vistas of thought to natural scenery, he retained a broad humanity which made him keenly interested in people. His boisterous laughter was the index to a rich sense of humour. Nor should it be forgotten that he had been a missionary and was always a devoted churchman who served his denomination well. Perhaps his most remarkable achievement, one at least for which many today in other lands bless his memory, lay in what he did at the end of the Second World War to reunite the disrupted fellowship of Old Testament scholars—a task he performed almost single-handed and at great cost in time and money to himself. It was only a great-hearted man and a man of imagination who could have done this. He brought new hope and courage to many and taught others a lesson in generosity. Scholar, teacher, missionary and churchman, his record will not easily be rivalled.

NORMAN W. PORTEOUS

PREFACE

WHEN I was invited at relatively short notice—owing to the withdrawal of the expected lecturer—to deliver the James Sprunt Lectures at Union Theological Seminary, Richmond, Virginia, I hesitated to accept, since I had so heavy a burden of other commitments. My warm friendship for Professor John Bright decided me to accept, and I then rationalized my acceptance by reflecting that the honour of such an invitation would be unlikely to come my way again, since disappointments through the withdrawal of acceptances are too rare to be counted on. The shortness of the time at my disposal between my acceptance and the date of the delivery of the lectures—during this interval I had already undertaken to deliver the Louis H. Jordan Bequest Lectures in Comparative Religion in the School of Oriental and African Studies in London—compelled me to deal with a broad subject, and I chose the general title of *The Faith of Israel*, though I realized that I could not cover the whole of this in seven lectures, even in general outline. In a number of scattered publications I have dealt with particular questions within this general field, and here I have passed over these lightly, with references to the places where I have dealt with them more fully. Other questions I have treated here more fully than I have elsewhere done, though still far less adequately than I could wish. Before I received the invitation from Richmond I had been invited by the late Principal of New College, London, to deliver the Drew Lecture on Immortality, and had announced my subject for a lecture a few months before the date of the James Sprunt Lectures. Since the subject I had chosen fell within the scope of the subject for these lectures I have embodied its material in the sixth lecture, and by permission of the Trustees of the Drew Lectures I have sometimes drawn verbally on my Drew Lecture.

In the footnotes I have tried to indicate to the interested reader who wishes to pursue various aspects of the subject where he will find relevant help. Yet I have tried to avoid excessive footnoting, and where possible I have referred the reader to the

9

fuller bibliographical information I have given elsewhere. It would have been easy to add a great many more references, thus making this book of greater service to the reader who wishes to go further, but only at the expense of making it too forbidding to the more general reader. As the latter is not likely to read the footnotes anyhow, and the former will find them more useful if quotations are left in their original languages, I have so left them.

It remains to acknowledge the great kindness I was shown at Richmond, not alone by Professor and Mrs Bright, whose guest I was, and by the President and the members of the Faculty, but by my audience of students and former students, whose reception of the lectures compensated me for my rashness in promising to deliver them and the pressure under which they had been prepared.

H. H. ROWLEY

Manchester University
August 1955

ABBREVIATIONS

A.A. = Alttestamentliche Abhandlungen
A.f.O. = *Archiv für Orientforschung*
A.J.S.L. = *American Journal of Semitic Languages and Literatures*
A.J.Th. = *American Journal of Theology*
A.N.E.T. = *Ancient Near Eastern Texts*, ed. by J. B. Pritchard
A.O. = Der Alte Orient
A.R.W. = *Archiv für Religionswissenschaft*
A.T.A.N.T. = Abhandlungen zur Theologie des Alten und Neuen Testaments
A.T.D. = Das Alte Testament Deutsch
B.A. = *The Biblical Archaeologist*
B.A.S.O.R. = *Bulletin of the American Schools of Oriental Research*
B.D.B. = *A Hebrew and English Lexicon to the Old Testament*, ed. by F. Brown, S. R. Driver, and C. A. Briggs
B.F.C.Th. = Beiträge zur Förderung christlicher Theologie
B.J.R.L. = *Bulletin of the John Rylands Library*
B.O.T. = De Boeken van het Oude Testament
B.W.A.N.T. = Beiträge zur Wissenschaft vom Alten und Neuen Testament
B.Z.A.W. = Beihefte zur *Zeitschrift für die alttestamentliche Wissenschaft*
Camb. B. = Cambridge Bible
C.B.Q. = *Catholic Biblical Quarterly*
Cent. B. = Century Bible
C.N.T. = Commentaire du Nouveau Testament
C.Q. = *The Congregational Quarterly*
C.R.A.I. = *Comptes rendus de l'Académie des Inscriptions et Belles Lettres*
C.Th. = Cahiers Théologiques
D.B. = *Dictionary of the Bible*, ed. by James Hastings
D.Bib. = *Dictionnaire de la Bible*, ed. by F. Vigouroux
D.L.Z. = *Deutsche Literaturzeitung*
E.B. = *Encyclopaedia Biblica*, ed. by T. K. Cheyne and J. S. Black
E.Bib. = Études Bibliques
E.R.E. = *Encyclopaedia of Religion and Ethics*, ed. by James Hastings
E.T. = *Expository Times*
E.Th.L. = *Ephemerides Theologicae Lovanienses*
E.Th.R. = *Études Théologiques et Religieuses*
H.A.T. = Handbuch zum Alten Testament, ed. by O. Eissfeldt
H.J. = *The Hibbert Journal*
H.K. = Handkommentar zum Alten Testament, ed. by W. Nowack
H.S.A.T. = Die Heilige Schrift des Alten Testamentes (Bonner Bibel)
H.S.A.T. = E. Kautzsch (ed. by), *Die Heilige Schrift des Alten Testaments* (4th ed. edited by A. Bertholet)

H.T.R. = *Harvard Theological Review*
H.U.C.A. = *Hebrew Union College Annual*
I.C.C. = The International Critical Commentary
J.A.O.S. = *Journal of the American Oriental Society*
J.B.L. = *Journal of Biblical Literature*
J.B.R. = *Journal of Bible and Religion*
J.E. = *Jewish Encyclopedia*
J.N.E.S. = *Journal of Near Eastern Studies*
J.Q.R. = *Jewish Quarterly Review*
J.R. = *Journal of Religion*
J.S.O.R. = *Journal of the Society for Oriental Research*
J.T.S. = *Journal of Theological Studies*
K.A.T. = Kommentar zum Alten Testament, ed. by E. Sellin
K.H.C. = Kurzer Hand-Commentar zum Alten Testament, ed. by
    K. Marti
Ned. T.T. = *Nederlands Theologisch Tijdschrift*
N.R.Th. = *Nouvelle Revue Théologique*
N.T.D. = Das Neue Testament Deutsch
N.T.T. = Norsk Teologisk Tidsskrift
O.T.S. = *Oudtestamentische Studiën*
P.A.A.J.R. = *Proceedings of the American Academy for Jewish Research*
P.R.E. = Herzog-Hauck, *Realencyclopädie für protestantische Theologie
    und Kirche*, 3rd ed.
R.B. = *Revue Biblique*
R.E.S.-B. = *Revue des Études Sémitiques et Babyloniaca*
R.G.G. = *Die Religion in Geschichte und Gegenwart*
R.H.P.R. = *Revue d'Histoire et de Philosophie religieuses*
R.H.R. = *Revue de l'Histoire des Religions*
S.A.T. = *Die Schriften des Alten Testaments in Auswahl*
S.B.T. = Studies in Biblical Theology
S.B.U. = *Svenskt Bibliskt Uppslagsverk*
S.D.B. = *Supplément au Dictionnaire de la Bible*, ed. by L. Pirot
S.J.T. = *Scottish Journal of Theology*
Symb.B.U. = Symbolae Biblicae Upsalienses
Th.L.Z. = *Theologische Literaturzeitung*
Th.R. = *Theologische Rundschau*
Th.W.B. = *Theologisches Wörterbuch zum Neuen Testament*, ed. by
    G. Kittel and G. Friedrich
Th.Z. = *Theologische Zeitschrift*
T.S.K. = *Theologische Studien und Kritiken*
T.U. = Tekst en Uitleg
U.J.E. = *Universal Jewish Encyclopedia*
U.U.Å. = Uppsala Universitets Årsskrift
V.T. = *Vetus Testamentum*
West. C. = Westminster Commentaries
Z.A.W. = *Zeitschrift für die alttestamentliche Wissenschaft*
Z.D.M.G. = *Zeitschrift der deutschen morgenländischen Gesellschaft*
Z.Th.K. = *Zeitschrift für Theologie und Kirche*

INTRODUCTION

In recent years there has been a revived interest in the Theology of the Old Testament, and in many countries works devoted to this subject have appeared in rapid succession.[1] Yet the task of writing such a work is harder today than it once was.[2] The critical work of the past century and a half has emphasized the diversity within the Old Testament, and has led to the study of the history of the religion of Israel. It has been recognized that the early beliefs and practices of Israel were not the same as those of the Judaism that prevailed on the eve of the Christian era. Hence it has sometimes been suggested that the Old Testament is no longer of importance to men.[3] To the historian of religion it may have a high value; but it is treated as no more vital to present-day religion than the study of the history of science to the man who wishes to make practical

[1] In *The Unity of the Bible*, 1953, pp. 4 ff., I have noted some of the many books and articles devoted to this theme. Since the publication of that work Vriezen's *Hoofdlijnen der Theologie van het Oude Testament* has appeared in a new and substantially enlarged edition (1955), and a German translation has been announced, while an English edition is in preparation. The first volume of a French work by P. van Imschoot, *Théologie de l'Ancien Testament*, I. *Dieu*, 1954, has appeared, and G. Pidoux has published a short study of *L'Homme dans l'Ancien Testament* (C.Th.), 1954. Moreover, C. Ryder Smith has published a study of *The Bible Doctrine of Sin*, 1953, Vriezen a study on the election of Israel, *Die Erwählung Israels nach dem Alten Testament* (A.T.A.N.T.), 1953, and G. Bernini has offered a contribution to the Theology of the Old Testament in a volume on penitential prayer, *Le Preghiere penitenziali del Salterio* (Analecta Gregoriana, lxii, Ser. Fac. Theol., A 9), 1953, and F. Asensio a contribution in a volume on the Biblical doctrine of election, *Yahveh y su Pueblo* (in the same series, A 8), 1953. While the present work has been in the press, E. Jacob's *Théologie de l'Ancien Testament*, 1956 (1955 on back of title page), has appeared.
[2] Cf. N. W. Porteous, *S.J.T.*, i, 1948, pp. 136 ff., and C. R. North, ibid, ii, 1949, pp. 113 ff., where some of the problems attaching to this task are discussed.
[3] G. E. Phillips (*The Old Testament in the World Church*, 1942, pp. 6 ff.) gives some examples of such an attitude, particularly on the Mission field. He cites, amongst much other evidence, the remark of a Chinese pastor: 'Intending missionaries or evangelists waste their time if they spend a lot of it studying the Old Testament . . . Reading the Old Testament is like eating a large crab; it turns out to be mostly shell, with very little meat on it' (p. 23). Similarly J. Woods (*The Old Testament in the Church*, 1949, p. 1) cites the observation that the Old Testament is 'a millstone about the neck of Christianity'. I have heard similar opinions expressed by missionaries, and a similar attitude to the Old Testament is not unknown in the West. It is curious to observe that in 1870, in the Introductory Lecture to his *Theology of the Old Testament*, G. F. Oehler lamented that a similar attitude was then common, but rejoiced that a revived interest in Old Testament Theology was beginning (Zondervan Press reprint edition, pp. 1 f.).

use of the scientific knowledge of today. To the scholar it may have an antiquarian interest, but for ordinary people it is treated as of no moment.

It is idle to try to rehabilitate the Old Testament by turning the back on all the scientific study that has been devoted to it, and by imposing upon it a dogmatic unity that is brought to it. The New Testament cannot be read back into the Old by the skilful selection of convenient texts and the ignoring of the rest, or by the resort to typology or the allegorizing of all that is inconvenient.[1] While it is true, as I have more than once argued,[2] that the Old Testament looks forward to something beyond itself, and the New Testament looks back to the Old Testament, so that in a real sense they belong to one another and form a single whole, the Old Testament is not to be read as a Christian book. It is an essential part of the Christian Bible, but it is not a part in which the meaning of the whole is to be found. A doctor may take a sample of our blood and test it, and form sound conclusions about the blood that is left in our veins; but the Bible is not to be treated in that way. Its unity is of a wholly different order. There is a unity in the life of an individual; yet it is impossible from the most careful study of the child to know the future course of his life. The unity of the Bible is of this latter kind. It is the unity of growth, and not a static unity, and each stage of the growth must be considered in relation to the whole, as well as in its uniqueness. Moreover, within the Old Testament we have the record of a long growth, so that no static unity can be found even in this part of the Bible. Ideas and practices which were outgrown within the period covered by the Old Testament figure in some parts of it. It is precisely this that makes the writing of an Old Testament theology so difficult. For how can the diversity of the ideas of the long process be reduced to the systematized unity of a theology? Is not that unity by its very nature a static unity, and therefore other than the dynamic unity of the process?

[1] On allegorical and typological interpretations of the Old Testament, cf. *The Unity of the Bible*, pp. 17 ff., and the literature there noted. To this may be added W. Zimmerli, *Evangelische Theologie*, xii, 1952, pp. 34 ff., F. Baumgärtel, *Verheissung*, 1952, and *Th.L.Z.*, lxxix, 1954, cols. 199 ff.
[2] Cf. especially *The Unity of the Bible*, pp. 95 ff. Cf. further H. W. Hertzberg, *Wendende Kirche im Neuen Testament*, 1950, and Baumgärtel, op. cit.; also J. Coppens, *Les Harmonies des deux Testaments*, revised ed., 1949, and *Vom christlichen Verständnis des Alten Testaments*, 1952.

That this dilemma must somehow be resolved is widely felt, and the number of books issued in recent years offering a study of Old Testament theology is eloquent testimony to the strength of the feeling. The essence of the problem is the necessity to retain a historical sense, and to have a firm grasp of the process that provides the material for our theology,[1] while yet not turning our theology back into a history. The Old Testament theologian must remember all the work done by the historian, and the study of the history of Old Testament religion must continue side by side with the study of the theology of the Old Testament.

Our problems have been increased by the fact that during the very years in which the demand for a study of the theology of the Old Testament has made itself heard, our materials for the study of the history of the religion have become more abundant. We have ever larger knowledge of the background of Semitic, and particularly Canaanite, religion which lay behind and around the religion of Israel,[2] and we see that much, even in Judaism, can no longer be regarded as special supernatural revelation given directly and specifically to Israel, but had its antecedents in Canaanite religion. To some who have approached the subject with simple evolutionary presuppositions this has seemed to yield the conclusion that Israel's religion developed naturally out of Canaanite religion.[3] Yet Canaanite religion could not of itself have yielded all that we find in the Old Testament, any more than the Old Testament of itself could have yielded all that we find in the New. A merely evolutionary view can dispense with the Incarnation, for which it can have no use, but it is bound to read back into the origins all that has come to light in the development, as it understands the development, or else to ignore in the development all that it does not find in the origins. My study of the Old Testament leads me to find both evolutionary and non-evolutionary factors in the story. Just because there is continuity, there is something carried forward from one moment

[1] Cf. W. A. Irwin, *J.B.R.*, xxi, 1953, pp. 9 ff.
[2] Cf. W. F. Albright, *Archaeology and the Religion of Israel*, 3rd ed., 1954, and M. Burrows, *What Mean these Stones?* 1941.
[3] Cf. G. E. Wright, *The Old Testament against its Environment*, 1950, p. 12: 'Has the God of Israel evolved from the gods of the nations, or Israelite monotheism from pagan polytheism? During the past century our preoccupation with the idea of development has led us to answer this question in the affirmative.'

to the next; yet new factors come in, and the mere passage of time could not produce from one moment all that we find in the next.[1] To these we shall return.

No more to be preferred is the view that Israel brought her religion with her from Sinai, and that in Canaan there was a long fight between this religion and Canaanite religion, until finally the faith of Sinai prevailed in Judaism. This is unduly to simplify the story. It would seem truer to say that at least three strands entered into the religious life of Israel. Israel's religion before Moses, while it derived from the general Semitic background, was different from Canaanite religion in character,[2] while after the settlement in Palestine Canaanite cultural and religious influence was continually felt. The third strand came at Sinai through Moses, and this was the unique and specifically Israelite element.[3] Many of the elements of the older religion persisted, and everything was not wholly new from the time of Moses. Nor was everything Canaanite finally resisted and excluded. Some Canaanite practices were incorporated into the religion of Israel and made the vehicle of the worship of Israel's God; other practices were resisted and rejected, because they were such that they could never be the vehicle of the religion which Moses established.[4] On the other hand, some of the older elements of Israel's pre-Mosaic religion, which were not eliminated by Moses, were gradually eliminated in the course of time. Moreover, the recognition of the significance of the work of Moses does not mean that the distinctive element in Israelite religion began and ended with him. It finds incipient in his work all the great ideas which characterized the religion, but it does not suppose that they were then left to develop of themselves. Rather does it find that the uniqueness of the work of Moses was continued by a unique succession of men, who brought into the life of Israel a con-

---

[1] For a criticism of a purely evolutionary understanding of the Old Testament cf. W. Eichrodt's review of H. E. Fosdick, *A Guide to the Understanding of the Bible*, 1938, in *J.B.L.*, lxv, 1946, pp. 208 ff., summarized in translation by W. F. Albright, pp. 205 ff.

[2] This is stressed by Wright, op. cit.

[3] Cf. Wright, ibid., p. 15: 'I find it necessary to agree with W. Eichrodt when he says that the source of the difficulty lies in the inability of the development hypothesis to take seriously the story of God's revelation and covenant at Mt. Sinai.'

[4] Wright observes (ibid., p. 13): 'Canaanite religion was the most dangerous and disintegrating factor which the faith of Israel had to face.'

tinuous influence which derived neither from the past nor from Canaan, but from God.

Any treatment of the religion of Israel, therefore, whether it is called a history of the religion or an Old Testament theology, must be marked by an historical sense, and by the recognition that ideas and practices of various origin, and at various levels of development, are to be found within the Old Testament. Nevertheless, there is a real unity, for without this it would be idle to speak in terms of the theology of the Old Testament. That unity is not here conceived of as the unity of the Judaism that emerged from the process, integrating into itself the various elements and imposing on them a unity which derived from itself, but as the unity of the development of the distinctive faith of Israel.[1] Within that faith there were incipient ideas and principles which became formulated with increasing clarity in due course. The genius of Israel's religion is to be found in the study of these. On the other hand, practices like blood revenge, polygamy, levirate marriage, and the massacre of conquered foes, were not specifically Israelite and were increasingly controlled or fell into insignificance as time passed. While all of these were religious in origin, and therefore properly belong to the study of the religious development of Israel, they can claim no place in an Old Testament theology.

Here, then, is a clear distinction between a history of Israelite religion and an Old Testament theology. For the former every religious idea and practice which marked any period of the story demands full consideration. For the latter all that is not of the essence of the faith of Israel is irrelevant. Here, however, we must beware of singling out all that is acceptable to ourselves, and building an edifice on that alone, while ignoring all that we do not like and labelling it irrelevant.

If we take the cases I have mentioned, we may find some instructive guidance. Blood revenge was gradually brought under control, and in the latter part of the story it falls wholly into the background. It was of very ancient origin and was derived from the general background of Semitic culture out of

---

[1] Cf. O. J. Baab, *The Theology of the Old Testament*, 1949, p. 25: 'While changing with the passage of time, yet . . . Hebrew religion throughout the centuries perpetuated itself as a distinctive way of life and belief.'

which Israel came,[1] and was not part of any new and special divine revelation given to Moses. Instead, as we trace its history in the Old Testament we find that it was brought more and more under control.[2] The distinction between murder and manslaughter was made,[3] and there was provision for sanctuary for the unwitting killer of his fellow,[4] with arrangements for adjudication, while in the latest strand of the law we find provision for the ending of all existing blood feuds at the death of the High Priest,[5] so that the manslaughterer could safely return to his home. Polygamy was not peculiarly Israelite, and is nowhere directly condemned or repudiated in the Old Testament, indeed, but there is little evidence of it in the later period of the Old Testament,[6] or in the Judaism of the New Testament. Levirate marriage, which sprang out of a wide background of primitive practice,[7] is still provided for in the Deuteronomic legislation,[8] but the only recorded examples of it in the Old

---

[1] Blood revenge was of very much wider than Semitic origin. Cf. L. H. Gray, in *E.R.E.*, ii, 1909, pp. 720 ff. On blood revenge in early Arabian society, cf. W. R. Smith, *Kinship and Marriage in Early Arabia*, New ed., 1903, pp. 25 ff., W. R. Patton, *A.J. Th.*, v, 1901, pp. 703 ff, and J. Obermann, in *The Idea of History in the Ancient Near East*, ed. by R. C. Dentan, 1955, pp. 253 ff. In its origin it allowed the revenge to fall on any member of the group to which the murderer belonged, and not necessarily on the murderer himself. It is possible that we have traces of this in the Old Testament in Gen. 34.30 and II Sam. 21.5 f.

[2] Cf. J. Pedersen, *Israel I–II*, E. Tr., 1926, pp. 395 ff., and A.-J. Baumgartner, in Westphal's *Dictionnaire encyclopédique de la Bible*, ii, 1935, pp. 816 f. Cf. also A. R. S. Kennedy, in *D.B.*, ii, 1899, p. 223 b: 'It is not too much to say that the aim of the Hebrew legislator, from first to last, was so to regulate the practice that the shedder of blood should be, as far as possible, protected from the hasty and unconsidered vengeance of the next of kin'.

[3] Cf. Ex. 21.12 ff., Deut. 19.6, 12. S. R. Driver, in *E.B.*, ii, 1901, col. 1746, observes: 'Already in the Book of the Covenant there is drawn the distinction (which is not yet found in Homer) between intentional and unintentional homicide, and the importance of the distinction is insisted on in all the Codes.' Mohammed made the same distinction, but A. H. Harley, in *E.R.E.*, ii, p. 733a, observes that 'the modern Bedawî has preserved the nomadic institutions of the tribal system and the blood-feud from the transforming influence Islam would otherwise have exercised. With him the laws of vengeance for murder and homicide are the same.'

[4] At first the altar (Ex. 21.14; cf. I Kings 1.50, 2.28 ff.). With the limitation of sacrifice to a single permitted altar came the provision of cities of refuge in Deut. 19.1 ff. and Num. 35.9 ff., together with rules for adjudication, so that the murderer might not be given the protection designed for the manslaughterer.

[5] Cf. Num. 35.25, 28; Josh. 20.6.

[6] Cf. W. P. Paterson, in *D.B.*, iii, 1900, pp. 264 f., where it is argued that there was an implicit protest against polygamy within the prophetic school.

[7] Cf. M. Burrows, *B.A.S.O.R.*, No. 77, February 1940, pp. 2 ff. For other references to literature cf. my *Servant of the Lord*, 1952, pp. 169 f.

[8] Cf. Deut. 25.5 ff. In *The Servant of the Lord*, p. 170, I suggest the probability that this passage reflects a limitation of a custom that was once wider in its range in Israel.

Testament are from the period before the establishment of the monarchy.[1] Similarly, while we read much of the massacre of conquered foes in the early period,[2] and find evidences of a similar custom amongst Israel's neighbours,[3] in the later period this ancient and widespread practice fell into desuetude.[4] The genius of Israel's religion is not to be found in these practices, or in others that could be mentioned, but in their control and elimination.[5] The theology of the Old Testament must be based on those elements of Israel's distinctive faith which, incipient at first, were developed in her history, and on those ideas and practices which, even though of older or alien origin, were accepted permanently into her faith and made its vehicle.

While, therefore, an Old Testament theology must be selective in its use of the Old Testament, it must not be arbitrarily selective. In the present lectures, which fall within the

[1] Cf. Gen. 38 and the book of Ruth. Neither in the case of Judah and Tamar, nor in that of Boaz and Ruth, do we have strictly levirate marriage, since in neither case was the man the brother-in-law of the woman.
[2] Cf. Num. 21.2; Deut. 2.34, 3.6; Josh. 6.17, 8.26, 10.28, 35, 37, 39, 40, 11.11, 12, 20, 21; I Sam. 15.3, 9, 20. On this practice cf. L. Delporte, *Recherches de Science Religieuse*, l, 1914, pp. 297 ff., and A. Fernández, *Biblica*, v, 1924, pp. 3 ff.
[3] Cf. The Moabite Stone, lines 14 ff., where Mesha says: 'And Kemosh said to me, Go take Nebo against Israel. And I went by night and fought against it from the break of dawn till the noontide, and I took it and slew all . . . seven thousand m[en] and . . . and women and . . . and damsels, for I had devoted it to Ashtarkemosh' (translation of G. A. Cooke, in *North Semitic Inscriptions*, 1903, p. 3). W. F. Albright (*From the Stone Age to Christianity*, 2nd ed., 1946, p. 213) says: 'The practice of devoting a recalcitrant foe to destruction as a kind of gigantic holocaust to the national deity was apparently universal among the early Semites.' Cf. S. R. Driver, *Notes on the Hebrew Text of the Books of Samuel*, 2nd ed., 1913, pp. 130 f.
[4] The word occurs in the later literature, indeed. It is used in Jer. 50.26, 51.3, to describe in prophecy the coming Chaldaean treatment of Jerusalem; in Isa. 34.5 to describe the coming divine judgement on Edom; in Isa. 43.28 to describe God's judgement on Israel; in Mal. 4.6 (Heb. 3.24) to describe the averted judgement on the earth; while in Zech. 14.11 Jerusalem is promised lasting security against such treatment. But none of these are historical accounts of Israel's practice of this ancient custom.
[5] In the Deuteronomic law the complete extermination of the Canaanites is represented as enjoined by Moses; cf. Deut. 7.24 ff., 20.17. That this was not historically carried out is clear from Judg. 2.3, 3.5 f. This Deuteronomic law was a reflection of the later attitude towards Canaanite religion, rather than a reflection of the current attitude towards the Canaanite people, who by that time had been merged through intermarriage (cf. Deut. 3.6) with the Israelite people. It is, indeed, probable that some of the above noted passages in Joshua are reflections into past history of this attitude, though there can be little doubt that at Hormah (Num. 21.2) and Jericho the ban was actually carried out. In Ex. 22.20 (Heb. 19) and Deut. 13.15 (Heb. 16) the ban is enjoined against Israelites who are guilty of religious disloyalty, but here again an ideal attitude, rather than a historical practice, is involved, and in any case this is quite different from the extermination of conquered foes referred to above.

field of Old Testament theology, there will therefore be no attempt to discuss all the material found in the Old Testament, or every belief which anyone in Israel ever had on the subjects under discussion. There will be selection in accordance with the dynamic principle already referred to. Moreover, since it is impossible to present a complete biblical theology within the compass of seven lectures, only a selection of the aspects of such a theology can be here treated.

Any arrangement of the material is open to question. We cannot treat fully of the Old Testament thought on God without considering its teaching on salvation; yet before the full thought on salvation can be examined, we must look at its teaching on sin, and this once more involves its thought on God. Whatever divisions of our subject are adopted, there is thus bound to be an imperfectly satisfying choice as to where material that is relevant to more than one section should be placed. For whereas our treatment must be linear, our subject is not. It treats of the relations between God and man and God and the world and of the relations between man and his neighbour, and these all subsist together and act and react on one another.

I do not propose to single out one key idea in terms of which to construct the whole, such as the covenant, or election, or salvation, partly because I think no one of these, or even all together, adequate, and partly because it is of the essence of the Old Testament to deal not so much in abstract ideas as in ideas which are embodied in concrete history. By this I do not mean that the Old Testament presents us with a theology of history.[1] For there is no claim that all history gives a satisfying knowledge of God or embodies his will. But what the Old Testament repeatedly maintains is that God came to men through the events of history to reveal his nature and his will. It is in significant moments of history that revelation is found, and for their detection and interpretation something more than the history itself, and more than a patient reflection on the facts, is required. In the first lecture it will be shown that history alone is not the most significant medium of revelation in the faith of

[1] Many writers use this expression, and G. Thils has published a long bibliography of works treating of this subject (*E.Th.L.*, xxvi, 1950, pp. 87 ff.). Cf. also R. Criado, *La Teologia de la historia en el Antiguo Testamento*, 1954 (extract from *XIV Semana Bíblica Española*, pp. 35 ff.).

Israel, and even in the great moments of history to which reference has been made there is something more than mere event.

The concepts of revelation and inspiration cannot here be
analysed.[1] Revelation is fundamentally the divine self-un-
folding, while inspiration lies in the use of human personality
for the declaration of the divine message.[2] Where there is
inspiration there must be personal factors, but revelation is not
necessarily given through persons. The Bible is throughout
based on the belief that God has unveiled to men something of
his own character and will, and that he has spoken through
men, in whose mouth he has put his own word. In Israel there
were many who claimed to have the word of God and to be
inspired by him, whose claim is denied by the sacred writers.
It is declared that their word had no deeper source than their
own heart.[3] Such a charge could always be made on both sides,
and if we had no more to go on than the unsupported claim to
inspiration, it would be hard to establish the genuineness of
inspiration, or to get behind the speaker to the God whose
word he claimed to utter.

The biblical faith is based neither on human reflection on
history, nor on human claims to be the mouthpiece of God, but
on both and more. For revelation through history and revelation through persons are not independent of one another, but
often linked intimately together and offering a check on one
another, so that while we must always speak of a faith, rather
than of a logical demonstration, it is a faith which is intellec-
tually respectable and for which there is solid evidence.[4]

From this it follows that the faith of Israel cannot be studied
in terms of ideas alone. Attention must constantly be drawn to
the concrete situation out of which the ideas sprang and to
which they were related, as well as to the divine revelation
which was given through the whole. In so far as there is revelation of God there is something timeless and of enduring validity;
yet this timeless element is mediated through a historical
moment and historical circumstances. It is precisely here that
the essential difficulty of writing on Old Testament theology
lies. It is so much easier to confine our attention to a history of

[1] Cf. H. Wheeler Robinson, *Inspiration and Revelation in the Old Testament*, 1946.
[2] Cf. what I have written on this in *The Authority of the Bible*, 1950, pp. 5 f.
[3] Cf. Jer. 23.16.
[4] Cf. *The Unity of the Bible*, pp. 8 ff.

Old Testament religion than to attempt this separation, where no simple rule of thumb can be relied on. Nevertheless, it seems to me to be of the utmost importance and urgency to attempt this task. For if God has indeed revealed himself, as the writers of both Testaments firmly believed, then it is important that men should apprehend this revelation. Behind the Bible, and behind those significant moments of history, and behind the great religious leaders of Israel, men believed that God stood, and therefore through all there was a fundamental unity which derived ultimately from him. Either this belief is wholly false, or the inner unity within the revelation should be sought in a theological study.

The Old Testament is not the whole of the Christian Bible, and I find a unity running through the revelation of which we have knowledge through both Testaments.[1] In these lectures, however, our attention must be confined to those elements of the revelation which were given to Israel during the period of the Old Testament. Even here the treatment must be incomplete and selective. It is offered as a contribution towards a theology of the Old Testament, supplementing some other studies which I have published,[2] though in no sense completing them.

At one point in the Coronation of Queen Elizabeth II, a copy of the Bible was presented to Her Majesty, with the words 'Here is wisdom; this is the royal law; these are the lively oracles of God.' It is in the faith that those words were not a hollow formula, but that the Bible, including the Old Testament, can be soberly so described, and that therefore it is of enduring significance to men, that these studies of its message are offered.

[1] Cf. what I have written on this in *The Unity of the Bible*.
[2] Cf. *The Relevance of the Bible*, 1941; *The Rediscovery of the Old Testament*, 1946; *The Biblical Doctrine of Election*, 1950; and *The Unity of the Bible*.

I

REVELATION AND ITS MEDIA[1]

'CANST thou fathom the secrets of God?'[2] asked Zophar scornfully. His question clearly expected a negative reply, and such
a reply is in the fullest harmony with the faith of Israel. The
biblical doctrine of God is not the achievement of the philosopher, arguing back to a first cause or an architect of the
universe, or seeking some pale abstraction of thought behind
all phenomena. It is not the personification of the powers of
Nature, or the blind acceptance of the gods from the remote
past. It rests on the belief that the God who is veiled from our
sight has revealed himself to men. There are, indeed, many
passages which call on men to seek God; but their thought is not
that by seeking man can find God for himself. Rather is it that
God can only reveal himself to those who will receive the
revelation, and will only give his fellowship to those who desire
it. The initiative is his, and the revelation can only come by
divine initiative. Yet it is no presumption to seek him humbly,
since he has called on men to seek him.[3] For his revelation of
himself is not forced on unwilling creatures, but given of his
grace to those who by eager sensitivity of spirit are open to
receive it.

[1] Much of the substance of this lecture is similar to that of the C. J. Cadoux
Memorial Lecture which I delivered at Bradford in 1949, and which was published in *C.Q.*, xxviii, 1949, pp. 248 ff.
[2] Job 11.7. R.V. reads: 'Canst thou by searching find out God?' S. R. Driver
declares this rendering impossible (cf. Driver-Gray, *Job* (I.C.C.), 1921, p. 107),
and in Driver and Gray's Commentary the verse is rendered: 'Canst thou find
out the immensity of God?' (ibid). P. (E.) Dhorme (*Job* (E. Bib.), 1926, p. 145)
observes that the word *ḥēḳer* denotes, not the process of investigation, but the
object of investigation, and renders: 'Trouveras-tu la nature d'Eloah?' The
Vulgate rendering, which follows the Septuagint, has *Forsitan vestigia Dei com-
prehendes*, understanding the word to mean 'footprints'; but this does not quite
get the meaning. The rendering of R.S.V., 'Can you find out the deep things of
God?' closely accords with that given above. A. S. Peake (*Job* (Cent.B.), p. 127),
has 'Canst thou find out the Almighty unto perfection?' Cf. F. Stier (*Ijjob*, 1954,
p. 57): 'Die Gottergründung willst du finden?'
[3] Cf. O. R. Sellers, *J.B.R.*, xxi, 1953, pp. 234 ff.

This belief is fundamental to the Bible from its very beginning. In the earliest account of the creation God makes his will known to man from the moment of his formation,[1] and later we find him walking in the garden seeking Adam.[2] He is represented as appearing to the patriarchs and speaking with them face to face.[3] That we are not to understand these narratives literally is made plain in the Bible itself. For to Moses God says: 'Thou canst not see my face: for no man may see me and live,'[4] while in the New Testament it is declared that 'No man hath ever seen God'.[5] In their vivid and picturesque narratives those ancient stories are declaring the belief of the writers that God has ever been willing to make himself known to men, and that the initiative in revelation has always been his. In the moment of his call Isaiah saw God in his vision,[6] and though there is no suggestion that any eye but his of all who were assembled in the Temple saw the vision, it was as real to him as any appearance recorded as given to the patriarchs. To concentrate on the naïveté of the form of the early stories of the Bible is to miss their spiritual profundity. They testify to the belief which penetrates the Bible as a whole, that God may be known to men because he desires to be known, and because he has chosen to reveal himself to them.

Similarly his will for men may be known because he has of his grace chosen to communicate it. He has not left man to stumble along in darkness, but has declared his will, and if men do in fact stumble blindly along, it is because they have been unwilling to receive his revelation or to obey his will. The great chapter in the book of Job which declares that wisdom will ever elude the search of men, says that God understands it and declares it to men, who can find it in finding him.[7] Revelation rather than discovery is the keynote of the Bible, though eager activity of spirit is enjoined upon men. How reasonable is this faith we shall see as we proceed. Our first task, however, is to examine the variety of the ways in which God was held to reveal himself, and what in the thought of the Old Testament were the media of revelation.[8]

[1] Gen. 2.16 f. [2] Gen. 3.8 f. [3] Gen. 12.7, 17.1 ff., 18.1 ff.
[4] Ex. 33.20. [5] John 1.18. [6] Isa. 6.1.
[7] Job. 28.23, 27 f.
[8] Cf. H. Wheeler Robinson, *Redemption and Revelation*, 1942, pp. 95 ff., L. Koehler, *Theologie des Alten Testaments*, 3rd ed., 1953, pp. 83 ff.

We may begin with the thought of revelation in Nature.
That biblical religion is not Nature worship scarcely needs to
be said. Some religions have personified the sun, the moon and
the stars, the winds and the streams and all the other powers of
Nature, and have given them worship. There are evidences in
the Old Testament that some in Israel followed this way, but
they stand condemned.[1] For nowhere is it the biblical faith
that worship is rightly to be given to them. The God of the
Bible is one who stands behind Nature and who controls it, but
who may use it to reveal something of his glory. 'The heavens
proclaim the glory of God, and the firmament declares his
handiwork.'[2] Amos speaks of God as 'him that made the
Pleiades and Orion, and turns deep darkness into the morning
and darkens the day into night; who calls for the waters of the
sea, and pours them out upon the face of the earth'.[3] Similarly
the first speech of God to Job from the whirlwind sets forth with
vivid brilliance the wonders of God's power as revealed in the
works of Nature,[4] and Ps. 104 has a similar theme. Deutero-
Isaiah asks 'Who measured the waters[5] in the hollow of his
hand, and meted out the heaven with the span, and contained
the dust of the earth in a measure, and weighed the mountains
in scales, and the hills in a balance?'[6] and continues 'Lift up
your eyes on high, and see who created these, leading out their
host by number';[7] while Hosea declares that it is he who gave
corn, wine and oil.[8]

In all this there is nothing that is peculiar to Israelite faith.
It is an element of her faith which she shares with many others.
Similarly, we find elsewhere, as well as in the Old Testament,
the thought that God uses his control of Nature to express his
displeasure. In the time of David, when drought afflicted the
land, it was believed that some sin must be its cause, and the
sin was traced to a deed of Saul's many years before.[9] When that
deed was atoned for by the execution of seven of Saul's descendants in Gibeah, God's favour was believed to be restored, and
he 'heard the entreaties for the land'.[10] The book of Deuteronomy
promises disaster when God is not obeyed. 'Thy heaven that is

[1] Cf. II Kings 17.16, 21.3, 23.5; Jer. 8.2; Ezek. 8.16; Deut. 4.19, 17.3 ff.
[2] Ps. 19.1 (Heb. 2).   [3] Amos 5.8; cf. Ps. 8.3 (Heb. 4).   [4] Job 38 f.
[5] The Dead Sea Scroll, DSIa or 1QIs[a], reads 'the water of the sea'.
[6] Isa. 40.12.   [7] Isa. 40.26.   [8] Hos. 2.8.   [9] I Sam. 21.1 ff.
[10] II Sam. 21.14.

over thy head shall be brass, and the earth that is under thee shall be iron. Yahweh will make the rain of thy land powder and dust: from heaven it will come down upon thee, until thou art destroyed.'[1] Amos complains that men have not taken warning from the disasters that God has sent, and have not realized that they were sent to call them to repentance and obedience. 'I have smitten you with blight and mildew: I have dried up[2] your gardens and your vineyards, and your fig trees and your olive trees hath the locust devoured: yet have ye not returned unto me, said Yahweh.'[3] Similarly when Joel describes the calamity brought upon the nation by the plague of locusts, he continues 'Rend your hearts, and not your garments, and return unto Yahweh your God: for he is gracious and compassionate, slow to anger, and plenteous in mercy, and repents of the evil. Who knows whether he will not turn and repent, and leave a blessing behind him?'[4]

Frequently the Israelites saw the hand of God in the natural phenomena that helped them in the hour of need. To them they were not chance coincidences, but the evidence that God was active on their behalf. When Joshua marched to the help of the Gibeonites, the fierce hailstorm that discomfited their foes heartened the Israelites and assured them that God was with them.[5] In the battle against Sisera, the sudden deluge that reduced the plain to a morass and rendered the chariots of the Canaanites a liability rather than an asset was the evidence of God's presence with his people in the battle, and Deborah sang 'The stars from their courses fought against Sisera. The torrent Kishon swept them away, That torrent that came to our aid,[6]

---

[1] Deut. 28.23 f.

[2] The Massoretic text has an infinitive 'to multiply', which R.V., following the Vulgate (*multitudinem*) renders 'the multitude of'. Most modern editors, however, follow Wellhausen's emendation (*Die kleinen Propheten*, 3rd ed., 1898, p. 80), which yields 'I have dried up', or 'laid waste'. Cf. A. van Hoonacker, *Les douze Petits Prophètes* (E. Bib.), 1908, p. 238.

[3] Amos 4.9.   [4] Joel 2.13 f.   [5] Josh. 10.10 f.

[6] The Hebrew word here is of very obscure meaning. The root means 'to be before' (either in time or place) or 'to come to meet', or 'to be opposed to'. The rendering of R.V. is 'that ancient river'. While this is a possible meaning, there seems no special reason why this particular river should be so described. Some editors render 'torrent of battles' (cf. K. Budde, *Richter* (K.H.C.), 1897, p. 47; so also E. König, *Hebräisches und aramäisches Wörterbuch*, 6th ed., 1936, p. 398 b). This was already found in older writers; cf. J. Simon, *Lexicon Manuale Hebraicum et Chaldaicum*, 2nd ed., 1771, p. 853: *torrens victoriarum*. G. A. Cooke (*The History and Song of Deborah*, 1892, p. 48, and *Judges* (Camb. B.), 1918, p. 64) renders 'onrushing torrent', and so R.S.V., but C.F. Burney (*The Book of Judges*, 2nd ed.,

the torrent Kishon.'[1] In the time of Samuel, we read that when the Israelites were gathered together at Mizpah and the Philistines came against them, 'Yahweh thundered with a great thunder on that day against the Philistines, and threw them into confusion.'[2] To the Hebrews, as to many others, not only was God behind the ordinary processes of Nature, the creator and sustainer of the universe; he was active within those processes, to use the more terrifying aspects of Nature to rebuke or to help his people.[3]

In a number of passages in the Old Testament we find reflected the belief that God sometimes revealed his will to men through the casting of the sacred lot, or through some form of divination.[4] Behind such an idea is the belief that man can find God's will by a technique, and we are in the world of magic. The line between magic and religion is not always easy to define, but broadly we may say that wherever there is the belief that by a technique man can control God, or control events, or discover the future, we have magic. Prophetic symbolism has sometimes been thought of as magic. When Zedekiah the son of Chenaanah made horns of iron and said 'With these shalt thou gore the Syrians',[5] he doubtless believed that by the act he was releasing power which would be active for the

---

1920, p. 147) is doubtful whether such a sense can be maintained. He prefers to follow A. B. Ehrlich (*Randglossen zur hebräischen Bibel*, iii, 1910, p. 85) and emend the text to read 'it faced them' (so also E. Sellin, in *Festschrift Otto Procksch*, 1934, p. 161, O. Grether, *Das Deboralied*, 1941, p. 27, and B. Ubach, *Josuè-Jutges-Rut* (La Biblia—Montserrat Bible), 1953, p. 236). A. Vincent (*Juges* (Jerusalem Bible), 1952, p. 56) follows the reading of LXX[A] and renders 'le torrent sacré', while A. Lods (*La Bible du Centenaire*, ii, 1947, p. 51) leaves the word untranslated. By its formation it should be an abstract noun, giving the sense 'torrent of confrontingness'. A cognate adjective in Arabic means 'first in attacking the foe, gallant, dauntless', and if this Arabic sense could be sustained in Hebrew this would give 'torrent of courage' or 'intrepid stream', and this sense was found by H. Ewald (*Die Dichter des Alten Bundes*, I i, 1839, p. 131). Without invoking Arabic, however, the sense of the root in Hebrew makes it possible to give this word the meaning of 'the quality of coming to attack', and so of 'intrepidity'. The phrase could then be rendered 'that hostile torrent', or 'that heroic torrent'. On the other hand, the cognate verb is sometimes used with the meaning of 'come to help' (cf. Ps. 59.10 (Heb. 11), 79.8; Deut. 23.4 (Heb. 5), and hence P. Cassel (*Richter und Ruth* (Lange's Bibelwerk), 1865, p. 57 b) (E. Tr. by P. H. Steenstra, 1871, p. 102 b) renders 'helpful stream'. This seems to be the most appropriate meaning for this context. The Kishon is hailed as the stream that rose to the aid of Israel.

[1] Judg. 5.20 f.   [2] I Sam. 7.10.
[3] For a study of the teaching of the Old Testament on Nature as the sphere of divine activity, cf. J. L. McKenzie, *C.B.Q.*, xiv, 1952, pp. 18 ff., 124 ff.
[4] Cf. E. Dhorme, *R.H.R.*, cviii, 1933, pp. 119 ff.
[5] I Kings 22.11.

fulfilment of his word. Similarly, when Jeremiah made a wooden yoke and wore it in the Temple,[1] he believed that his act was a prophecy, and that it released power, just as the prophetic word was believed to release power. Wheeler Robinson distinguishes between prophetic symbolism and magic by observing that the prophet was acting under a constraint which he believed to be of God, and that he was not therefore seeking to control God by a technique, but was releasing power whose source was God.[2] When the profession of action under divine constraint was a cover for what had no deeper origin than the prophet's own desire, as is sometimes declared to be the case in relation to the false prophets,[3] we have nothing more than magic.[4] But since the same act could be magic or prophecy according to the degree of sincerity of the prophet's heart, the line between magic and religion is manifestly hard to determine, since sincerity cannot be measured by any simple tests.

There are passages in which Urim and Thummim are referred to as a means of finding the will of God,[5] and it is possible that in some other passages where the sacred lot is referred to, it was by Urim and Thummim that it was consulted. In this connexion the most instructive passage is found in I Sam. 14.41, where, however, the Hebrew text has suffered some loss, and we must resort to the Greek text for a clearer notion. We read that Saul put a question to God and found no answer. He then framed the question differently, but again received no answer.[6] He then decided to cast lots to find out where the trouble lay. He first asked that if the evil lay in himself or Jonathan the answer might be Urim, but if it lay in the people it might be Thummim.[7] When the answer was Urim a further

[1] Jer. 27 f.
[2] Cf. *Old Testament Essays* (read before the Society for Old Testament Study), 1927, p. 14; *J.T.S.*, xliii, 1942, pp. 132 f.; and *Redemption and Revelation*, 1942, p. 250 Cf. also L. H. Brockington, in *Studies in History and Revelation*, ed. by E. A. Payne, 1942, p. 41. On Prophetic Symbolism cf. also D. Buzy, *Les Symboles de l'Ancien Testament*, 1923; A. Regnier, *R.B.*, xxxii, 1923, pp. 383 ff.; W. F. Lofthouse, *A.J.S.L.*, xl, 1923–4, pp. 239 ff.; and G. Fohrer, *Die symbolischen Handlungen der Propheten* (A.T.A.N.T.), 1953.
[3] Cf. Jer. 23.16, 26.
[4] On magic in the Old Testament cf. A. Lods, in *Old Testament Essays*, 1927, pp. 55 ff.
[5] Cf. I Sam. 28.6.   [6] I Sam. 14.37.
[7] I Sam. 14.41. The Hebrew omits several words, jumping from the first occurrence of the word 'Israel' to the third. The word *tummîm* was then meaningless, and it was therefore pointed by the Massoretes as *tāmîm*, and is rendered in R.V. '(shew) the right'. The sense of the verse can be seen in R.S.V.

inquiry was necessary to determine whether it was in Saul or in Jonathan.[1] Here we see that there were always two possible answers, though there was a third possibility, that no answer should be given. The Urim seems to have been the inauspicious answer, the word Urim coming from a root meaning 'to curse'[2] rather than from the root meaning 'light' as the Greek translators understood it. Hence when the question was susceptible of the answer Yes or No, it is probable that Urim meant No and Thummim Yes. But where the question offered alternatives of a different kind, it was necessary to prescribe beforehand how the reply would be understood. The precise nature of Urim and Thummim can only be conjectured, but the view which seems to me most probable is that they were two flat stones, one side of which was the auspicious side and one the inauspicious, so that if they both fell with the same side upward the answer was given, while if they revealed different sides there was no answer.[3] Be that as it may, the sacred lot provided a mechanical means of finding out the will of God, though its possibility of no answer meant that it was recognized that man could not compel God to answer.

Divination was much more practised in Babylonia than it was in the official religion of Israel.[4] In Babylonia there were many classes of diviners, who claimed to be able to discover the

---

[1] I Sam. 14.42.

[2] This derivation was suggested by J. Wellhausen, *Prolegomena to the History of Israel*, E.Tr. by Black and Menzies, 1885, p. 394 n. In its favour is the consideration that Urim and Thummim would then be of the same formation, both from geminate verbs. Cf. A. R. Johnson, *The Cultic Prophet in Ancient Israel*, 1944, p. 9 n. For a different view cf. E. Dhorme, *La Religion des Hébreux Nomades*, 1937, p. 237. R. Press (*Z.A.W.*, li (N.F. x), 1933, p. 229) deprecates the attempt to establish the etymology in the light of the significance of the Urim and Thummim, but agrees that Urim gave the inauspicious answer.

[3] So H. P. Smith, *The Religion of Israel*, 1914, p. 122, and Oesterley and Robinson, *Hebrew Religion*, 2nd ed., 1937, p. 166. A similar device was used in Chinese divination; cf. H. Doré, *Recherches sur les superstitions en Chine*, I ii (Variétés sinologiques, N. 34), 1912, p. 243. A less probable suggestion is that they were in the form of dice (cf. A. R. S. Kennedy, in *D.B.*, iv. 1902, p. 840 a), and still less probable that one stone was called Urim and one Thummim (cf. G. F. Moore, in *E. B.*, iv, 1907, col. 5236), since in that case the use of plural names would not be expected.

[4] Cf. F. Lenormant, *La Divination et la science des présages chez les Chaldéens*, 1875; M. Jastrow, *Die Religion Babyloniens und Assyriens*, ii, 1912, pp. 203ff.; L. W. King, in *E.R.E.*, iv, 1911, pp. 783 ff.; A. Boissier, *Choix de textes relatifs à la divination assyro-babylonienne*, 1905, and *Mantique babylonienne et mantique hittite*, 1935; E. Dhorme, *R.H.R.*, cxiii, 1936, pp. 125 ff., cxvi, 1937, pp. 5 ff.; A. Guillaume, *Prophecy and Divination*, 1938, pp. 37 ff.; G. Contenau, *La Divination chez les Assyriens et les Babyloniens*, 1940; A. Haldar, *Associations of Cult Prophets among the Ancient Semites*, 1945, pp. 1 ff.

will of God or the future course of events by studying the liver
of slaughtered animals or some other phenomena. That
divination was practised in Israel is clear from the denunciations
of it which stand in the Bible,[1] and it may well be that there
were many varieties of diviners.[2] It has been claimed that the
prophets belonged to divining orders,[3] and that Amos was one
who practised hepatoscopy.[4] This seems to me to be without
warrant,[5] and we should distinguish between the popular
religion, which took over practices and beliefs current in the
world in which Israel was set, and the religion of the Old
Testament. It is hard to think that the greater prophets, who
brought so rich a contribution to the faith of Israel, practised
the divination which stands condemned both in the law and in
the prophetic books themselves.[6] Nevertheless, it must be remembered that Joseph is said to have had his divining cup,[7] and
therefore to have resorted to hydromancy. And there is no hint
of any condemnation of Joseph. Such traces of divination as
figure without condemnation, however, cannot be supposed to
be characteristic of the religion of the Old Testament, and even
the resort to the sacred lot is not the characteristic means of
learning the will of God. Where these things figure, they are
survivals of older and widespread ideas and practices which

---

[1] Lev. 19.26; Deut. 18.10; I Sam. 15.23, 28.3; II Kings 17.17, 21.6. References
to the practice of divination may be found also in Isa. 3.2; Micah 3.11;
Jer. 27.9, 29.8; Ezek. 13.6, 9, 22.28; Zech. 10.2. Cf. T. Witton-Davies, *Magic,
Divination and Demonology among the Hebrews and their Neighbours*, 1898, and E.
Dhorme, *R.H.R.*, cxiii, 1936, pp. 125 ff., cxvi, 1937, pp. 5 ff.

[2] Dhorme (*R.H.R.*, cviii, 1933, pp. 119 f.) brings Joshua's extended spear at Ai
(Josh 8.18), Jonathan's shooting of arrows to give a message to David (I Sam.
20.18 ff.), and Elisha's use of arrows in his death-bed scene (II Kings 13.14 ff.)
into relation with divination.

[3] Cf. A. Haldar, op. cit., pp. 108 ff.

[4] Cf. M. Bič, *V.T.*, i, 1951, pp. 293 ff. On hepatoscopy cf. G. Contenau, *La
Divination chez les Assyriens et les Babyloniens*, 1940, pp. 235 ff. That Amos was a
cultic official has been affirmed by I. Engnell (*S.B.U.*, i, 1948, cols. 59 f.). Already,
in *Studies in Divine Kingship in the Ancient Near East*, 1943, p. 87, he had argued that
the word *nōkēdh*, which is used of King Mesha in II Kings 3.4 and of Amos in
Amos 1.1, is proved by its use in Ugaritic (cf. *Syria*, xv, 1934, p. 241) to denote a
cultic official. Cf. Haldar, op. cit., pp. 79, 112. J. Bright (*The Kingdom of God*,
1953, p. 60 n.) observes that 'even granting that the words may on occasion have
had a cultic significance, this is no proof that they must always do so'. Cf. O.
Eissfeldt, in *The Old Testament and Modern Study*, ed. by H. H. Rowley, 1951, pp.
123 f. P. Haupt (*J.B.L.*, xxxv, 1916, pp. 280 ff.) denied that Amos had anything
at all to do with sheep.

[5] Cf. A. Murtonen, *V.T.*, ii, 1952, pp. 170 f.

[6] That some prophets practised divinatory arts is, indeed clear from Micah 3.11;
Ezek. 13.6, 9, 22.28.

[7] Gen. 44.2, 5.

Israel shared with many other peoples. We read little of Urim and Thummim in the later portions of the Old Testament,[1] save as a part of the priestly insignia.[2] They survived, indeed, but as fossils, though they may still have been occasionally consulted,[3] as we find that even in the New Testament the sacred lot is occasionally resorted to.[4] Mechanical and technical means of finding the will of God must be included amongst the media of revelation in Old Testament thought and practice, but they have a relatively insignificant place, and are survivals from a pagan past.

In a variety of ways God was believed to reveal himself through the experience of men. Dreams were sometimes the medium of such revelation.[5] In Jacob's dream at Bethel God appeared unto him and spoke to him.[6] To Abimelech he appeared in a dream and warned him against approaching Abraham's wife.[7] It is possible that the story of the divine direction to the patriarch to listen to Sarah's voice and to send Ishmael away was intended to be understood as given in a dream,[8] since we read that Abraham rose in the morning and acted on the direction.[9] To Joseph dreams in which the future was forecast were given,[10] and Pharaoh's baker and butler had their fortunes indicated in dreams,[11] which, however, they were unable to understand without an interpreter. Similarly, Pharaoh had dreams in which God indicated the coming series of good and bad years,[12] but he again had no clue to the meaning of the dreams until the divinely inspired Joseph interpreted them to him. At the beginning of his reign Solomon received a

---

[1] Cf. A. R. S. Kennedy, in *D.B.*, loc. cit., p. 840 b: 'It cannot be a mere coincidence that the use of Urim and Thummim is never mentioned in the historical narratives after the time of David.' In the Talmud it is observed that Urim and Thummim were lacking in the Second Temple (TB Yoma 21 b), and this was probably a deduction from the non-mention of them in later historical narratives. It is more likely to be a deduction than a tradition.

[2] A. R. S. Kennedy, ibid., says: 'That the Urim and Thummim should reappear in the scheme of the Priestly Code is not surprising. It is part of its ideal reconstruction of the theocracy that the High Priest should be at all points fully equipped for his office as the Divine vicegerent in the theocracy . . . In any case it is clear from the principal passage, Ex 28³⁰, that it is rather a symbolical than a practical significance that is attached to the mysterious contents of the "pouch of judgment (or decision)".'

[3] In Ezra 2.63, Neh. 7.65, the possibility of the future use of Urim and Thummim is recognized, but we have no mention of any actual consultation.

[4] Cf. Acts 1.26.   [5] Cf. 1 Sam. 28.6.   [6] Gen. 28.10 ff.

[7] Gen. 20.3.   [8] Gen. 21.12 f.   [9] Gen. 21.13.

[10] Gen. 38.5 ff.   [11] Gen. 40.5 ff.   [12] Gen. 41.1 ff.

divine message in a dream at Bethel.[1] In the book of Daniel we
again find dreams figuring as the medium whereby the future
was divinely unfolded.[2] Here, once more, heathen kings needed
the help of Daniel to find the significance of their dreams,[3] and
even Daniel did not find the meaning of the vision of the four
beasts by his own skill in interpretation, but by the angelic
explanation which was itself part of the dream.[4]

There are passages which indicate that the prophets sometimes received their messages through dream experience.
Jeremiah seems to discount this source of revelation,[5] and to
link it more particularly with the false prophets of his own day.
He complains that they caused men to forget God by the dreams
which they recounted, and continues: 'The prophet who has a
dream let him tell the dream; but he who has my word, let him
speak my word faithfully.'[6] The possession of the word of God
would here seem to be contrasted with the dreaming of a dream.
In a familiar passage in the book of Numbers, however, while
Moses is contrasted with others in that God spoke to him
directly, and not in dreams,[7] it is recognized that to other
prophets genuine revelation from God could come through
dreams.[8] In all this, however, there is still nothing fundamentally unique in Israelite thought. Amongst other peoples
dreams have been held to be the medium of revelation, especially if the dream was experienced in a sacred spot, and the
interpretation of dreams has been elevated into a technique.[9]

Sometimes revelation was found to come through some
chance experience, though here the experience was rather the
occasion than the source of the message. Amos saw a basket of
summer fruit, and his mind sprang from the word *summer*,
ḳaiṣ, to the word *end*, ḳēṣ, and a message of judgement was given
to him.[10] Similarly, at his call Jeremiah saw an almond tree in
blossom, and as he lingered to look on its beauty his mind
passed from the word for *almond tree*, shāḳēdh, to the word
waking, shōḳēdh, and a message to men was born in his mind.[11]
In these cases the prophet was sure that it was by divine

---

[1] I Kings 3.4 ff.
[2] Dan. 2.1 ff., 4.4 ff., 7.1 ff., 8.1 ff., 10 ff.   [3] Dan. 2.25 ff., 4.8 ff.
[4] Dan. 7.16 ff.   [5] Jer. 23.27.   [6] Jer. 23.28.   [7] Num. 12.6.
[8] On the dream cf. E. L. Ehrlich, *Der Traum im Alten Testament* (B.Z.A.W. No. 73),
1953.
[9] Cf. R. Follet, *Verbum Domini*, xxxii, 1954, pp. 90 ff.
[10] Amos 8.1 ff.   [11] Jer. 1.11 f.

activity within him that the transition of thought came. Not always did the transition arise from some word play, as in these cases. When Amos saw the man standing by the wall with the lead in his hand,[1] or when Jeremiah saw the cauldron boiling over as the wind from the north fanned the flame,[2] or the potter at his wheel,[3] or the fig seller with two baskets of figs of very different quality,[4] these things became parables charged with a message to men, which the prophets believed to be a message from God.

Here, once more, we have something not unrelated to what may be found amongst other peoples. Professor Guillaume has cited examples from Arabia, where one who was appealed to for guidance on some problem let his eye light on any chance thing and found in it the clue to the answer.[5] Here this method was made a technique. The question was put to the technician and he used this method to discover the answer. There are cases in the Old Testament of resort to prophets with a question to which an answer from God is sought. When Saul went to Samuel to ask where his father's lost asses were,[6] or when Jeroboam sent his wife to Ahijah to inquire whether their child would recover,[7] it may be that the prophet employed some technique to discover the answer, though of this we have no information. Certainly in the cases found in the prophetic books, there is no reason to suppose that some question was presented to the prophet and that he let his eye seek the answer in this way. In all of them the initiative came from God, who sought the prophet through some simple, or even chance, experience.

To Hosea the divine revelation came through a more sustained and more poignant experience. Few Old Testament

---

[1] Amos 7.7 ff. The word *'anāk* is rendered by 'plumbline' in the English Versions, and this meaning is defended by J. Morgenstern, *Amos Studies*, i, 1941, p. 83, and V. Maag, *Text, Wortschatz und Begriffswelt des Buches Amos*, 1951, p. 66. Cf. also K. Cramer, *Amos* (B.W.A.N.T., iii, 15), 1930, p. 45. The LXX understood the word to mean 'adamant', and this is defended by A. Condamin, *R.B.*, ix, 1900, pp. 586 ff., where it is argued that the picture is of one with a sword in his hand. H. Junker (*Biblica*, xvii, 1936, pp. 359 ff.) objects to the rendering 'plumbline', on the ground that this is used only in building and not in destruction. He therefore holds that what is in mind is molten lead, poured out as a destroying stream. A. van Hoonacker (*Les douze Petits Prophètes* [E. Bib.], p. 266) took a similar view, but changed the word *ḥômath* ('wall') to *ḥammath* ('heat') to accord with it.
[2] Jer. 1.13 ff.   [3] Jer. 18.1 ff.   [4] Jer. 24.1 ff.
[5] Cf. *Prophecy and Divination*, pp. 117 ff.   [6] I Sam. 9.6.   [7] I Kings 14.1 ff.

questions have been more discussed, or have received a wider variety of answers, than that of Hosea's marriage.[1] To discuss it here is impossible, and I must be content to indicate that I accept the view that the wife whom Hosea deeply loved was unfaithful to him, and that her infidelity brought him intense anguish yet without destroying his love, so that he found God approaching him through his agony to illumine his mind with an understanding of the depth of the divine love for Israel that is unsurpassed in the Old Testament. Not by the things that he saw, but by the things that he suffered, he was lifted into the heart of God.

In all this there is nothing to suggest that every experience is sent by God or reflects his will. The prophets continually declared that much was directly contrary to the will of God. The murder of Abel,[2] of Uriah,[3] or of Naboth[4] could not be thought of as anything but an offence against God. Not all human experience is the medium of divine revelation. It is when God chooses to make it the medium of revelation that it may become so, and before it can become so there is needed a man of sensitive spirit to receive the revelation.

Similarly, in the life of the community, while it was believed that God could use the corporate experience to express his warning or approval, it is nowhere suggested that all human history reflects his will, or that history in itself is the medium of revelation. For its interpretation a prophetic person was needed, just as much as for the dream. It was believed that God could speak thus to men, not only by his control of the forces of Nature, but by the fortunes of the nation at the hands of its neighbours. The Deuteronomic school believed that defeat in war and oppression at the hands of alien powers could be the instrument of divine rebuke for disloyalty and apostasy,[5] and the prophets of the pre-exilic age frequently promised conquest and suffering at the hands of the great contemporary powers as the consequence of the disobedience to God which they discerned in the life of their times. They were not teaching a

[1] For a brief indication of the variety of answers and of the writers who have given them, cf. *The Servant of the Lord*, p. 115 f. This is treated more fully in a paper to be published in *B.J.R.L.*, September, 1956.
[2] Gen. 4.6.   [3] II Sam. 11.14 ff.   [4] I Kings 21.8 ff.
[5] Cf. Deut. 28.7 ff., and the recurring formula in the framework of the book of Judges, indicating that foreign oppression followed religious infidelity.

passive resignation to all as the will of God, but seeking to make the experience spiritually profitable, and to rouse men to the active seeking for God and obedience to his will.

Yet another medium of revelation was the written word. In the story of Sinai the first tables of stone were written by the finger of God,[1] but when these were destroyed by Moses in his anger they were rewritten by the hand of Moses.[2] Their content was still the revelation of God's will. In the time of Josiah a lawbook was found in the Temple,[3] and it immediately became the basis of the reform which Josiah seems already to have begun, as the religious side of his bid for freedom when the Assyrian empire was tottering to its fall. The lawbook was believed to have divine authority, and to express God's will for the nation. When Ezra came from the Persian court to Jerusalem he carried a lawbook in his hand,[4] and while he had authority from the Persian king to put its provisions into effect, it was believed to derive its real authority from God. Both of these lawbooks are believed to be embodied in the Pentateuch, and many other books beside the Pentateuch gradually came to be regarded by the Jews as sacred, until the collection which we know as the Old Testament came into being. Of the variety and richness of its contents there is no need to speak here. It preserved the work of historians, prophets, singers and sages. But beyond that it was believed to preserve the word of God. It was not merely an anthology of the wisdom of Israel. It was treasured as a religious collection, through which God spoke to men.

The prophet Jeremiah appears to have been an enthusiastic supporter of Josiah's reform,[5] and to have gone through the land advocating the acceptance of the lawbook that had been found. But he became less enthusiastic later, when he realized that just as false prophets could speak a word which had no deeper foundation than their own hearts, so a written word could be made the vehicle of human thoughts while purporting to be the word of God. He spoke of the lying pen of the scribes which falsified the word,[6] and saw that a written word was open to abuse no less than a spoken. Like all the prophets he

---

[1] Ex. 31.18.   [2] Ex. 34.1, 4.   [3] II Kings 22.8.   [4] Ezra 7.14.
[5] Cf. *Studies in Old Testament Prophecy* (ed. by H. H. Rowley), 1950, pp. 171 ff.. where this disputed question is discussed.
[6] Jer. 8.8.

was more eager to see the submission of heart and life to the will of God than any formal observance of rites and ceremonies, and he looked for the day when God's word should be inscribed on men's hearts, and belong to the very texture of their personality.[1] To him the final revelation of God was not to be sought in a book, but in personality. Nevertheless we must include the written word in the media of revelation in Old Testament thought. To the Jews this whole collection brought the revelation of God, and the Pentateuch was especially sacred as the vehicle of the expression of his will. The Christian Church accepted the Old Testament from Judaism, and continued to regard it as a far more significant medium of revelation than any of those others so far mentioned.

The sacred book is not peculiar to Israel, however, and other religions regard the written word as the medium of revelation. Especially is this so with Mohammedanism, which carries the belief in the verbal inspiration of the Qur'an to the extreme.

I have said that to Jeremiah the final revelation of God was to be sought in personality, and he looked forward to the day when that revelation would be universal. Meanwhile, such revelation was found in outstanding personalities. For certain purposes the king was, or at any rate should be, the instrument of God's will. When he was *en rapport* with the spirit of God, the national well-being was thought to be assured. The spirit of God was believed to be in him, directing him. He was the anointed of God and as such he represented God to the nation in some aspects of its life. He also represented the nation before God, and its life was bound up intimately with his.[2] Not all kings were thus *en rapport* with the spirit of God, and many stand

---

[1] Jer. 31.31 ff. This passage is denied to Jeremiah by some modern editors (so B. Stade, *Geschichte des Volkes Israel*, 2nd ed., i, 1889, pp. 646 f. n., R. Smend *Lehrbuch der alttestamentlichen Religionsgeschichte*, 2nd ed., 1899, pp. 249 ff., and B. Duhm, *Jeremia* (K.H.C.), 1901, pp. 254 f.). Others, however, defend its authenticity, and I am of their number (so F. Giesebrecht, *Jeremia* (H.K.), 1894, p. 165, A. S. Peake, *Jeremiah and Lamentations* (Cent. B.), ii, pp. 68 ff., 101 ff., A. W. Streane, *Jeremiah and Lamentations* (Camb. B.), 1913, p. 195, L. E. Binns, *Jeremiah* (West. C.), 1919, pp. 241 ff., J. Skinner, *Prophecy and Religion*, 1922 pp. 320 ff., G. A. Smith, *Jeremiah*, 3rd ed., 1924, pp. 374 ff., P. Volz, *Jeremia* (K.A.T.), 2nd ed., 1928, p. 284, F. Nötscher, *Jeremias* (H.S.A.T.), 1934, p. 236, W. Rudolph, *Jeremia* (H.A.T.), 1947, pp. 170 f.). Peake (op. cit., p. 70) expresses 'an unshaken conviction that though in its present form we may owe it to Baruch, the prophecy itself comes from Jeremiah and from no other, and is the worthy crown of his teaching.'

[2] On the position of the king and its significance cf. J. Pedersen, *Israel III-IV*, 1940, pp. 76 ff.

condemned. They are condemned not merely because they were bad men, but because by being such they failed to fulfil the true function of their kingship.

Beside them were priests, who again by their function were designed to be media of revelation. There were bad priests, as there were bad kings, who did not fulfil their function, and we are accustomed to think of priests as inherently evil. We should not forget that there were bad prophets, who also stand condemned, and we should not think of prophets only at their best and of priests only at their worst. The priest was not merely the technician of sacrifice. The sacred lot was consulted through him.[1] He was also the custodian of sacred tradition, able to give guidance in innumerable ways to men in the ordinary affairs of life. To him men went for *tôrāh*, for instruction in the way of God.[2] The statutes and ordinances of God were in his charge, in days before any written word was available to them. He was the arbiter of justice in a wide variety of cases, and the administration of justice was a religious function in Israel.[3] For justice truly administered was the expression of the will of God.

More significant than king or priest for us, however, is the prophet. Like the king and the priest, he was not peculiar to Israel.[4] The Egyptian story of Wen-amon brings before us a prophet similar to some of the early Israelite prophets, who was found at Byblos in the eleventh century B.C.[5] Moreover, we now have evidence of prophets at Mari much earlier than this.[6] The beginnings of prophecy in Israel were not all very exalted. The ecstatic groups which figure in the story of the time of the founding of the monarchy were not composed of

---

[1] Cf. I Sam. 14.36 ff.

[2] On the meaning of *tôrāh*, cf. H. Wheeler Robinson, in *Law and Religion*, ed. by E. I. J. Rosenthal, 1938, pp. 50 ff., and G. Östborn, *Tōrā in the Old Testament*, 1945.

[3] Cf., e.g., Ex. 18.16.

[4] Cf. A. Neher, *L'Essence du Prophétisme*, 1955, pp. 17 ff., and N. H. Ridderbos, *Israëls Profetie en 'Profetie' buiten Israël*, 1955.

[5] The story of Wen-amon may be found in English translation in A. Erman, *The Literature of the Ancient Egyptians*, E.Tr. by A. M. Blackman, 1927, pp. 174 ff., or in *A.N.E.T.*, 1950, pp. 25 ff. (translated by J. A. Wilson).

[6] Cf. A. Lods, in *Studies in Old Testament Prophecy*, ed. by H. H. Rowley, pp. 103 ff.; M. Noth, *B.J.R.L.*, xxxii, 1949–50, pp. 194 ff., and *Geschichte und Gotteswort im Alten Testament*, 1950; F.M.Th. de Liagre Böhl, in *Ned.T.T.*, iv, 1949–50, pp. 82 ff.; W. von Soden, *Die Welt des Orients*, 1950, pp. 397 ff.; and H. Schmökel, *Th.L.Z.*, lxxvi, 1950, cols. 64 ff.

men of the stature of the greater prophets. When Saul was caught up into a prophetic frenzy, he stripped off his clothes and rolled about on the ground all night naked.[1] When we find him liable to break out into fits of uncontrolled passion indistinguishable from madness, so that he could hurl javelins at people who happened to be before him, the same verb is used which elsewhere describes the behaviour of the prophet.[2] If this were all there were to prophecy, it would not provide a very impressive medium of divine revelation. There would not appear to be much to differentiate this type of prophecy from that of the Baal prophets who danced about and gashed themselves with knives.[3] The Hebrew prophets were the devotees of Yahweh as the Baal prophets were the devotees of their god, and both believed that they were acting under the influence of their deity.

The essence of prophecy is not to be found in its forms of manifestation,[4] however, and when we come to the higher prophecy which is found in the great figures of the Old Testament, it is not of the behaviour of the prophet that we think. Some modern writers have claimed that all the prophets were ecstatic,[5] and that every oracle was received by the prophet in some abnormal experience. While this seems to me very improbable, it is undeniable that even the great prophets acted sometimes in ways that would be thought strange today. When Jeremiah appeared in the Temple wearing a wooden yoke,[6] his behaviour was similar to that of Zedekiah the son of Chenaanah, who appeared before Ahab wearing horns of iron.[7] Isaiah walked the streets of Jerusalem naked and barefoot,[8] and Ezekiel performed many strange acts. But when we think of the prophets we think rather of the content of their message than of the forms whereby it was proclaimed. When the Old Testament offers us any clear indication of the essence of prophecy, it does so in terms of the utterance of the divine word. When Aaron is

---

[1] I Sam. 19.24.   [2] I Sam. 18.10 f.   [3] I Kings 18.28.
[4] Cf. my study of 'The Nature of Old Testament Prophecy in the Light of Recent Study', in *The Servant of the Lord*, pp. 91 ff.
[5] Cf. H. Gunkel, *The Expositor*, 9th series, i, 1924, p. 538; 'The fundamental experience in all types of prophecy is ecstasy'; W. Jacobi, *Die Ekstase der alttestamentlichen Propheten*, 1920, p. 4; 'Die Ekstase zum Wesen des Propheten gehört'. On this view cf. the reserves I have expressed in the above mentioned article. Cf. also P. van Imschoot, *Théologie de l'Ancien Testament*, i, pp. 170 ff.
[6] Jer. 27 f.   [7] I Kings 22.11.   [8] Isa. 20.2 f.

called the prophet of Moses, with Moses playing the part of
God to him, it is made clear that this means that Moses will
give Aaron the content of his message, which Aaron will then
deliver.[1] The prophet is described as one who is privileged to
stand in the council of God,[2] and who therefore understands
his will. At his call Jeremiah is assured that God has put his
words in his mouth,[3] and when Jeremiah condemns the false
prophets it is because they speak their own word and not God's.[4]
The essential function of the prophet was conceived to be the
mediation of a word which he received by divine inspiration.
He was the mouthpiece of God bringing some *ad hoc* word
relevant to the circumstances of the moment when he delivered
it. But since the inspiration came through the organ of the
prophet's personality, it bore the marks of that personality as
well as of the God who was its source. Hence not all the prophets were of the same stature, and there are varieties of level
even within the prophetic books.

Other religions provide examples of prophetic personality,
and we may recognize a genuine prophetic character in Con-
fucius and Buddha and Zoroaster and Mohammed. What gives
to Old Testament prophecy its unique quality is the richness of
the divine revelation mediated through its greater figures. The
prophets were far from perfect men, and we have no need to
idealize them to heighten their glory. They were men who
knew the intimacy of fellowship with God to whom something
of his spirit was given, men who looked on the world in the
light of what they had seen in the heart of God, men who spoke
because they had to and not because they wanted to, upon
whom the constraint of God had been laid, and men who
delivered a word not alone relevant to the needs of the hour,
but of enduring importance to men. Just as we must penetrate
beneath the outward behaviour of the prophet to his inner
spirit, so we must strip his word of that which ties it to the
situation of his day and perceive its enduring content which
may be clothed afresh in the terms of our contemporary situation, before we can realize his true significance.

---

[1] Ex. 7.1; cf. 4.16.
[2] Cf. Amos 3.7; Jer. 23.18, 22.   [3] Jer. 1.9.
[4] Jer. 23.16, 21, 26. On the false prophets cf. G. von Rad, *Z.A.W.*, li (N.F.x),
1933, pp. 109 ff., K. Harms, *Die falschen Propheten*, 1947, and G. Quell, *Wahre und
falsche Propheten* (B.F.C.Th., xlvi,1), 1952.

None of the media of revelation so far mentioned is unique in kind in the Old Testament. We may regard the content of the revelation as superior to that given in other religions, and at the content we shall look in the succeeding lectures. But there is nothing unique about the media. Revelation in Nature or through divination, through a written word or through experience, or through inspired leaders, can be found elsewhere, and it is often thought that there is nothing unique in biblical revelation, save in the loftiness of its content. We think of it as prophetic religion because it was mediated through Moses and the prophets and through our Lord; and we think of it as revelation which came through history. What is less often realized is that there is a unique medium of revelation found in the Bible. This is a combination of historical and personal factors which dovetail into one another. To this I have more than once directed attention,[1] and it is both relevant and important to do so again here. Beyond revelation through prophetic personality, which is found constantly in the Old Testament, we find revelation through a complex of personality and event in certain moments of special significance in the biblical story.

The first of these concerns the Exodus from Egypt. We may read this simply as a historical event, and find in it one of the biblical examples of the activity of God on the plane of history. We then see in the story no more than the Israelite idea that God had come to their help, just as other peoples have often believed their God came to their help. In the days of the Spanish Armada our fathers cried 'He blew with his winds and scattered them'. In the deliverance from Egypt the wind is said to have played a part,[2] and the sceptic may dismiss the one claim as the other by supposing that a chance circumstance of Nature happily coincided with the need of people, who then turned their good fortune into a supposed act of God. But the deliverance from Egypt was quite different in character from the deliverance from the Armada, and while I am prepared to find the hand of God in many events of history, I am not prepared to ignore the peculiar elements in the story of the deliverance under Moses in order to equate it with what is essentially different.

[1] Cf. *The Authority of the Bible*, pp. 12 ff., and *The Unity of the Bible*, pp. 16, 66.
[2] Ex. 14.21a, 26 f.

The story of the deliverance from Egypt does not begin at the point where the Israelites stood before the sea with the pursuing hosts of Pharaoh behind. It begins with the divine commission to Moses to go into Egypt to bring the people out.[1] In the wilderness this man had a great spiritual experience which left him in no doubt that Yahweh was sending him into Egypt to bring the Israelites out. I am not concerned to explain or to rationalize the incident of the Burning Bush, but merely to recognize the essential fact that Moses was sure God was calling him to this task. To some scholars Moses has seemed an unhistorical character,[2] but it seems incredible to me that he could have been created by chance tradition. In many ways tradition may have developed the story, but in its broad lines it seems to me to bear the marks of its own truth. Moses is said to have belonged to the people who were oppressed in Egypt, and to have fled from Egypt into the wilderness. This might seem to offer some explanation of his return to lead the people out, but it offers no explanation of his doing so in the name of a God called Yahweh. The Bible itself declares that the people in Egypt would not recognize this as the name of their God,[3] and this is borne out by the fact that after their deliverance they make a covenant with this God. Yahweh sends Moses into Egypt and adopts the oppressed Israelites as his people. Such a story is hardly likely to have been invented by the Israelites.[4] Had they invented the story they would have been more likely to ascribe their deliverance to the God they had hitherto

---

[1] Ex. 3.7 ff.

[2] Cf. H. Winckler, *Die Keilinschriften und das Alte Testament*, 3rd ed., 1903, p. 209; E. Meyer, *Die Israeliten und ihre Nachbarstämme*, 1906, p. 451, n.; G. Hölscher, *Geschichte der israelitischen und jüdischen Religion*, 1922, pp. 64 ff. M. Noth allows him but a small and nebulous place in history. He says (*Geschichte Israels*, 2nd ed., 1954, p. 128): 'Mose mit dem Sinaivorgang geschichtlich nichts zu tun gehabt hat. Ihn als den Organisator und Gesetzgeber Israels zu bezeichnen, ist danach geschichtlich kaum haltbar. Auch darin also bleibt der Sinaivorgang für uns geheimnisvoll, dass wir keine menschliche Gestalt zu nennen wissen, die in das dort Geschehende handelnd oder deutend eingegriffen hätte.'

[3] Ex. 6.3.

[4] P. Volz, when he published the first edition of his *Mose* (1907), was uncertain whether any historical event lay at the foundation of the religion of Israel. He said (p. 88): 'Unsicher ist, ob die Religionsstiftung auf irgend einem geschichtlichen Ereignis fusst und auf welchem'. In the second edition (1932), however, he revised his opinion, and said: 'Die mosaische Religion und damit die gesamte alttestamentliche Religion ist eine geschichtliche Religion, nicht eine Naturreligion. Sie ist an einem bestimmten Ort zu einer bestimmten Zeit vom einem bestimmten Person in einem bestimmten Verband gegrundet worden. Sie beruht auf geschichtlichen Tatsachen' (p. 72).

worshipped. Had the mission of Moses arisen merely from his own heart and his sympathy with his suffering fellows, he might have been expected to present himself before them in the name of their God. Instead he went with the confidence that he was sent by Yahweh. Arrived in Egypt he promised them a deliverance which he was powerless to achieve, and which was not to be achieved by their efforts. Indeed, their efforts play no part whatever in the story. He speaks as a prophet, announcing a word of God. His word is not like that of many a commander before a battle, promising the help of God, and stimulating men to superhuman bravery, so that while they might attribute their deliverance to God they could not but feel that they, too, had had some part in it. His word promises a deliverance which neither he nor they can bring to pass. When they are actually on the way out of Egypt and Pharaoh pursues them, Moses again promises deliverance, but not by his own hand or theirs. The people do not turn to fight Pharaoh and vanquish him. If they had done so, we may be sure their traditions would have cherished the memory of it. The deliverance came by the timely help of wind and wave, clearing a way across the sands by which they could escape but covering it again before the chariots of Pharaoh could follow them to the other side. To regard this timely help as a chance coincidence offers no explanation of the return of Moses to Egypt, or the confidence he had known that Yahweh would deliver the people. Neither could his confidence control the powers of Nature and bring about the timely help. Both sides of this story must be remembered. There was the prophetic personality of the man who appeared in the name of God to promise a deliverance he and the Israelites were helpless to effect; and there was the historic event of the deliverance which responded to his prior promise. There was more than the chance coincidence of help in the nick of time. There was also the strange fact that this timely help vindicated the prior faith of a man who profoundly believed that he was the mouthpiece of God. Discount either side of this and the story is left more incredible than it is in the Bible. No people would invent the story that their fathers had been oppressed slaves in a foreign land if it were not true. No people would invent the story that it had been delivered by a God it had not hitherto worshipped if it had not strong grounds for believing that it was true. And no man would needlessly complicate his task of delivering a company of slaves by the strange story that he had been sent by a god whose name they had never acknowledged as the name of their god unless he had been profoundly convinced that this was true. Discount the call of Moses, and we are left with no reasonable explanation of his strange errand, or basis for his confidence of success that no material power was at any point invoked to achieve.

This story, in which personal and impersonal factors are woven together, in which God's control of Nature and activity in history are combined with his activity through prophetic personality, carries in its texture a revelation of the character of God at which we must look in the next lecture. Moses, who had announced the delivery, also interpreted its significance; but the significance is not artificially imposed upon the story. Nor does this story stand alone, though it is by far the most important in the whole of the Old Testament. We may look more briefly at two other examples.

In the time of Deborah, the Israelites north and south of the Vale of Esdraelon were being reduced to subjection piecemeal by their Canaanite neighbours.[1] This prophetess, acting under a constraint which she believed to be of God, took the lead in bringing together a gathering of many Israelite tribes from both sides of the vale, in the confidence that God would aid them. Their foes were far better armed and equipped with dreaded chariots, and all the advantages apparently lay with them. Yet in the battle a great and resounding victory was won by the Israelites. At first sight this might seem to be an ordinary case of using religion to stir the valour of men, and so to create a morale that then issued in victory. Here, however, the most important factors were not the human factors, and though human valour was displayed the victory was primarily due to natural forces which came to the help of Israel. A sudden deluge turned the plain into a morass, and rendered the chariots a liability, and the Kishon was rapidly turned into a flood which swept away those who tried to cross it. It was not Sisera's bad generalship, or Israelite military genius, which gained the victory, but forces wholly beyond man's control. And once more these conditions occurred in response to the prophetic

[1] Judg. 4 f.

word of Deborah, as well as in the moment of Israel's need. It is easy to offer a psychological explanation of victories· gained under the impetus of religious enthusiasm kindled by a prophet. But no psychological explanation will suffice here, since the weather is not subject to psychological control. Nor will any theory of coincidence suffice, since coincidence could not explain the prior faith and promise of Deborah.

The second example is the deliverance of Jerusalem from Sennacherib in the time of Hezekiah. When the foe had overrun all the surrounding country and his armies proudly stood before the gates of the city demanding surrender, Isaiah counselled the king not to yield and promised deliverance.[1] No calculation of resources could have inspired his confidence, nor can the prophet be supposed to have been a rabid nationalist who blindly trusted in the fortunes of his people. Isaiah could often denounce his own people, and more often uttered the unpopular word than the popular. He had opposed the rebellion against Assyria, and had warned that it could lead to no good. Yet when disaster was almost complete, he had confidence. That confidence was wholly prophetic confidence. That is to say, it was confidence born of a constraint which he believed to be of God, and it was confidence in God. He did not summon men to activity and heroism, but to quiet waiting for the salvation which God would achieve.[2] Here, as in the case of the deliverance from Egypt, the people of the city played no real part in the deliverance. All they were called to do was to have confidence and see the salvation of God. This time it was brought about by a plague which broke out in the camp of Sennacherib and carried off large numbers of his troops.[3] This is not the only time in history in which sickness has determined the issue of a campaign, nor even the only time when this has happened in that particular part of the world.[4] Like wind and weather, plague was beyond human control, and Isaiah's confidence could not bring it about. But here, once more, no theory of a chance coincidence can offer an explanation. It

---

[1] Isa. 37.21 ff.   [2] Isa. 30.15.
[3] Isa. 37.36, where the destroying angel is symbolic of the plague, just as in II Sam. 24.16, the sparing of the city of Jerusalem from the plague which had spread elsewhere through the land is symbolized by the stopping of the angel at the threshing floor of Araunah.
[4] Cf. G. A. Smith, *The Historical Geography of the Holy Land*, 22nd ed., pp. 157 ff.

cannot explain the prior faith and promise of Isaiah, who spoke not in his own name, but God's, and not as one who could invoke God's name to give a spurious authority to his own wishes, but as one whose whole prophetic career proved the sincerity of his faith.

In both of these examples, though in different ways, as also in the example of the Exodus, we find personal and impersonal factors woven together in what the Hebrews believed to be God's manifestation of himself. The medium of revelation here is not to be found in the separate factors, but in their combination into a single complex.

Such a complex we find also in the New Testament. My theme in these lectures is the Old Testament, but I may be forgiven if I occasionally pass over into the New, since I am persuaded that the two Testaments belong together. Christians see in Jesus one who is a prophet and more than a prophet, through whom the revelation of God comes in human personality. That revelation is given not only in his life and word, however, but also in his death—a death which was brought upon him by the action of his enemies. This does not mean that death was the interruption and frustration of his work. On the contrary, it was its crown and climax. Before it took place he had foreseen it, and had assured his disciples that it would be charged with unique power.[1] That his death has been charged with unique power is a matter of history. Once again, therefore, we have the prior word of one who claimed to speak the word of God and the vindication of his word in a subsequent history, which his word could not control unless it really was the word of God. Those who put him to death expressed in that act the evil purpose of their own hearts, and believed that they were extinguishing him and his claims. Not through natural forces or disease did the factors independent of the prophetic personality of Jesus come in here, but through the malevolence of other men. The supreme revelation of the love of God and the supreme demonstration of the power of God in salvation, subsequently proved in the experience of countless millions of men, came in this combination of person and event, and the pattern of revelation is similar to that of the manifestations of God's power at which we have looked in the Old Testament.

[1] Mark 8.31, 9.31, 10.45, and parallels; cf. John 12.32.

Moreover, this revelation is not unrelated to that given in the Old Testament. It is both impossible and unnecessary here to speak of all the ways in which Old Testament hopes are fulfilled in Christ and his Church. In the Old Testament we find the prophetic delineation of the Suffering Servant,[1] whose mission should be fulfilled by the organ of his death, and who was charged with the task of carrying the light of the true religion through all the world.[2] His death is described as a sacrifice,[3] superior to any offered in the Temple in that it was the offering of one who was without moral blemish,[4] and wider in its efficacy in that it availed for Gentiles who confessed that his sufferings should really have been theirs.[5] In remarkable ways this finds its realization in Christ, whose death has been the organ of his world-wide mission, and before whose Cross multitudes have felt that the words the prophet put in the mouths of men who saw the sufferings of the Servant were alone adequate to express their confession. There is the prophetic anticipation and the subsequent fulfilment in history that the prophet himself was powerless to effect by any human means, and personal factors and factors objective so far as the prophet himself was concerned are interwoven together. In the other cases the prophetic word and the vindication in history were closely linked in time. Here they were widely separated in time, but the pattern of revelation was the same. The fulfilment of the prophetic hope came in the person of Jesus, in whose life and death we have found the supreme example of the same pattern in swifter succession.[6]

Moreover, it is not without significance that the sacrifice of the Servant stands in the prophetic canon. The sacrifices prescribed in the law continued until this prophecy of a greater and more efficacious sacrifice was fulfilled in Christ. To his followers his death gathered into itself the meaning of all lesser

---

[1] Isa. 52.13–53.12.   [2] Isa. 49.5.

[3] Isa. 53.10. We have not merely the use of the word '*āshām* in this verse, but the sacrificial character of the thought of the whole song; cf. *The Unity of the Bible*, pp. 55 f.

[4] Isa. 53.9.   [5] Isa. 53.4 f.

[6] It is important to observe that this is not merely a simple prediction and its fulfilment. The prediction gathers into itself various elements of Old Testament thought, and is linked with both the sacrificial and the missionary ideas found elsewhere. The fulfilment gathers into itself not alone this passage, but others also, and the response to the thought and promise of the Old Testament is highly complex. Cf. *The Unity of the Bible*, pp. 90 ff.

sacrifices and they were no longer needed. Jewish Christians continued to sacrifice as Jews, but Gentile Christians were not brought into relation with the sacrifices of the Jerusalem Temple. For the Church sacrifice was superseded in the sacrifice which fulfilled the promise of the Old Testament, and the sacrifices of the law were no longer necessary. For the Jew also the sacrifices of the law soon ceased because the Temple itself was destroyed and it was no longer possible to offer them. For the Church the supersession of sacrifice was based on the authority of a new revelation which came with the same marks of divine origin as the old revelation, and which fulfilled the promise of the old revelation itself. The faith of the Church that no other sacrifice was needed has been for nearly nineteen centuries shared by Judaism, but only because the cruel hand of circumstance denied Jews the possibility of sacrifice on the one spot allowed by the law. Here, once more, a faith which was born in men who believed they were acting under divine guidance has been confirmed by a subsequent event, which their faith had no part in bringing about, and we have something of the same pattern of revelation that we have found in these other examples.

God has revealed himself in many ways, and in the thought of the Old Testament that variety is reflected. If we leave out of account divination, which figures but little and decreasingly there, we are left with ways whereby God still speaks to men. His voice is still heard in Nature and in history, in individual experience and in the personality of men and women who are attuned to his spirit. Through each of these separately his voice may be heard, and much of the message of the Old Testament was mediated through prophetic personality. Of greater significance than any of these separately, however, is that combination of factors dovetailing into one another, wherein the most distinctive medium of revelation in biblical thought and experience is to be found.

II

THE NATURE OF GOD

THE thought of the Old Testament is centred in God.[1] Yet there is nowhere any effort to prove that God exists. For the God of the Old Testament is the God of experience and not of speculation. It was not because some postulate of thought led men to think of a first cause that they turned to the thought of God. They no more questioned his being than they questioned the reality of the world around them and of themselves. The philosopher may raise doubts about the reality of all things, but the plain man is content to base his belief in the reality of the world on his experience, however illusory the philosopher may tell him it is. So the Hebrew was content to base his belief in the existence of God on what seemed to him to be the experience of God granted to himself or to his people, and especially on the experience of God given to the nation in the great moments of its history. At some of those moments we looked in the previous lecture, and they provided impressive reasons for believing in God.

It is true that from time immemorial the ancestors of the Israelites, like most other peoples in the world, had taken the existence of some god or gods for granted. But the faith of the Old Testament is not based on such a thought. It is based on the belief that God had played a part in Israel's history, and had chosen her for himself, and that he had declared his will to her. He was a postulate of experience rather than of thought. When Amos felt the impulse to prophesy, he found it as in-

---

[1] On the subject of this lecture cf. W. Eichrodt, *Theologie des Alten Testaments*, i, 3rd ed., 1948, pp. 81 ff.; L. Koehler, *Theologie des Alten Testaments*, 3rd ed., 1953, pp. 2 ff.; P. Heinisch, *Theology of the Old Testament*, E. Tr. by W. Heidt, 1950, pp. 48 ff.; M. Burrows, *An Outline of Biblical Theology*, 1946, pp. 54 ff.; Th.C. Vriezen, *Hoofdlijnen der Theologie van het Oude Testament*, 2nd ed., 1954, pp. 159 ff.; O. J. Baab, *The Theology of the Old Testament*, 1949, pp. 23 ff.; O. Procksch, *Theologie des Alten Testaments*, 1950, pp. 420 ff.; P. van Imschoot, *Théologie de l'Ancien Testament*, i, *Dieu*, 1954.

escapable as the catch at the heart on hearing the roar of the
lion in the open country. 'When the lion roars, who will not
fear? When the Lord Yahweh speaks, who can but prophesy?'[1]
No man who hears the roar of the lion near him will turn to
philosophy to ask whether there is any such objective reality as
the lion; and no man who has had experience of God is concerned to ask whether the philosopher will allow him to believe
in God. Where we find atheism in the Old Testament, it is
rather a practical atheism than a theoretical atheism. 'The
wicked, in the haughtiness of his countenance, saith, He will
not require it. All his thoughts are, There is no God'.[2] This is
not a speculative denial of the existence of God, but the
thought that God is not interested in men and can be left out
of account. A few verses below in the same psalm the wicked
says in his heart 'God has forgotten; he hides his face, he will

[1] Amos 3.8.

[2] Ps. 10.4. The rendering here substantially follows R.V. There is, however, an
extraordinary variety of interpretation of this verse in modern translations and
commentaries. R.S.V. has 'In the pride of his countenance he does not seek him;
all his thoughts are, "There is no God".' This is in substantial agreement with
A.V., and a similar view is taken by W. O. E. Oesterley (*The Psalms*, i, 1939,
p. 143), save that he adds here two words from the previous verse and renders:
'The wicked contemneth, in the pride of his countenance, Yahweh, seeketh
(him) not.' Some editors take the words rendered 'in the pride of his countenance'
to refer to God, and so render 'According to the height of his anger he will not
require'; so G. R. Berry, *The Book of Psalms*, 1934, p. 36, following B. Duhm,
Die Psalmen (K.H.C.), 1899, p 31 (cf. H. Pérennès, *Les Psaumes*, 1922, p. 20,
C. Mercier, in *La Bible du Centenaire*, iii, 1947, p. 9, and E. Podechard, *Le Psautier:
Traduction . . . et explication . . .*, i, 1949, p. 48). This view agrees with R.V. in
finding the thought to be that God will not punish the wrongdoer, rather than
that the latter will not seek God. W. E. Barnes, *Psalms* (West. C.), i, 1931, p. 45,
renders: 'The wicked in his angry pride careth not'; similarly J. Calès, *Le Livre
des Psaumes*, i, 1936, p. 153 (*in arrogantia sua non curat de eo*). In substantial agreement with R.V. are F. Baethgen, *Die Psalmen* (H.K.), 1897, p. 26, A. B. Ehrlich,
Die Psalmen, 1905, p. 20, C. A. Briggs, *Psalms* (I.C.C.), i, 1907, p. 77, H. Gunkel,
Die Psalmen (H.K.), 1926, p. 31, F. Zorell, *Psalterium ex hebraeo latinum*, 2nd ed.,
1939, p. 22, C. Lattey, *The Psalter in the Westminster Version*, 1945, p. 15, F. M. Th.
Böhl, *De Psalmen* (T.U.), i, 1946, p. 50, B. Bonkamp, *Die Psalmen*, 1949, p. 76,
E. A. Leslie, *The Psalms*, 1949, p. 221, E. Pannier and H. Renard, *Les Psaumes*
(Pirot-Clamer, La Sainte Bible), 1950, p. 92, and R. Tournay and R. Schwab,
Les Psaumes (Jerusalem Bible), 1950, p. 90; cf. also H. Schmidt, *Die Psalmen*
(H.A.T.), 1934, p. 15. It is curious to find R.S.V. rejecting the interpretation of
R.V., while the new Biblical Institute Latin translation turns from the Vulgate.
Exacerbavit Dominum peccator; secundum multitudinem viae suae non quaeret, to agree
closely with R.V. in its rendering *Ait impius in superbia mentis: 'Non vindicabit; non
est Deus': haec est omnis cogitatio eius* (*Liber Psalmorum cum Canticis Breviarii Romani*,
2nd ed., 1945, p. 14). A. F. Kirkpatrick, *Psalms* (Camb. B.), 1906 ed., p. 52,
observes that decisive for the understanding of 'he will not seek' of God's visitation
of man's wickedness is verse 13, which R.S.V. renders: 'Why does the wicked
renounce God, and say in his heart, "Thou wilt not call to account"?', where
the same verb is used. Similarly Gunkel, op. cit., p. 38.

not notice.'[1] It is an atheism born in the will and not in the mind.[2] Hence the answer of the Old Testament writers is not to offer reasons for belief in God, but to rebuke the wicked will and to invoke punishment rather than instruction. To them the proof of God's existence was not in man's reasoning but in God's own activity.

The fact of God is less important than the character he is perceived to have.[3] The belief in the existence of God is common to many religions, however that belief may have been reached. Where they differ is in their conception of the nature and character of God. In Israel, as we shall see, the profoundest elements of the conception of God were found in the texture of the revelation, rather than in men's thought about God. Those elements were developed in the teaching of the prophets, who claimed that they were the mouthpiece of God, but their seeds were found long before the rise of the eighth and seventh century prophets in one of those combinations of personal and impersonal factors at which we looked in the previous lecture, and to which we shall have to return.

First, however, we may observe that a variety of terms for God may be found in the Old Testament. In its opening words we read 'In the beginning God created'.[4] Here the term used for God is 'Elôhîm, a word which is of plural form, and which is sometimes used of foreign deities and translated *gods*.[5] In the great majority of its occurrences, however, it is rendered God, and refers to the Israelite deity. Of itself, therefore, its use neither demands nor excludes a monotheistic view. It is probable that the term took its rise in a polytheistic *milieu*, but in the most ancient texts of the Bible it is already used of a single God,

[1] Ps. 10.11.

[2] J. Bonsirven (*Le Judaïsme palestinien au temps de Jésus-Christ*, i, 1934, p. 114) cites some passages in I Enoch (38.2, 41.2, 45.2, 46.7, 63.7, 48.10) which refer to those 'who deny the name the Lord of Spirits'. B. Gärtner (*The Areopagus Speech and Natural Religion*, 1955, p. 104 n.) observes against Bonsirven that these were not atheists, as is shown clearly by I Enoch 46.7, but 'men who show their despite of the One God by unrighteous works and worship of other gods'. There is here nothing which goes beyond what we find in the Old Testament. In fairness to Bonsirven it should be added that he does not affirm that these passages condemn speculative atheism, but contents himself by posing the question whether they do.

[3] Cf. G. R. Berry, 'The Old Testament Teaching concerning God', *A.J.Th.*, v, 1901, pp. 254 ff.; also J. Lindblom, in *Werden und Wesen des Alten Testaments* (B.Z.A.W., No. 66), ed. by J. Hempel, 1936, pp. 128 ff.

[4] Gen. 1.1.

[5] Cf. Ex. 18.11, 20.3, I Sam. 4.8, Ps. 86.8, and frequently.

and is construed with a singular verb. This does not, of course, prove that he is thought of as the only existing deity, and indeed there can be little doubt that in historical times many in Israel used this term of their God without any idea of denying the reality of other gods. To this we must return when we consider the rise of monotheism. For the moment it must suffice to note that the use of the plural word '*Elôhîm* does not of itself imply the recognition of more than one god wherever it is found, or rule out such a recognition. A singular form, '*Elōah*, is found frequently in the book of Job[1] and occasionally outside.[2]

Amongst many other terms for God found in the Bible we may note '*Ēl, Shaddai,* and '*Elyôn,* the last two sometimes found in combination with the first. In most of our texts there can be no doubt that all of these terms are used with reference to the God of Israel. It is certain, however, that there was a stage when they were thought of as separate and distinct deities.[3] Moreover, incorporated in proper names are elements consisting of the names of other gods who are known to us from the texts which have come down from Israel's neighbours. So far as we have any knowledge of these neighbours, from Egypt to Babylonia, they were polytheistic, with the exception of the Pharaoh Ikhnaton of Egypt, who seems to have imposed, for a short time, a form of monotheism on an unwilling people.[4] Of

---

[1] It stands forty-two times in the book of Job.

[2] E.g., in Isa. 44.8, Hab. 3.3, Ps. 50.22, 139.19.

[3] O. Eissfeldt, *Z.D.M.G.*, lxxxviii, 1934, p. 179, says: 'Die vom A.T. gebrauchten Appellativa für "Gott" El und Elim, Eloah und Elohim sowie die in ihm erwähnten Götternamen Baal und Aschera-Astarte, Dagon und Milkom und viele andere kommen in den Jahrhunderte älteren Ras Shamra-Texten vor, und viele der hier genannten Götter werden auch ihrem Wesen nach genauer charakterisiert.' Cf. E. Dhorme, *La Religion des Hébreux nomades*, 1937, pp. 333 ff.; also H. S. Nyberg, *A.R.W.*, xxxv, 1938, pp. 329 ff.

[4] S. A. B. Mercer, *J.S.O.R.*, x, 1926, pp. 14 ff., denies that Ikhnaton was a monotheist, and L. A. White, *J.A.O.S.*, lxviii, 1948, pp. 91 ff., attributes to him little originality. Others recognize a genuine monotheistic character in his religion. So W. F. Albright, *From the Stone Age to Christianity*, 2nd ed., 1946, p. 167. Indeed Albright thinks this was the source of Mosaic monotheism (ibid., p. 206). This seems to me highly improbable, even if I could agree in using the term 'monotheism' of Moses without qualification. A Lods (*R.H.P.R.*, xiv, 1934, pp. 173 ff.), while allowing that thought in the wider ancient East may have prepared the ground for the prophetic movement in Israel, denies that it can explain the monotheism which was attained in Israel. Cf. also W. W. von Baudissin 'Zur Geschichte des Monotheismus bei semitischen Völkern', in *D.L.Z.*, xxxv, 1914, cols. 5 ff., where such apparent monotheism as was expressed in non-Israelite texts is described in terms of the universal character attributed to individual gods, rather than a general monotheism (col. 8).

the polytheism of the Canaanite neighbours of Israel we have ample witness since the Ras Shamra texts became known. It is not, therefore, surprising to find remnants of polytheism in the speech of Israel, though here we observe that syncretism has been at work to equate the once separate deities with Israel's God. Thus, in the familiar passage in Ex. 6.2, we read 'I am Yahweh: and I appeared unto Abraham, Isaac, and Jacob as El Shaddai', where we have a clear case of such syncretism. Here the God of the patriarchs is identified with the God in whose name Moses came, though they bear different names. In a similar way missionaries in China identified the God of the Bible, Yahweh, with the ancient Chinese deity, Shang Ti, and used Shang Ti to render *'Elôhîm*, wherever it occurs with the meaning *God* in the Old Testament. In Christian circles Yahweh has gathered Shang Ti into himself, and has filled with a new content the old name. In Israel the name *Shaddai* fell largely out of use, and was replaced by the name of Moses' God. Where it remained, it was generally in poetry; and the same is true of *'Elyôn*. We never find any opposition between the God of Moses and the God of the patriarchs, or any undercurrent of feeling that the identification was not complete.

One example of syncretism finds much resistance, however. The Canaanites used the term *Ba'al*, or *Lord*, for their gods, and in the post-Settlement period Israelites worshipped at Canaanite shrines according to Canaanite rites, and used this term when they would have affirmed that they were worshipping the God of Israel. There was always an undercurrent of feeling, however, that Israel's God was not *Ba'al*, and in times of national tension this found open expression. One of Gideon's first acts was to break down the local *Ba'al* altar.[1] Yet through long periods this syncretism continued with little opposition, and in the Israelite religion that ultimately emerged not a little of the ritual that was of Canaanite origin appears to have found a place.[2] Yet the term *Ba'al* was repudiated, and Hosea sets God and *Ba'al* in sharp opposition to one another. This

---

[1] Judg. 6.25 ff.

[2] Cf. H. F. Hahn, *Old Testament in Modern Research*, 1954, p. 111: 'The Ras Shamra texts strongly suggested some connexion between the sacrificial ritual of the Hebrews and that of the Canaanites'; p. 112: 'The similarity of the Ugaritic rituals to several aspects of the cultus described in the Priestly Code was the most striking fact discovered in the Ras Shamra texts'.

seems odd, since the meaning of the term is not exceptionable, and another term *'Adhōnai*, of comparable meaning and also associated with Canaanite religion, familiar to us in its Greek form *Adonis*, not only continued to be used unchallenged, but was actually substituted for the proper name of Israel's God in the reading of the Old Testament,[1] giving rise to the rendering *Kyrios* in the Greek, *Dominus* in the Latin, and LORD in the English versions.

The proper name of Israel's God is familiar to us in the hybrid form *Jehovah*. This is a mediaeval coinage,[2] and it consists of the consonants of the Hebrew name for God, but vowel sounds similar to those of *'Adhōnai*. How the name was really pronounced before its pronunciation was avoided we can never know with certainty. It is commonly thought that it was pronounced *Yahweh*, and this has become conventional in modern works of scholarship.[3] If it is used, it must be used with reserve, and with recognition of the fact that God has not thought it important that his name should be preserved. None can know with assurance more than the consonants of the name of the God in whose name Moses went into Egypt to lead the Israelites out.

[1] L. Finkelstein, *H.T.R.*, xxxv, 1942, p. 296, says that the substitution was made in the third century B.C.

[2] Its origin is often attributed to Petrus Galatinus in 1518, but G. F. Moore has shown that the form is older. For his researches into the antiquity of this form, and the various other forms, such as Jahvoh, Jova, Johovah, Johavah, etc., cf. *A.J.Th.*, xii, 1908, pp. 34 ff., *A.J.S.L.*, xxv, 1908–9, pp. 312 ff., xxviii, 1911–12, pp. 56 ff. On the date of Petrus Galatinus, *De arcanis catholicae veritatis*, commonly given as 1520 (so *B.D.B.*, 1907, p. 218 a), and occasionally as 1516 (so F. Prat, in *D.Bib.*, iii, 1903, col. 1224), cf. *A.J.Th.*, loc. cit., p. 34, and *A.J.S.L.*, xxviii, pp. 58 f. Cf. also *P.R.E.*, 3rd ed., ix, 1901, p. 811, for evidence of the use of the form 'Jehovah' by Wessel in the fifteenth century. F. Prat (loc. cit., col. 1225) attributes it to Raymond Martin, whose *Pugio fidei* was written *c.* 1270, and published in 1651. Moore (*A.J.Th.*, loc. cit.) holds that the form is not to be attributed to Martin, but to the copyists, but since one MS. is dated 1381, the form was certainly older than Galatinus, and was probably common in the fourteenth century. B. Smalley (*The Study of the Bible in the Middle Ages*, 2nd ed., 1952, p. 350) states that the form Jehovah was already known to Christians in the late thirteenth century.

[3] On the original pronunciation of the Tetragrammaton there is a considerable literature, and many views have been propounded. It will suffice here to refer to O. Eissfeldt, *Z.A.W.*, liii (N.F. xii), 1935, pp. 59 ff., A. L. Williams, ibid., liv (N.F. xiii), 1939, pp. 262 ff. (maintaining that the pronunciation was 'Jāhôh'), J. A. Montgomery, *J.B.L.*, lxiii, 1944, pp. 161 ff. (holding that it was pronounced 'Yā-hû'), and D. D. Luckenbill, *A.J.S.L.*, xl, 1923–4, pp. 247 ff. (arguing for 'Jāhô'), and A. Murtonen, *A Philosophical and Literary Treatise on the Old Testament Divine Names El, Eloah, Elohim and Yahweh*, 1952, pp. 54 ff. J. Obermann (*J.B.L.*, lxviii, 1949, pp. 301 ff.) argues that Yahweh was not originally a proper name, but a *nomen agentis*, meaning 'Sustainer, Maintainer, Establisher'.

It has been claimed that this name was known at Ras Shamra, where it stood in the form *Yw the son of El*.[1] This view is not unchallenged, and it is most improbable that we have here the name of Israel's God.[2] In any case this God plays no prominent part in Ras Shamra mythology, and it could scarcely have been under the influence of this religion that the Israelites made Yahweh the sole God whose worship was held to be legitimate for them. More commonly it is held, on evidence found in the Old Testament itself, that Yahweh was worshipped by the Kenites before he was worshipped by Israel.[3] The evidence for this is not irresistible, and many scholars dispute it,[4] but it seems on the whole probable. There is evidence to connect the father-in-law of Moses with the Kenites,[5] and it is stated that he was a priest.[6] If he was, as this theory believes, a priest of Yahweh, Moses' contact with the worship of Yahweh is explained. This does not mean that the religion of Israel is to be equated with the religion of the Kenites, and treated as a development from it. What is important is not so much the name of the deity as the character of the religion that was associated with it, and the character of the religion of Yahwism established by Moses was different from any Kenite Yahwism. Just as Christianity in China has taken over the name Shang Ti, but filled it with a meaning it never had in China before the Gospel was taken there, so the name Yahweh, if it were a

[1] R. Dussaud, *R.H.R.*, cv, 1932, p. 247, *C.R.A.I.*, 1940, pp. 364 ff., and *Les Découvertes de Ras Shamra et l'Ancien Testament*, 2nd ed., 1941, pp. 171 f.; H. Bauer, *Z.A.W.*, li (N.F. x), 1933, pp. 92 ff.; O. Eissfeldt, *Ras Schamra und Sanchunjathon* 1939, pp. 17 f.; A. Vincent, *La Religion des Judéo-Araméens d'Éléphantine*, 1937, pp. 27 f.; Ch. Virolleaud, *La Déesse 'Anat*, 1938, p. 98; A. Murtonen, op. cit., pp. 49 f.

[2] Cf. R. de Vaux, *R.B.*, xlvi, 1937, pp. 352 f.; A. Bea, *Biblica*, xx, 1939, pp. 440 f.; W. F. Albright, *From the Stone Age to Christianity*, 2nd ed., pp. 197, 328, C.H. Gordon, *Ugaritic Grammar*, 1940, p. 100; W. Baumgartner, *Th.R.*, N.F. xiii, 1941, pp. 159 f.; R. de Langhe, *Un Dieu Yahweh à Ras Shamra?* 1942; and J. Gray, *J.N.E.S.*, xii, 1953, pp. 278 ff.

[3] Cf. B. Stade, *Geschichte des Volkes Israel*, i, 1887, pp. 130 f.; K. Budde, *Religion of Israel to the Exile*, 1899, Chapter i; W. Vischer, *Jahwe der Gott Kains*, 1929; J. Morgenstern, *H.U.C.A.*, xv, 1940, pp. 127 ff.; A. J. Wensinck, *Semietische Studiën*, 1941, pp. 23 ff. In my *From Joseph to Joshua*, 1950, pp. 149 ff., this view is presented as probable.

[4] Cf. E. König, *Geschichte der alttestamentlichen Religion*, 1912, pp. 162 ff.; W. J. Phythian-Adams, *The Call of Israel*, 1934, pp. 72 ff.; T. J. Meek, *Hebrew Origins*, 1936, pp. 86 ff. (2nd ed., 1950, pp. 93ff.); M. Buber, *Moses*, 1947, pp. 94 ff.; and C.H.W. Brekelmans, *O.T.S.*, x, 1954, pp. 215 ff.

[5] He is called a Midianite in Ex. 3.1, 18.1, but a Kenite in Judg. 4.11. It is probable that the Kenites were a Midianite clan.

[6] Ex. 3.1.

Kenite divine name, was filled with a new significance. This, however, was not a significance which Moses or the Israelites brought to it, but a significance which was given to it in the texture of the revelation which is associated with Moses. If the name of God was shared with the Kenites, the conception of the character of God could hardly have been shared, since the Israelite conception was born of her own experience of God in the deliverance from Egypt. For this reason we have no need to discuss the problem of the meaning of the name Yahweh. This has been much discussed, and a variety of views advanced. But etymology is not finally important here for Old Testament theology, since not etymology but experience filled the term with meaning.

While, therefore, various names were used for God, names which originally denoted different deities, they were all used for the one God of Israel, and from the time of Moses it was recognized that Israel should have no other god. This does not mean that no other gods were actually worshipped, for the Bible itself tells us that men often worshipped other gods, and they are condemned for this again and again. It does, however, mean that one element of the distinctive religion of Israel, which Moses established, was that Israel's God, Yahweh, was the sole legitimate object of her worship. In so far as she worshipped other gods, for whatever reason, she was disloyal to the spirit of her own religion.

In having but one legitimate God there was nothing unique. Many nations and tribes have had each their own god, to whom they have given exclusive worship—worship more exclusive than Israel gave to Yahweh throughout long periods. What was unique was the way Israel—or at least those elements of the nation that were led by Moses[1]—came to worship Yahweh. Israel believed that Yahweh had chosen her to be his people, and her pledge of loyalty to him was her response to his election and deliverance of her from Egypt. This is fundamental for the understanding of the Old Testament, and here are to be found the seeds of all the great distinctive principles of its teaching. Through his experience at the Bush Moses went

---

[1] It is a common view that not all the tribes were led out of Egypt by Moses. For my view on this question, and a full discussion of some other views, cf. *From Joseph to Joshua*.

into Egypt in the name of Yahweh to lead the people out. He was as sure as any of the prophets that he went with a divine commission, and that this commission sprang out of the divine compassion for Israel. 'I have indeed seen the suffering of my people in Egypt, and have heard their cry because of their taskmasters.'[1] Here Yahweh was choosing Israel and adopting her to be his people. In accordance with this Hosea says 'I am Yahweh thy God from the land of Egypt';[2] and Ezekiel 'Thus saith the Lord Yahweh: on the day when I chose Israel, and lifted up my hand[3] unto the seed of the house of Jacob, and made myself known to them in the land of Egypt, when I lifted up my hand unto them, saying, I am Yahweh your God.'[4] While there are passages which represent the election of Israel as going back earlier than the time of Moses,[5] this is less fundamental to the thought of the Old Testament than the election through Moses.[6] In any case it was through the work of Moses that God's choice of Israel was renewed and confirmed,[7] and through the deliverance of the Exodus that his claim upon her was established. Of some aspects of that deliverance I have spoken in the previous lecture. It was not achieved by human valour, but by the activity of God, and all that was asked of them was faith to believe in the deliverance promised by Moses in the name of God.

For the study of the faith of Israel it does not matter whether this story is reliable or not, since Israel believed it, and on it erected her faith that God was active in history and in her experience. I have already given my reasons for believing that in its broad outlines this story is true, and that while many of the details may have been enhanced in the tradition, beneath

---

[1] Ex. 3.7.   [2] Hos. 12.9 (Heb. 10).
[3] This is the gesture signifying an oath; cf. Gen. 14.22.
[4] Ezek. 20.5.   [5] Cf. e.g., Isa. 41.7 f.; Ps. 105.43.
[6] Cf. K. Galling, *Die Erwählungstraditionen Israels*, 1928, where a careful study of these traditions is offered. Cf. also E. Jacob, *La Tradition historique en Israël*, 1946, p. 148: 'Jérémie n'ignore pas les traditions patriarcales, mais il ne les considère pas comme faisant partie de l'histoire du salut; l'histoire d'Israël commence à Moïse', and p. 152: 'L'élection ne remonte pas à l'époque patriarcale, mais à la sortie d'Egypte'; similarly A. G. Hebert, *The Throne of David*, 1941, p. 29 n.; C. R. North, *The Old Testament Interpretation of History*, 1946, p. 50. On the measure of validity in both traditions cf. *The Biblical Doctrine of Election*, pp. 19 ff.
[7] Cf. C. G. Montefiore, *The Old Testament and After*, 1923, p. 76; 'It is very generally now believed either that Yahweh only became Israel's God in the Mosaic age, and then by an act of deliberate choice, or that, even if Yahweh was known in Israel before Moses, he was, as it were, chosen and accepted afresh after the escape from Egypt.'

them lies a substance which is as secure as anything in ancient history. Israel found various elements in the character of God revealed here, and if the story is in substance reliable, then those elements are true not for Israel alone. It is therefore not to be surprised at that here in the story of the Exodus and its outcome we have the seeds of the teaching about God which characterizes both Testaments, and which is still valid for the modern world.

To Israel God was personal, and his personality expressed itself in will. He was active in history, and not a mere spectator of its course. He controlled the forces of Nature, and could make himself known through prophetic personality. The Old Testament sometimes calls Moses a prophet.[1] He is not seldom denied any place in a study of the Old Testament prophets.[2] For this denial there is no justification.[3] He was much more than a prophet, indeed, but he was also as truly a prophet as any of the great figures of the eighth and seventh centuries. He was admitted to the counsel of God, and became the mouthpiece of God to men, as much as they; and indeed, through him there came a more fundamental revelation of the will of God than through any other. His personality was vital to the whole experience of Israel in the Exodus. It was not that they experienced deliverance, and then somehow believed that God had delivered them, and afterwards through meditation on that deliverance evolved a theology. The deliverance was first promised before it was achieved, and then interpreted by the man who had been vindicated in the deliverance. It was history announced in advance in the name of God, and the prophet who then interpreted it in retrospect had not completed his prophetic work in the prior announcement. He continued that work by both interpreting the history and directing the response to the deliverance.

Many modern minds are disturbed by the miraculous element in the story of the deliverance from Egypt and elsewhere in the Old Testament. On the other hand it is sometimes alleged that critical scholarship is based on the denial of the

---

[1] Num. 12.6 ff.; Deut. 18.15, 34.10; Hos. 12.13 (Heb. 14).
[2] P. Volz, in his *Prophetengestalten des Alten Testaments*, 1938, devotes a chapter to Moses, but this is uncommon in modern studies of Old Testament prophecy.
[3] Cf. K. Marti, *The Religion of the Old Testament*, E.Tr. by G. A. Bienemann, 1914, p. 63 f.: 'He is only rightly understood when he is conceived as a prophet.'

possibility of miracle.[1] Let me say with clarity and candour that I am a critical scholar and that I neither begin nor end with any such denial. If miracle be defined as divine activity within the world,[2] a belief in its possibility would seem to be fundamental to a belief in God. He cannot be excluded from the world he has made, or reduced to the position of a spectator of the interplay of forces which he had once set in motion. In the faith of Israel he was too real and personal to be reduced to impotence in his own world, or regarded as one who idly watched while men worked out their own destiny, and this faith is integral to any worth-while faith in God. Many of the miracles recorded in the Old Testament are examples of divine activity through natural events, such as the deliverance from Egypt through wind and wave,[3] from Sisera through storm,[4] or from Sennacherib through plague.[5] Others are examples of divine activity through events which were contrary to the order of Nature, such as the passage through walls of water at the Red Sea,[6] the standing still of the sun in the time of Joshua,[7] the recovery of an axe-head by Elisha by the device of throwing wood into the water,[8] or the delivery of the three youths from Nebuchadnezzar's fire.[9] In some cases these stories are dramatic representations of simpler facts, as may be seen by a study of the context in which they are set; or wonder tales that grew round the name of a hero; or parabolic stories that were made the vehicle of a message.[10] The miracle stories can neither be uncritically accepted as historical, nor uncritically rejected as fancy. Each example must be examined for itself, in the light of the character of the narrative in which it stands and the purpose for which it appears to have been written. But that there is a truly miraculous element in the story I am fully persuaded.

[1] Cf. *The New Bible Handbook*, ed. by G. T. Manley, 2nd ed., 1949, pp. 40 ff., where it is argued that modern critical scholarship is based on, and permeated by, unbelief in the possibility of miracle.

[2] Such divine activity is never a mere demonstration of power for its own sake, but always to serve the purpose of God. A. Richardson (*A Theological Word Book of the Bible*, 1952, p. 152) defines miracle as 'an event which happens in a manner contrary to the regularly observed processes of nature'. This is too narrow a definition. It confines itself to the unusual form of the phenomenon, and relates it neither to God nor to the purpose of God, and it ignores the fact that some of the biblical 'miracles', such as the deliverance in the battle of Taanach, involved nothing which was contrary to the ordinary processes of nature.

[3] Ex. 14.21.   [4] Judg. 5.21 f.   [5] II Kings 19.35.   [6] Ex. 14.22.
[7] Josh. 10.13.   [8] II Kings 6.6.   [9] Dan. 3.25 ff.
[10] Cf. *The Relevance of the Bible*, pp. 103 ff.

We have not merely the working out of human impulses and the chance interplay of natural forces. We have the activity of God in inspiration and revelation, and the evidence of his presence in Nature and history.

In tales of wonder there is nothing distinctive of Israel's religion. Similar tales are widely current elsewhere, and, indeed, on a more liberal scale. In stories of the activity of gods in human affairs, there is nothing in itself unique. Many peoples have believed their gods took part in the affairs of men, usually to defend the interests of their worshippers, but sometimes to punish them for their offences. What is distinctive of Israel's faith is the belief that God revealed his character in his activity, and that there was a moral purpose governing it. This is not to suggest that there was some moral law to which God himself was subject, but that God was conceived of as a moral being, and that in the revelation of himself the moral law was unfolded. Most religions prescribe some moral code for men. But the gods are often thought of as exempt from that code. In the popular stories of the Greek and Roman gods, the gods are represented as behaving often in ways that would be immediately condemned in men. In Israel it was perceived in germ in the beginning, and with increasing clearness as time passed, that what God is they who worship him should become. Thus the religion of Israel is ethical in its essence, and not merely in its demands.

This is clear from the time of its foundation through Moses. After he had led the people out of Egypt by a deliverance to which their prowess had contributed nothing, they pledged themselves to God by voluntary consecration, as their response in gratitude for his saving act. Unlike fear, sorrow, and joy, which have no necessarily ethical quality, gratitude is a fundamentally ethical emotion, and it is not surprising that a religion so founded should have had an ethical quality. The ethical character of Old Testament religion is commonly associated with the prophets of the eighth and seventh centuries. Those prophets emphasized and developed the ethical demands of religion, indeed, but the beginnings of ethical religion in Israel did not have to wait till the eighth century. Israel did not at Sinai realize all the implications of her faith, and often long subsequently lived on a low ethical plane, as the prophets so clearly and insistently declared. But the seeds of ethical religion were planted at Sinai, and were later watered by prophetic teaching. Nathan made it plain to David that there were rights of man which a king could not violate with impunity,[1] and Elijah renewed this declaration to Ahab.[2] But neither prophet stood merely as the champion of human rights. They stood as champions of the will of God; for man's ultimate rights were based on the will of God. Hence all sin of man against man was conceived of as primarily sin against God. And when the great prophets of the eighth and seventh centuries declaimed against the social injustice of their age, their message was born of their perception of the character of God. It was because they realized that God was a God of justice and righteousness that they demanded justice and righteousness from men. Here was something deeper than an abstract theology, a mere formulation of belief about God. It was a vital theology. It was a demand that men should reflect the character that God was perceived to have. And that character was the character that he revealed in his acts.

That Israel thought of God as creator, and as all-powerful, all-knowing, and present everywhere does not need to be elaborated here. This is not because it is not true or important, but because it is of less significance than the revelation of his character. His creatorship is declared on the first page of the Bible, and his knowledge of the inmost thoughts of men is declared again and again. The account of creation given in the first chapter of the Bible is often contrasted with the story of creation and of the Garden of Eden that follows. The naïveté of the anthropomorphism of the second story and of associated stories is emphasized, and it is pointed out that in the story of the Tower of Babel, God is represented as having to come down to see what is going on,[3] and in the Garden of Eden he takes a walk in the cool of the day.[4] Despite the cruder anthropomorphism we find in these passages, it should not be overlooked that in the story of the Garden of Eden we can hardly presume that when God asks Adam what he has been doing,[5] he is ignorant of the answer until Adam confesses. In the following chapter Cain avoids confessing his sin, but finds that God

---

[1] II Sam. 12.7 ff.   [2] I Kings 21.10.   [3] Gen. 11.5.
[4] Gen. 3.8.   [5] Gen. 3.11.

already knows.[1] His power to control the forces of Nature and the kingdoms of men is assumed everywhere. He uses wind, and storm, and plague to effect his purpose; he humiliates Pharaoh and employs the proud might of Assyria to do his will. He is also present everywhere, present with Joseph in Egypt, with Moses in the wilderness, with Jonah at sea. There is no place from which he is excluded. All of this is taken for granted everywhere in the Bible, and there is no need to cite texts to establish it.

Nor need we linger over some other qualities of God, which figure constantly in the thought of the Old Testament. The glory of God is frequently mentioned,[2] and he is conceived of in terms of the highest exaltation as one before whom men are constrained to bow in reverence and adoration. He is far above men, clothed in majesty, and nowhere does he act without dignity or fail to inspire awe. His wisdom, too, is always manifest. His means are ever appropriate to his ends. He uses the forces of Nature to serve his purposes without making them any the less natural, and equally he uses the thoughts and actions of men without making them the less human. When he makes the Assyrian the rod of his anger,[3] the Assyrian is all unconscious of the fact,[4] and is merely following the evil bent of his heart. He bears full responsibility for his action, even though that action, despite its evil character, is integrated into the purpose of God. In his patience and long-suffering God uses the conflicting desires and purposes of men to achieve his will, without destroying human freedom or converting man into a mere puppet in his hands. The inscrutability of the divine wisdom is often brought out, and notably in the book of Job, where Job is rebuked for passing judgement on God on the basis of his ignorance.[5] Similarly in the great Wisdom chapter in the book of Job,[6] which seems to be independent of the rest of the book, the only home of wisdom is declared to be in God. Man by his searching cannot find it, until God in his grace reveals it.[7]

Leaving aside these qualities of God, important as they are

[1] Gen. 4.9 f.
[2] For a study of the concept of the glory of God in the Old Testament cf. B. Stein, *Der Begriff Kᵉbod Jahweh und seine Bedeutung für die alttestamentliche Gotteserkenntnis*, 1939, and G. von Rad, in *Th.W.B.*, ii, 1935, pp. 240 ff.
[3] Isa. 10.5.   [4] Isa. 10.7.   [5] Job 38 f.   [6] Job 28.   [7] Job 28.23, 27 f.

for any full understanding of biblical theology, we turn to his moral attributes. For it is in these that the distinctive elements of the faith of Israel lie.

In Egypt God had revealed himself as a compassionate and a saving God. He had pity on the sufferings of Israel and he saved her by the exercise of his power. It is sometimes supposed that it was to Hosea that Israel owed the thought of God as gracious and merciful. Yet clearly it went back far behind Hosea to the event of the Exodus, and in a passage which is held by many critical scholars to antedate the time of Hosea we read 'Yahweh, Yahweh, a God compassionate and gracious,[1] slow to anger, and abundant in mercy[2] and truth.'[3] Hosea, indeed, developed this thought of God, and with an intensity born of his own tragic experience declared the constancy of God's love, and pressed on men the demand of that love for an answering love and loyalty.[4] Here again the demands of God

[1] The Hebrew word here is *ḥannûn*, the adjective from *ḥēn*, which is often rendered 'grace', or 'favour'. On the relations between this word and *ḥesedh* cf. W. F. Lofthouse, *Z.A.W.*, li (N.F. x), pp. 29 ff.; also P. Bonnetain, in *S.D.B.*, iii, 1938, cols. 727 ff. W. L. Reed (*J.B.L.*, lxxiii, 1954, pp. 36 ff.) argues that *ḥēn* meant inner good will, while *ḥesedh* means the overt act which results from it. It is difficult to think that this is adequate.

[2] This is the Hebrew word *ḥesedh*, which has no precise equivalent in English. G. A. Smith (*Jeremiah*, 3rd ed., 1924, p. 104) says that 'troth' is the nearest English equivalent, while N. H. Snaith (*Distinctive Ideas of the Old Testament*, 1944, p. 95; cf. J. Bright, *The Kingdom of God*, 1953, p. 28 n.) defines it as 'covenant love', and A. R. Johnson (cf. *J.B.L.*, lxvi, 1947, p. xxx) proposes 'devotion'. Cf. now A. R. Johnson, 'ḤESED and ḤĀSÎD', in *Interpretationes ad Vetus Testamentum pertinentes* (Mowinckel Festschrift = *N.T.T.*, lvi, 1–2 Hefte), 1955, pp. 100–12. None of these words is adequate. A. Lods (*The Prophets and the Rise of Judaism*, E.Tr. by S. H. Hooke, 1937, p. 89) says: 'Ḥèsèd, a very comprehensive word, which, for want of an adequate equivalent, we are obliged to translate, now by piety, now by mercy, love or grace: it corresponds fairly closely to the Latin *pietas*, meaning not only the feeling of a faithful believer towards God, or of a son towards his father, but also the feeling of God or of a leader towards his subordinates, and in a general way, the natural feeling which prompts a man, apart from the constraint of law, to be kind and indulgent towards the members of his family or tribe.' Cf. T. H. Robinson, in *The Psalmists*, ed. by D. C. Simpson, 1926, pp. 36 f., and A. Neher, *L'Essence du Prophétisme*, 1955, pp. 264 ff. In the present passage it is used of the divine initiative in grace. Cf. also below p. 70, n.1.

[3] Ex. 34.6. This verse is assigned to the J source of the Pentateuch by J. E. Carpenter, *The Composition of the Hexateuch*, 1902, p. 517; C. Steuernagel, *Einleitung in das Alte Testament*, 1912, p. 150; S. R. Driver, *Exodus* (Camb. B.), 1918 ed., p. 367; A. H. McNeile, *Exodus* (West. C.), 2nd ed., 1917, p. 217; Oesterley and Robinson, *Introduction to the Books of the Old Testament*, 1934, p. 37; A. Weiser, *Einleitung in das Alte Testament*, 2nd ed., 1949, p. 81. By some scholars, however, it is attributed to a Redactor; so W. H. Bennett, *Exodus* (Cent. B.), pp. 256 f., O. Eissfeldt, *Hexateuch-Synopse*, 1922, pp. 54 ff., 158*, G. Beer, *Exodus* (H.A.T.), 1939, p. 160, and C. A. Simpson, *Early Traditions of Israel*, 1948, p. 215.

[4] Cf. F. Buck, *Die Liebe Gottes beim Propheten Osee*, 1953.

spring out of his character. But this character was not first revealed in the eighth century B.C. Already when Israel was suffering in Egypt, he loved her and had pity on her, and his love both expressed his own character and laid its constraint upon Israel.

Yet if he was a saving God in the Exodus, he was by no means always represented as such. There were many occasions when he delivered his people, but beside them we must remember the occasions when the prophets predicted woe for them. In the prophetic teaching this was never thought of as due to some temporary whim of God, or to his anger at some ritual offence. There are stories in the Old Testament which tell of God's anger with the whole nation because some individual had violated a *tabu* either in conscious disobedience, as in the story of Achan,[1] or in ignorance, as in the account of the battle of Michmash, when Jonathan nearly lost his life.[2] But these do not stand in the prophetic teaching; and while they are not without value, as will be seen below, they are not in themselves stories distinctive of Israel's religion. They reflect ideas which were common in the world in which Israel lived. The great prophets, however, unfolded God's moral purpose for the world. When Israel did not reflect his character in her internal life, but by the evils that were rampant revealed her sorry state, then her way could not prosper. This was not simply because God was offended with her. It was the expression of his moral character and his love. For in the teaching of the prophets the only foundation for man's well-being lies in obedience to the will of God. If God were indifferent to the lives of men he would not be a moral being; and if he were indifferent to their well-being he would not be a God of love. Hence the discipline of events was thought of as designed to bring Israel back into the way of God's will, so that she might reap blessing, and the disasters foretold by the prophets were as much the expression of the character and will of God as the deliverance from Egypt had been. Israel's election did not mean that she was the pampered favourite of God. It brought her high privilege; but it also laid heavy responsibility on her, and was charged with constraint, which she could only disclaim to her hurt.

[1] Josh. 7.1.   [2] Sam. 14.27, 37 ff.

Nor could the disasters foretold by the prophets be thought of as arbitrary and unrelated to the evils the prophets denounced. The people that would not walk in the way of God's will could not know true well-being. If it would not submit itself to him in spirit, it could not know his guidance, and therefore its way could not prosper. For the life of a people issues from its spirit. It was therefore idle to expect that in external affairs it would prosper when in internal affairs it was plainly not subject to his guidance. The social evils which marked the life of the nation were symptoms of its diseased spirit, and until spiritual health was renewed in a return to God and to obedience to his will, disease would continue to afflict all its life. In the book of Deuteronomy this is clearly taught, and it is declared that the disobedient nation will meet disaster in war and innumerable other ills.[1] In the framework of the book of Judges we find the same doctrine, and it is implicit in much of the teaching of the prophets. That it is not the whole truth, and that desert and fortune cannot be rigidly equated, should be remembered. Yet broadly it is true that the way of wisdom and well-being is the way of obedience to the will of God. To this, however, we shall have to return. Here all that concerns us is the recognition of God's moral character in the discipline of his people, which is as much an expression of his love for her as was his deliverance at the Red Sea.

It is manifest that the thought of God as saving did not rest at the point where it began in the Exodus. There he saved Israel from her bondage, and from the lash of the taskmaster. But in the prophetic teaching he was seeking to save her from herself. He desired her truest well-being, and therefore he desired her to reflect his will. So by the discipline of events he sought to open her eyes to her folly, that she might renounce her way. Here again, therefore, we find in the revelation associated with the Exodus the seeds of something that was deepened in the prophetic teaching.

From this it is clear that the justice and the love of God are not attributes to be set over against one another, between which there was a tension. His discipline of Israel was not simply the expression of God's justice, overcoming and setting aside his love for the time being. It was as much the expression of his

[1] Deut. 28.15 ff.

love as of his justice. When Amos announces the discipline which God was about to send, he made it clear that it was the expression of God's love. 'You only have I known[1] of all the families of the earth; therefore will I visit upon you your iniquities.'[2] Similarly, the wrath of God and his love are not to be set over against one another. His wrath was the expression of his love, no less than his justice was. For love is not soft indulgence; nor is the wrath of God a display of temper. It is his holy intolerance of that which is not merely antithetical to his own character, but also hostile to man's deepest interest. His justice visits man's iniquity upon him, because that iniquity is man's own worst foe. The words rendered *righteousness* and *justice* are often used forensically in Hebrew. Their use in relation to God means that he is utterly blameless, and that if there were a court before which he could be arraigned, his acts would stand the utmost scrutiny.[3] God's acts conform to the principles which he lays down for men.

Nor are these all the moral attributes of God. His holiness is often predicated.[4] This was at first thought of as a numinous quality attaching to God and to persons and things that were separated from common use. In the Canaanite fertility cult

---

[1] The meaning here is clearly 'loved' or 'chosen'. The mediaeval Jewish commentator Rashi rendered by the former, and Ḳimḥi by the latter. I. Engnell (*Israel and the Law* (Symb. B. U.), vii, 2nd ed., 1954, p. 26) has the latter. Cf. K. Cramer, *Amos* (B.W.A.N.T., iii, 15), 1930, pp. 55 ff. For a discussion of this verse cf. A. Neher, *Amos*, 1950, pp. 34 ff.

[2] Amos 3.2.

[3] Cf. G. Quell and G. Schrenk in *Th.W.B.*, ii, 1935, pp. 176 ff. (E.Tr. by J. R. Coates, *Righteousness*, 1951); K. H. Fahlgren, *Ṣᵉdāḳā, nahestehende und entgegengesetzte Begriffe im Alten Testament*, 1932; A. Descamps, 'Justice et Justification', in *S.D.B.*, iv, 1949, cols. 1417 ff.; F. Nötscher, *Die Gerechtigkeit Gottes bei den vorexilischen Propheten* (A.A., vi, 1), 1915; R. Leivestad, *Guds straffende rettferdighet*, 1946; A. H. van der Weijden, *Die 'Gerechtigkeit' in den Psalmen*, 1952; J. H. Ropes, ' "Righteousness" and "the Righteousness of God" in the Old Testament and in St. Paul', *J.B.L.*, xxii, 1903, pp. 211 ff.; W. F. Lofthouse, 'The Righteousness of Jahweh', *E.T.*, l 1938–9, pp. 341 ff.; N. H. Snaith, *The Distinctive Ideas of the Old Testament*, 1944, pp. 51 ff.; H. Cazelles, 'A propos de quelques textes difficiles relatifs à la justice de Dieu dans l'Ancien Testament', *R.B.*, lviii, 1951, pp. 169 ff., 189 ff.; J. A. Bollier, 'The Righteousness of God: a word study', *Interpretation*, viii, 1954, pp. 404 ff. On the term *mishpāṭ* cf. H. W. Hertzberg, *Z.A.W.*, xl, 1922, pp. 256 ff., xli, 1923, pp. 16 ff., and J. van der Ploeg, *O.T.S.*, ii, 1943, pp. 144 ff. Cf. also Cramer, op. cit., pp. 146 ff. T. W. Nakarai (*The Shane Quarterly*, xiii, 1952, pp. 51 ff.) insists on the necessity of keeping *ṣᵉdhāḳāh* and *mishpāṭ* quite separate.

[4] On the concept of holiness in the Old Testament cf. O. Procksch, in *Th.W.B.*, i, 1932, 88 ff.; J. Pedersen, *Israel III–IV*, 1940, pp. 264 ff.; N. H. Snaith, op. cit., pp. 21 ff.; H. Ringgren, *The Prophetical Conception of Holiness* (U.U.Å., 1948:12), 1948.

there were sacred prostitutes, to whom the term holy was applied. Such a conception is not characteristic of the religion of Israel, though there were many Israelites who rose no higher. In the faith of Israel a moral content was given to the term. This is associated especially with the teaching of Isaiah, who is fond of calling God 'The Holy One of Israel', though again it was not without preparation before his time. In the story of the call of Moses,[1] the prophet feels a profound awe in the presence of God, who is portrayed not alone in terms of power and separateness from man, but in terms of goodness and mercy, sending Moses on his gracious errand of deliverance from oppression. There is a moral quality in the holiness of God, as well as the numinous quality which communicated itself to the very ground on which Moses stood. In the story of the call of Isaiah,[2] the prophet trembles exceedingly in the presence of the thrice holy God. Yet what makes him tremble is not the consciousness of his humanity in the presence of divine power, but the consciousness of his sin in the presence of moral purity. His dread is due to the realization that sin could not live in that presence. Either he must perish with his sin, or it must perish that he might live. And when one touched his lips with a live coal from the altar, it was this miracle of the renewal of the springs of his moral nature that was achieved. The holiness of God is thus seen to be the antithesis of all moral stain, that quality in God which is not only a rebuke to all in man which is contrary to His will, but in whose presence sin cannot live.

Again, the faithfulness, or truth, of God is often insisted on in the Old Testament. By this is not meant his loyalty to his people or to his covenant, for which the term *ḥesedh* is commonly used—though the meaning of that word is not exhausted in the term loyalty. Rather is it here meant, by the terms *'emûnāh* and *'emeth*[3] that God is not arbitrary in character, but self-consis-

---

[1] Ex. 3.1 ff.   [2] Isa. 6.1 ff.

[3] On this concept cf. F. Asensio, *Misericordia et Veritas* (Analecta Gregoriana, xlviii, Series Fac. Theol., Sect. B, No. 19), 1949, pp. 1 ff., 197 ff.; J. C. C. van Dorssen, *De derivata van de stam 'mn in het Hebreeuwsch van het Oude Testament*, 1951; also P. Bonnetain, in *S.D.B.*, iii, 1938, cols. 1255 ff., G. Quell, in *Th.W.B.*, i, 1932, pp. 233 ff., P. Humbert, *Problèmes du livre d'Habacuc*, 1944, pp. 149 f., and E. Perry, *J.B.R.*, xxi, 1953, pp. 252 ff. P. Joüon (*Mélanges de l'Université de St.-Joseph*, v, Part 1, 1911, pp. 406 ff.) argues that when *'emeth* is parallel to *ḥesedh*, it means 'grace' rather than 'faithfulness'.

tent and to be relied on. He does not resort to the exercise of his power to cover fickleness, which man is therefore powerless to question. In him there is no fickleness, but in all that he is and all he does he is to be trusted. It is true that there are many passages where God is said to repent of having done something. This term is not used in a moral sense, however, implying that God recognized that he had been at fault. There is certainly an element of anthropomorphism in the term, and it is used at various levels of meaning in the Old Testament. In general terms it may be said to mean that God changed his mind, not because of fickleness in himself, but because of failure in men or because of man's repentance. Just as in prophecy there was a contingent element,[1] so that if men profited by the warning it could serve its purpose without the necessity for the judgement announced, so in grace there was a contingent element, so that if men failed to respond to the grace of God they forfeited its fruits. To represent either process anthropomorphically as a change of God's mind, as though he rued the judgement or the blessing that he purposed, is not to conceal the fact that in either case the real cause is to be sought in man and not in God.

There are, indeed, passages in the Old Testament which suggest that God is arbitrary, such as that in which we are told that he moved David to number the people and then punished him, and, indeed, his people with him, for doing so.[2] But it has been already said that the Old Testament is not to be read as on a flat level, and that within its pages we have depicted a long process of development. In the particular instance noted it should be remembered that a later writer reflects a more developed theology in ascribing the moving of David to number the people to Satan instead of to God.[3] In any case such a passage as the former of these represents ideas that were abandoned, rather than the enduring thread of the religion of the Old Testament. It was the belief in God's faithfulness which was more significant and which persisted.

Yet again, in the complex of events connected with the Exodus it is clearly brought out that God is an electing God.[4]

---

[1] Cf. Jer. 18.7 f.; Joel 2.12 ff.   [2] II Sam. 24.1 ff.   [3] I Chron. 21.1.
[4] On this concept cf. K. Galling, *Die Erwählungstraditionen Israels*, 1928; H. H. Rowley, *The Biblical Doctrine of Election*, 1950; Th. C. Vriezen, *Die Erwählung Israels nach dem Alten Testament* (A.T.A.N.T.), 1953.

This was firmly held throughout the Old Testament, and indeed the thought of him as an electing God is vital to the teaching of both Testaments, though it has fallen into the background in much modern thought. God chose Israel for himself, and sent Moses to bring her out of Egypt in his name. He did not choose her because she was strong or cultured or good; but precisely because she was weak and helpless and downtrodden. Only so could he reveal those elements of his character which he purposed to reveal, and which we have seen to belong to the very texture of the revelation. There was thus nothing arbitrary in his election. It was the revelation of his character. There was nothing in it to foster self-esteem in the elect, though there were many in Israel who preened themselves on it. In the same way many Christians have shown a spirit of pride and superiority to others, though the New Testament says 'God commendeth his own love toward us, in that while we were yet sinners Christ died for us.'[1] In both Testaments need rather than worth is what calls forth the election, and the election is not something that merely confers a favour on the elect. It demands a response, and a response in service. At Sinai God's election of Israel found that response in the Covenant.[2] Of the importance of the idea of the Covenant[3] in the thought of the Old Testament there can be no doubt, but of its

[1] Rom. 5.8.

[2] On the meaning of the Covenant in the Old Testament cf. R. Valeton, *Z.A.W.*, xii, 1892, pp. 1 ff., 224 ff., xiii, 1893, pp. 245 ff.; R. Kraetzschmar, *Die Bundesvorstellung im Alten Testament*, i, 1894; P. Karge, *Geschichte des Bundesgedankens im Alten Testament* (A.A., ii, 1–4), 1910; E. Lohmeyer, *Diatheke*, 1913; J. Pedersen, *Der Eid bei den Semiten*, 1914, pp. 21 ff., and *Israel I–II*, E.Tr., pp. 263 ff.; G. Quell, in *Th.W.B.*, ii, 1935, pp. 106 ff.; J. Begrich, *Z.A.W.*, lx (N.F. xix), 1944, pp. 1 ff.; P. van Imschoot, *N.R.Th.*, lxxiv, 1952, pp. 785 ff. W. Eichrodt has built his *Théologie des Alten Testaments*, 2nd and 3rd ed., 1948, largely in terms of Covenant. Cf. also L. Koehler, *Theologie des Alten Testaments*, 3rd ed., 1953, pp. 43 ff., O. Procksch, *Theologie des Alten Testaments*, 1950, pp. 572 ff., and P. van Imschoot, *Théologie de l'Ancien Testament*, i, 1954, pp. 237 ff.

[3] It is generally agreed that the tradition of a Covenant goes back to the earliest sources. In Ex. 24.9 ff. we read that Moses and the elders ascended the sacred mountain and there partook of a sacred meal in the presence of God. This passage is ascribed to J by Carpenter (loc. cit.), S. R. Driver (op. cit., p. 254), Oesterley and Robinson (loc. cit.), McNeile (op. cit., p. 148), H. Trabaud (in *La Bible du Centenaire*, i, 1941, p. 103), to E by C. Steuernagel (*Einleitung in das Alte Testament*, 1912, p. 150), and to the earliest layer of E by Baentsch (*Exodus-Leviticus* (H.K.), 1905, p. 216) and Beer (op. cit., p. 126), while Eissfeldt (op. cit., p. 152*) assigns it to the source L, which is the oldest of all the sources into which he analyses the Pentateuch. This passage refers to a covenant meal, and C. R. North (*The Old Testament Interpretation of History*, 1946, p. 30) says this may well be the oldest story of the Covenant we have. Procksch, however (op. cit., p. 83), assigns it to P, the latest strand of the Pentateuch. This is very unlikely.

character there is often much misunderstanding. It was not a commercial bargain or a legal contract,[1] but rather Israel's pledge of loyalty to him who had first chosen and saved her. It laid no obligations on God, who had already of his free grace both pledged himself to Israel and given the evidence of his devotion to her in the deliverance he had wrought.[2] On Israel's side it was as unconditional as God's deliverance of her had been.

The fruits of Israel's deliverance would be shared by future generations. They would not alone inherit the freedom from Egypt, but would also inherit the revelation of God's character given to Israel in the experience which had been hers. For Israel was enjoined to cherish the memory of the Exodus, and indeed always did so. Yet the election was not the automatic inheritance of all the generations of the Israelites. 'Now therefore, *if ye will truly obey my voice, and keep my covenant*, ye shall be my own treasure among all peoples.'[3] From his side God pledged himself never to repudiate the bond which his own love had forged; but from her side Israel could break it. And if she broke it, it would be broken. Any generation which declined to make its own the Covenant by the renewal of its own loyalty to God would repudiate its election and declare that it no longer wanted the bond between Israel and God to continue. Yet it is everywhere made clear that any generation which so repudiated the Covenant could only disgrace itself. Nowhere is it supposed that each generation should decide *de novo* whether it desired the bond to continue. Rather was it taught that on

---

[1] G. E. Wright, *The Challenge of Israel's Faith*, 1944, p. 73 (English ed., 1946, p. 90), speaks of the Covenant in terms of a contract. Against this conception of it cf. E. Lohmeyer, op. cit., p. 54, and R. B. Y. Scott, *The Relevance of the Prophets*, 1944, p. 12.

[2] Cf. C. H. Dodd, *E.Th.R.*, xxiii, 1948, pp. 11 f.: 'God's Covenant is a *diathēkē*, and not a *synthēkē*; that is to say, God fixes the terms of the Covenant and offers it to man that he may accept it: the acceptance is also essential'. Cf. Procksch, op. cit., p. 92.

[3] Ex. 19.5. This verse is assigned to the earliest source of the Pentateuch, J, by S. R. Driver (*Exodus* (Camb. B), p 170), and by Oesterley and Robinson (op. cit., p. 37). Eissfeldt (op. cit., p. 146*) assigns it to E, and G. Beer (*Exodus* (H.A.T.), p. 97) to the oldest layer of E. A. Weiser (*Einleitung*, 2nd ed., p. 89) thinks this chapter is from E with some J additions, while Carpenter (op. cit., p. 517) assigns verses 3b–6 to the JE Redactor. All of these therefore assign the verse to an early date. Some other scholars would put it later. So B. Baentsch (op. cit., p. 172), C. Steuernagel (loc. cit.), McNeile (*Exodus* (West C.), 2nd ed., p. 110), Trabaud (loc. cit., p. 94), and C. A. Simpson (op. cit., p. 199), who assign it to the D Redactor.

every generation rested the moral obligation to renew the
Covenant in its own life, since each generation inherited a
blessing which imposed its claim upon it.

The election therefore called for loyalty and obedience,
without which it was repudiated. It called for *ḥesedh* from
Israel, which may be simply, if inadequately, defined as a
devotion to God which was a fitting response to his devotion
to her, and an initiative in unselfish service to men that was a
reflection of God's initiative in service to Israel.[1] Without this
quality any generation would declare more effectively than by
any verbal repudiation that it no longer desired to be the people
of God. It would proclaim its unwillingness to reflect the
character of the God whose will for men was revealed in his
character, and would thus be withholding the only response
which could give reality to the Covenant.

Yet even so, God could not lightly give up his people, but by
the warning voice of the prophets and by the discipline of
experience sought to reclaim their loyalty. The electing grace
which lay at the heart of Israel's deliverance from Egypt and
which called forth the first response in the Covenant would
renew its claim so long as Israel's repudiation was not final and
complete. With brilliantly effective anthropomorphism Jeremiah expresses the divine reluctance to give up the Israel that
from her side repudiated him in terms of his rising up early in
the morning to send the prophets to her with his message in
eager yearning to bring her back to himself in loyalty.[2] Equally
moving is the almost heart-broken cry which Hosea speaks of
God as uttering 'How can I give thee up, Ephraim? how can I
surrender thee, Israel? . . . my heart is turned within me, my
compassions are stirred together.'[3]

That reluctance to give up Israel shows itself in the continuance of the election in the Remnant,[4] when the nation as a

---

[1] The word *ḥesedh* has been much discussed. It will here suffice to refer to N.
Glueck, *Das Wort ḥesed im alttestamentlichen Sprachgebrauche* (B.Z.A.W., No. 47),
1927; W. F. Lofthouse, *Z.A.W.*, li (N.F. x), 1933, pp. 29 ff.; J. A. Montgomery,
H.T.R., xxxii, 1939, pp. 97 ff.; N. H. Snaith, op. cit., pp. 94 ff.; F. Asensio, op.
cit., pp. 32 ff.; H. J. Stoebe, *V.T.*, ii, 1952, pp. 244 ff.; and the very long article
by P. Bonnetain on 'Grace' in *S.D.B.*, iii, 1938, cols. 701–1319, where a full
bibliography will be found. Also now A. R. Johnson, in *Interpretationes ad Vetus
Testamentum pertinentes* (Mowinckel Festschrift=*N.T.T.*, lvi, 1–2 Hefte), 1955,
pp. 100 ff. (issued while the present work was in the press).
[2] Cf. Jer. 7.13, 25, 11.7, 25.4, 26.5, 29.19, 32.33, 35.14, 44.4.
[3] Hos. 11.8.   [4] On the concept of the Remnant cf. below, pp. 103 ff., 117 ff.

whole is disloyal. Everywhere the claim of the election is for loyalty and service, and only in so far as it finds this response does it fulfil its purpose. It brings privilege, indeed, but it also involves responsibility, and no thought of the Old Testament teaching on election that fails to do justice to both sides can rightly unfold its teaching about God.

It is often said that monotheism is characteristic of the three religions which derive in various ways from the Old Testament, Judaism, Christianity, and Islam, and that it is found nowhere else. Such unity as is found in other faiths is different from the personal unity of the Godhead found in these religions. How far it is legitimate to describe the faith of Israel as monotheistic, however, is a question that calls for some consideration. By many writers Israelite monotheism is thought to have had its beginnings in the eighth century prophets[1] and to have been attained only by Deutero-Isaiah,[2] and to have marked the later religion of the post-exilic period, but not to have been a feature of the faith of the Old Testament as a whole. By others it is maintained that full monotheism was achieved in the teaching of Moses.[3] It seems more probable that the truth lies between these two positions, and that the seeds of monotheism are to be found in the work of Moses though not its full achievement.[4] If this is so, we have here one more example of the rich significance of the revelation given through the Exodus and through Moses, where, as with the other elements of the character of God there revealed, we have a revelation which is only incipient, but which became clearer and fuller through the inspired work of the prophets.

It is hard to find any evidence that Moses either believed or

---

[1] Cf. I. G. Matthews, *The Religious Pilgrimage of Israel*, 1947, p. 129. A. Causse, *Les Prophètes d'Israël et les religions de l'Orient*, 1913, p. 62, attributed the beginnings of monotheism to Elijah.

[2] Cf. R. H. Pfeiffer, *J.B.L.*, xlvi, 1927, p. 194.

[3] Cf. F. James, *A.Th.R.*, xiv, 1932, pp. 130 ff.; W. F. Albright, *From the Stone Age to Christianity*, 2nd ed., p. 206. R. de Vaux goes further, and maintains that the patriarchs were monotheists; cf. *Initiation Biblique*, ed. by A. Robert and A. Tricot, 2nd ed., 1948, pp. 827 f.

[4] Cf, H. H. Rowley, *E.T.*, lxi, 1949–50, pp. 333 ff.; also G. E. Wright, *Theology Today*, iii, 1946, pp. 185 f. It is to be observed that already in the J document, which is commonly dated in the ninth century, and therefore long before the time of Amos, we find Yahweh described as 'the judge of all the earth' in Gen. 18.25. This does not necessarily imply monotheism, and may not go beyond monarchical theism, Yahweh being regarded as the supreme, and not the only, God.

taught that Yahweh was the only existing God, and that he was therefore not alone the God of Israel but of all men. On the other hand, it does not seem sufficient to note that at Sinai it was affirmed that Yahweh was alone the legitimate object of Israelite worship, and that there was no denial of the existence of other gods. For there were in the story the seeds of monotheism. The bringing out of Israel is not represented as a contest between Yahweh and the gods of Egypt. Those gods are ignored as negligible. Yahweh's will alone counted, and his power could not be challenged, while all the forces of Nature were obedient to his will. He could choose for himself what people he would. Whether other gods exist is neither affirmed nor denied.[1] But that they mattered is implicitly denied.

Yet whatever degree of monotheism was attained then was lost later, when in the popular worship other gods were not alone recognized as legitimate for other peoples, but were actually worshipped in Israel. Hence we find the need for the teaching of the great pre-exilic prophets, in which there is a clear but implicit monotheism,[2] and that of Deutero-Isaiah, in which speculative monotheism is explicitly set forth. Repeatedly it is here declared that Yahweh alone is God, and that all other gods are non-existent and their idols symbols of unreality.[3] Moreover, the same prophet taught the corollary of monotheism in universalism.[4] If there is but one God, then he must be the God of all men. Here again is something which finds its seeds in earlier teaching, and which meets us in many forms in the pre-exilic writers. Suffice it to mention the familiar passage attributed to both Isaiah[5] and Micah,[6] in which the age

---

[1] G. R. Berry, *A.J.Th.*, v, 1901, p. 262, objects to the use of the term monolatry to describe the religion of Moses, since there is no explicit recognition of the reality of other gods. He prefers to describe it as a practical monotheism. So also B. Baentsch, *Altorientalischer und israelitischer Monotheismus*, 1906, p. 87.

[2] Cf. Amos 4.13, 5.8, 9.7. In I Kings 8.60 and II Kings 19.15, 20, explicit monotheism is attributed to Solomon and Hezekiah. It is doubtful if we have here the *ipsissima verba* of Solomon and Hezekiah, however. In the former passage there are marks of the influence of the Deuteronomic style on the prayer, which may with probability be ascribed to the Deuteronomic editor of the books of Kings in their present form. The same editor may have similarly given its present form to the prayer of Hezekiah. The last event recorded in the books of Kings occurred in 561 B.C., and it is probable that the books were completed shortly after this date. This brings the probable date of these passages very close to the date of Deutero-Isaiah, when we have explicitly formulated monotheism.

[3] Cf. Isa. 44.6, 8, 45.5 f., 18, 21, 22.

[4] Cf. Isa. 42.6, 45.22, 49.6.

[5] Isa. 2.2 ff.   [6] Micah 4.1 ff.

of universal peace, when men will no longer need swords and spears, is declared to be the age when all men will first go up to the house of Israel's God and will learn his way.

It is indeed surprising, and not easily to be accounted for on simple evolutionary lines, that Israel attained a monotheistic faith. She was never a powerful nation, and her monotheism was in no sense the reflection of the prestige of the nation in the prestige of its God. Assyria imposed the recognition of her gods as the suzerains of the gods of conquered peoples, and the prowess of her armies was thought to reflect the power of her gods, whose prestige in turn was enhanced by their exploits. But in Israel it was not so, and the prophet who most specifically formulates a monotheistic faith was the spokesman of a people living in exile. Her monotheism is not the expression of national pride, since the prophets were the spokesmen of judgement rather than of a superficial patriotism. It is the gift of revelation, begun in Moses and continued in the prophets, whereby God was making himself known, first to the people of his choice, and then through them to all his creatures.

The character of God is an inexhaustible subject, and even his character as unfolded in the revelation given in the Old Testament cannot be compassed in a single lecture. That great and enduringly valid glimpses of that character may be found here will emerge from what has been said. He is a compassionate and a saving God, one who chooses men for his holy purposes and who calls them to privilege and service, a gracious and holy God, righteous and faithful, one who is alone and without rival and therefore the only legitimate object of the worship of all men, and, moreover, one whose resources are ever equal to his own wise purposes—all this and more is writ large upon the Old Testament.[1] It belongs to the faith of Israel, and to the faith which Israel has mediated to the world.

---

[1] Cf. J. Lindblom, loc. cit., p. 135: 'Gott ist einer, ein Gott nicht nur der Schöpfung, sondern vor allem der Geschichte, der als souveräner, heiliger, persönlicher Wille den Geschichtslauf einem weltgeschichtlichen Ziel planmässig entgegenleitet. Gott hat das Volk Israel für hohe Zwecke auserwählt und ist zu diesem Volke, bzw. seinen einzelnen Gliedern, in echt persönliche Beziehungen getreten. Das persönliche Handeln Gottes ist von ethischen Gesetzen bestimmt und wurzelt dem Menschen gegenüber in den heiligen Liebe und dem heiligen Zorn. In seinen Forderungen dominiert ebenfalls das Sittliche und Persönliche'.

III

THE NATURE AND NEED OF MAN[1]

Man is the creature of God. Both of the accounts of creation with which the Bible opens proclaim this faith. In the second account, which is believed to belong to the earliest of the main sources of the Pentateuch, we find God moulding man's body of the dust of the earth, and breathing into it the breath of life, so that it becomes a living soul.[2] The animals are also termed living souls,[3] and it would seem that there is nothing to dis-

[1] On the subject of this lecture cf. W. Eichrodt, *Das Menschenverständnis des Alten Testaments* (A.T.A.N.T.), 1944 (E.Tr. by K. and R. Gregor Smith, 1951); C. Ryder Smith, *The Bible Doctrine of Man*, 1951, *The Bible Doctrine of Sin*, 1953, and *The Bible Doctrine of Salvation*, 1941; G. Pidoux, *L'Homme dans l'Ancien Testament* (C.Th.), 1953; also the relevant sections of the theologies of the Old Testament noted above, p. 48 n., and W. Rudolph, 'Das Menschenbild des Alten Testaments', in *Dienst unter dem Wort* (Festgabe für H. Schreiner), 1953, pp. 238 ff.

[2] Gen. 2.7. It would be better to render by 'living being'; cf. E. F. Sutcliffe, *Scripture*, v, 1952, pp. 47 f.

[3] Gen. 2.19. Here the same phrase is used as in 2.7, but it is generally held to be a gloss. So H. Gunkel, *Genesis* (H.K.), 5th ed., 1922, p. 11, H. Holzinger, *Genesis* (K.H.C.), 1898, p. 29, J. Skinner, *Genesis* (I.C.C.), 1910, p. 68, and O. Procksch, *Genesis* (K.A.T.), 1924, p. 27. The same phrase is elsewhere used in P of the animal world (Gen. 1.20, 24, 30, 9.12, 15, 16; also in Ezek, 47.9), but A. R. Johnson (*The Vitality of the Individual in the Thought of Ancient Israel*, 1949, p. 23 n.) differentiates this syntactically from the phrase found in Gen. 2.7, and observes that whereas *nephesh* is used elsewhere by itself to denote a human being, there does not appear to be any example of its use *by itself* with exclusive reference to the animal world. It is to be noted, however, that it is used of animals in Deut. 12.23 f., where R.V. renders by 'the life', but where Briggs renders '(for the blood is the) living being, (and thou shalt not eat the) living being (with the flesh)' (*B.D.B.*, p. 659 b). Here the *nephesh* or 'living being', stands for an animal, but not for the totality of its being; it stands only for the non-fleshly element of its make up. J Moffatt (*The Old Testament: a New Translation*) renders 'the blood is the soul', and similarly Buber and Rosenzweig (*Die fünf Bücher der Weisung*): 'das Blut ist die Seele'. It is clear that animals and men were recognized to be animated bodies, and if man is defined merely in terms of an animated body, as is not seldom done by modern writers, it is hard to see what distinction from the animals is allowed for. It is true that in Gen. 2 it is not said that God breathed into the animals the breath of life, but neither is it said that he did this for woman. In Gen. 7.22, however, the phrase 'everything in whose nostrils was the breath of life' clearly includes the animals. On the much discussed term *nephesh* cf. C. A. Briggs, *J.B.L.*, xvi, 1897, pp. 17 ff., H. Wheeler Robinson, in *Mansfield College Essays* (presented to A. M. Fairbairn), 1909, pp. 269 ff., E. D. Burton, *A.J.Th.*, xviii, 1914, pp. 68 ff., and M. Lichtenstein, *Das Wort nephesh in der Bibel*, 1920.

tinguish man from the animals in the fundamental nature of his being. Yet in the continuation of the story it becomes clear that man is conceived of as having a moral nature, such as is attributed to none of the lower creatures. In the first account of creation, man is represented as the crown and climax of it all, and he is said to be created in the image of God.[1] By many writers this is understood to mean that man is in the physical likeness of God.[2] This seems to me on every ground improbable.[3]

It is true that we find much anthropomorphic language in the Old Testament. Reference has already been made to Jeremiah's representation of God as 'rising early in the morning' to send his prophets to Israel. Most of the anthropomorphisms we find in the Bible are mere accommodations to human speech, or vivid pictures used for their psychological effect rather than theological in significance. We can still speak of the hand of God, or of his eye, or of bowing before his feet, of the voice of God or his heart, though we should deny these terms any more than metaphorical value. In some passages the anthropomorphism is expressed with a naïve picturesqueness, such as those in which we read of God moulding Adam's body,[4] building woman from his rib,[5] taking a walk in the Garden of Eden,[6] or coming down to see what men were doing at Babel.[7] There are passages which represent God as appearing before men in human form,[8] and others where he sends an angel to represent him[9]—the angel often turning into God himself in the course of the narrative.[10] Yet in the teaching of the Old Testament God is nowhere conceived of as essentially of

---

[1] Gen. 1.27.

[2] Cf. A. Jeremias, *Das Alte Testament im Lichte des Alten Orients*, 4th ed., 1930, p. 53; P. Humbert, *Études sur le Récit du Paradis et de la Chute*, 1940, pp. 153 ff.; B. D. Eerdmans, *The Religion of Israel*, 1947, p. 309; L. Koehler, *Th.Z.*, iv, 1948, pp. 16 ff.; C. R. North, *The Thought of the Old Testament*, 1948, p. 27; C. Ryder Smith, *The Bible Doctrine of Man*, 1951, pp. 29 f. Th.C. Vriezen (*O.T.S.*, ii, 1943, pp. 86 ff.) thinks that both corporal and spiritual qualities are involved; cf. esp. p. 99.

[3] Cf. *The Unity of the Bible*, pp. 75 ff.

[4] Gen. 2.7.   [5] Gen. 2.21.   [6] Gen. 3.8.   [7] Gen. 11.7.

[8] Cf. Gen. 12.7, 17.1, 18.1, 32.30.

[9] Cf. Gen. 16.7 ff., 26.11, Ex. 3.2, Judg. 6.11 f.

[10] Cf. Gen. 16.13, 31.12, Ex. 3.4 ff., Judg. 6.14 ff. On this cf. A. R. Johnson, *The One and the Many in the Israelite Conception of God*, 1942, pp. 32 ff., and W. G. Heidt, *Angelology of the Old Testament*, 1949, pp. 69 ff.; also earlier G. F. Oehler, *Theology of the Old Testament*, Section 69 (Zondervan reprint, pp. 129 ff.).

human form. Rather is he conceived of as pure spirit, able to assume a form rather than as having in himself a physical form.[1]

It is probably this conception of God which lies behind the prohibition of images in the Bible. This we find in the familiar Decalogue of Ex. 20,[2] and also in the passage in Ex. 34,[3] which is often referred to as the Ritual Decalogue, and which is commonly held to be older than the other. Attention is sometimes drawn to the fact that in the one passage we have the prohibition of graven images and in the other of molten.[4] In neither is there the slightest suggestion that any other sort of image, other than the one specified, was permitted. What both aim to do is to forbid the making of any images, since God would have none of them. By many scholars the Decalogue of Ex. 20 is attributed to a late period in Israel's history,[5] and the existence of images through long periods is held to be evidence that this provision was unknown. It would not be in place to argue this question here, but I have elsewhere argued it and given reasons for believing that the Decalogue of Ex. 20 dates from the time of Moses, and that the other represents what was originally a pre-Mosaic form of Decalogue.[6] Both were associated with the worship of Yahweh, and they provide strong reason to believe that integral to the worship of Yahweh from its very beginning was the repudiation of images.[7]

Nevertheless it is certain that long after the time of Moses

[1] Cf. A. R. Johnson, *The One and the Many in the Israelite Conception of God*, 1942, pp. 18 f.
[2] Ex. 20.4.   [3] Ex. 34.17.
[4] Cf. E. Kautzsch, in *D.B.*, Extra Vol., 1904, p. 641 b: 'Such a carved image appears to have been for long regarded as unobjectionable, whereas the molten image is already prohibited in the Jahwistic section of which Ex. 34[17] forms a part.'
[5] Cf. A. H. McNeile, *Exodus* (West. C.), pp. lvi ff., H. P. Smith, *The Religion of Israel*, 1914, p. 187, A. Lods, *Israel*, E.Tr. by S. H. Hooke, 1932, pp. 315 f., and J. N. Schofield, *The Religious Background of the Bible*, 1944, p. 144, where the Decalogue is attributed to the prophetic age; and C. Steuernagel, *Einleitung in das Alte Testament*, 1912, pp. 259 ff., G. Hölscher, *Geschichte der israelitischen und jüdischen Religion*, 1922, p. 129, J. Meinhold, *Der Dekalog*, 1927, pp. 13 ff., and G. Beer, *Exodus* (H.A.T.), 1939, p. 103, where it is assigned to the exilic age or later.
[6] Cf. *B.J.R.L.*, xxxiv, 1951–2, pp. 81 ff. Many other scholars have recognized the Decalogue of Ex. 20 to be Mosaic; so, amongst others, A. Dillmann, *Handbuch der alttestamentlichen Theologie*, 1895, pp. 108, 228 f.; E. Kautzsch, in *D.B.*, Extra Vol., 1909, p. 634 b; H. Gressmann, *Mose und seine Zeit*, 1913, pp. 471 ff.; R. Kittel, *Geschichte der Hebräer*, 6th ed., i, 1923, p. 383, 445 ff.; P. Volz, *Mose und sein Werk*, 2nd ed., 1932, pp. 20 ff.; W. Eberharter, in *S.D.B.*, ii, 1934, cols. 341 ff.; A. Weiser, *Einleitung in das Alte Testament*, 2nd ed., 1949, pp. 94 f.
[7] Cf. R. H. Pfeiffer, *J.B.L.*, xlv, 1926, pp. 211 ff.

images of various kinds were made in Israel.[1] Here we have to remember two things. In the first place, customs that are eradicated in one age have a tendency to creep back, as Jer. 44 sufficiently illustrates. There we read how the practices associated with the worship of the Queen of Heaven crept back after being eradicated, and people attributed all the troubles that had come upon them to the cessation of these old customs. It would not therefore be surprising if in the conditions depicted in the period of the Judges usages which had been abandoned at Sinai tended to return. In the second place, we know that in the period following the settlement there was a constant tendency towards syncretism with the Canaanite religion, and the practices of a religion which did not repudiate images invaded Israel. There is no evidence that Moses made any visible image of Yahweh, in whose name he had led the people out of Egypt. There is no evidence that any image of Yahweh stood in the shrine of Shiloh, or in the Jerusalem Temple,[2] though Ezek. 8.10 is evidence that idols were not unknown even within its sacred precincts. There is evidence that a brazen serpent existed in the Temple until it was destroyed by Hezekiah,[3] and that men worshipped it, but the serpent was a widely current emblem of the fertility cult, and it was not specifically Yahwistic in its significance. Its creation was attributed to Moses in tradition,[4] but there is no suggestion whatever that it was regarded as an image of Yahweh. Moreover, the fact that when images were made by Jeroboam,[5] they were made in the form of well-known Canaanite symbols, though they may have been treated as images of Yahweh, suggests that there was no specifically Yahwistic form of image that could be

---

[1] Cf. Judg. 3.19, 8.27, 17.3 f., 1 Sam. 21.9, II Kings 21.7.

[2] Cf. E. Sellin, *Introduction to the Old Testament*, E.Tr. by W. Montgomery, 1923, p. 41: 'The absence of any images, which is so indubitably attested as regards the sanctuaries of Shiloh and Jerusalem, must, after all, have had some reason.'

[3] II Kings 18.4.

[4] Num. 21.8 f. This is probably an aetiological story 'told to explain a symbol that actually owed its origin to other than Yahwistic belief' (G. B. Gray, *Numbers* (I.C.C.), 1903, p. 275). It seems likely that it was a pre-Davidic Jebusite symbol, which was already in Jerusalem when the Israelites captured it; cf. *J.B.L.*, lviii, 1939, pp. 113 f., and *Festschrift für Alfred Bertholet*, 1950, pp. 461 ff.

[5] It is not certain that Jeroboam's bulls were images, indeed. Some scholars believe that they were empty pedestals, in contrast to the bulls on which Hadad stood. Cf. H. T. Obbink, *Z.A.W.*, xlvii (N.F. vi), 1929, pp. 267 f.; W. Eichrodt, *Theologie des Alten Testaments*, 3rd ed., i, p. 50; W. F. Albright, *From the Stone Age to Christianity*, 2nd ed., pp. 228 ff.; J. Bright, *The Kingdom of God*, 1953, p. 50.

employed. Where we find images, they are either of syncre-
tistic origin, or are a popular continuance of such ancient, pre-
Mosaic symbols as the *teraphim*.[1]

It is true that when the opposition to syncretism first appears
it does not attack images. Gideon, who broke down a Baal
altar in protest against the syncretism of his day,[2] later himself
made an ephod, which appears to have been an image of some
form.[3] When Micah restored the silver which he had stolen, it
was converted into an image,[4] which was later served by the
grandson of Moses,[5] and ultimately carried to the shrine of
Dan.[6] Not until we come to Hosea do we find any protest
against the sacred bulls.[7] But that does not prove that bull
images were legitimate in the worship of Yahweh, any more
than the other things against which Hosea protested were, or
ever had been, integral to Yahwism as such. It would rather
seem that it was characteristic of Yahwism from its origin that
it had no idol symbols of its own, and that when finally idols
were eliminated with the completeness and rigidity that
marked later Judaism we have a development that was in line
with the essential spirit of the religion.

If, then, God is not thought of as having any physical form
and on that ground unable to be represented by any material
image, it is hard to suppose that any biblical writer, and least
of all the author of Gen. 1, with its exalted conception of God,
could think of man as being formed in the physical likeness of
his Creator. Moreover, immediately after the statement that
man was made in the image of God we read of man's sexual
division and the command to be fruitful and multiply.[8] It
cannot be supposed for a moment that any writer of the Old
Testament thought of God in sexual terms, or in terms of
physically reproductive powers.[9] The only elements of man's
physical make up which are mentioned, therefore, are elements

---

[1] On the *teraphim* cf. *B.J.R.L.*, xxxiv, 1951–2, p. 104 n., and the literature I there
cite; also the valuable note in A. R. Johnson, *The Cultic Prophet in Ancient Israel*,
1944, pp. 31 f., and the further literature there cited.
[2] Judg. 6.28 ff.
[3] Judg. 6.27. Cf. *B.J.R.L.*, loc. cit., pp. 102 f. n.
[4] Judg. 17.3.
[5] Judg. 18.30. The Hebrew text says the priest was the grandson of Manasseh,
but the *n* is suspended, and is almost certainly an intrusion into the text, as
rabbinical writers, as well as modern scholars, are agreed.
[6] Judg. 18.14 ff., 30.   [7] Hos. 8.5, 10.5, 13.2.   [8] Gen. 1.28.
[9] Cf. J. Hempel, *Z.A.W.*, lvii (N.F. xvi), 1939, pp. 75 ff.

which he could not be supposed to share with God. It is hard to see, then, how the passage can be held to express his physical likeness to God. Moreover, the distinction between man and the lower creation was not so much the difference of his physical form as the fact of his spiritual nature. It was this that he shared with God as against the lower creation.[1]

Like the animals he has a physical body which is vitalized so long as there is breath in it. Yet it is not a complete statement of the biblical view of man to say that he is an animated body. Animals too are animated bodies, and the cessation of breath for man and animals spells death.[2] In biblical thought there is something in man's make-up which he does not share with the animals, and which gives him a measure of kinship with God. This is to be found in his spiritual nature. He was made for God's fellowship and obedience. In the story of the Garden of Eden he is represented as made for that fellowship, which is only broken by his disobedience. No command of God is laid upon the animals, as it is laid upon man, and to none of them is moral freedom attributed.

It is characteristic of the thought of the Old Testament that man may understand and do the will of God, may have fellowship with God and walk in his way. He is not alone the creature of God. He is created for God's service. That he was created in the image of God is the mark of his spiritual exaltation in the purpose of God, and of the honour that God conferred upon him. One of the most familiar of the psalms says that man was made but little lower than God.[3] When this passage is cited in the New Testament it takes the form 'little lower than the angels',[4] and this was the rendering of the Authorized Version in the Old Testament. This may serve to remind us that in biblical thought man is not the only spiritual being made for the fellowship and obedience of God. There are passages such

---

[1] Cf. S. R. Driver, *Genesis* (West. C.), 1904, p. 15: 'What is meant by the "image of God", which man is thus said to bear? . . . It can be nothing but the gift of *self-conscious reason*, which is possessed by man, but by no other animal'. Cf. also E. Sellin, *Theologie des Alten Testaments*, 2nd ed., 1936, p. 58, F. Ceuppens, *Genèse I–III*, 1946, pp. 46 f., F. Horst, *Interpretation*, iv, 1950, pp. 259 ff., G. E. Wright, *The Interpreter's Bible*, i, 1952, p. 368 a, W. Hess, *Benediktinische Monatsschrift*, xxix, 1953, pp. 371 ff.
[2] Cf. Ps. 104.29.   [3] Ps. 8.5 (Heb. 6).
[4] Heb. 2.7. Similarly LXX and Vulgate. But Jerome rendered *minues eum paulo minus a Deo* (cf. H. de Sainte-Marie, *Sancti Hieronymi Psalterium iuxta Hebraeo*, 1954, p. 15).

as the Prologue to the Book of Job which depict God as presiding in a heavenly court,[1] and there are others which speak of him as dispatching messengers to do his will—either invisible spirits such as the lying spirit to which Micaiah referred,[2] or beings who appeared in human form and spoke with men.[3] The theological problems involved in the thought of a lying spirit being in the court of God, or in the account of Satan's presenting himself there to give his report, need not detain us. Any treatment of the Old Testament as on a flat level of inspiration and authority would mean that these passages would provide serious problems, but a historical view makes it possible to regard them as outgrown beliefs.

In the thought of the inter-testamental period there was developed the conception of a court of evil, set over against God's court, to which such evil spirits were relegated, and where they were presided over by Satan or Beliar.[4] In the later teaching of the Old Testament we find that some of the principal angels of God's court are given names, such as Gabriel[5] and Michael,[6] and they are regarded as the guardians of the nations and entrusted with standing commissions by God. This speculation and movement in the direction of dualism may owe something to Zoroastrian influence in the Persian period,[7] but it is to be emphasized that its seeds were already found in Israel, where in all periods good and evil spirits were thought of as existing. And if evil spirits are represented as being in the court of God, it is significant that in the cases referred to, the initiative in their evil is represented as lying with them and not with God. If they were permitted to carry out their purposes, it was that God might use them to serve his own, just as he is represented as using men's purposes to further his own. When Assyria

---

[1] Job 1.6, 2.1.   [2] II Kings 22.21 ff.
[3] Cf. Gen. 16.7 ff., 19.1 ff., 22.11 ff., 32.1; Ex.3.2; Num. 22.22 ff.; Judg. 6.11 ff., 13.3 ff.; II Kings 1.3.
[4] Cf. my *Relevance of Apocalyptic*, 2nd ed., 1947, pp. 63, 65 f., 70, 95, 156; also E. Langton, *Essentials of Demonology*, 1949, pp. 119 ff.
[5] Dan. 8.16, 9.21.   [6] Dan. 10.13, 21, 12.1.
[7] On Persian influence in later Jewish thought cf. E. Stave, *Über den Einfluss des Parsismus auf das Judentum*, 1898; E. Böklen, *Die Verwandtschaft der jüdisch-christlichen mit der parsischen Eschatologie*, 1902; L. H. Mills, *Avesta Eschatology compared with the Books of Daniel and Revelation*, 1908; J. Scheftelowitz, *Die altpersische Religion und das Judentum*, 1920; E. Meyer, *Ursprung und Anfänge des Christentums*, ii, 4th ed., 1925, pp. 189 ff.; W. O. E. Oesterley, *The Jews and Judaism during the Greek Period*, 1941, pp. 85 ff.; W. F. Albright, *From the Stone Age to Christianity*, 2nd ed., pp. 275 ff.

is described as the rod of God's anger,[1] it is recognized that her heart was evil and her act such as to call down punishment upon her,[2] even though God could use it to serve his own purposes.

If angels are thought of as created to serve God in heaven, man is thought of as created to serve him on earth. God's command is laid upon him in the moment of his creation. The command is not something hard and irksome, that subjects man to any harsh domination by God. 'Be fruitful and multiply . . . and have dominion.'[3] 'Of every tree of the garden thou mayest freely eat: but of the tree of knowledge of good and evil thou shalt not eat.'[4] Not yet is this the full understanding of the will of God. Higher words are found in the Law and the Prophets. 'Thou shalt love the Lord thy God with all thine heart, and with all thy soul, and with all thy might.'[5] 'Cease to do evil: learn to do good. Seek justice, keep the oppressor within bounds,[6] give the fatherless their rights, take up the cause of the widow.'[7] Here and in countless other passages it is assumed that the will of God is the law for man. At the same time it is realized that obedience to God is not alone man's duty; it is also his privilege, and it brings him blessing. 'If ye will truly obey my voice . . . ye shall be my own special treasure.'[8]

In the Garden of Eden the blessing of obedience was the fellowship of God, which was broken by disobedience. Yet it is clear from many passages that the enjoyment of God's fellowship was believed to be still open to men, and the attainment of the goal of manhood depended upon it. When we are inclined to dismiss the naïve simplicity of the Paradise story, we should not forget that it enshrined ideas which could be expressed less naïvely, and which are so expressed elsewhere in the Bible, and that those ideas are not to be dismissed because of the form of the story through which they are presented.[9] The calamity that befell man in that story was that he was thrust forth from the presence of God and no longer enjoyed the free intercourse with

---

[1] Isa. 10.5. [2] Isa. 10.7, 12. [3] Gen. 1.28. [4] Gen. 2.16 ff. [5] Deut. 6.5.
[6] Here R.V. has 'relieve the oppressed'. The verb may mean 'pronounce blessed', or 'cause to go straight'. If the former sense is found, as in R.V., the word that follows has to be revowelled to make it passive. But the latter sense seems more appropriate here, the word that follows the verb being then given its normal sense of 'oppressor'. R.S.V. renders 'correct oppression', but the form of the Hebrew noun is commonly used of an agent.
[7] Isa. 1.16 f. [8] Ex. 19.5.
[9] Cf. G. Lambert *N.R.Th.*, lxxvi, 1954, pp. 919 ff.; also J. L. McKenzie, *Theological Studies*, xv, 1954, pp. 541 ff.

his Maker that he had hitherto enjoyed. That this was expressed in terms of physical companionship should not blind us to its enduringly valid teaching that God's fellowship is man's highest privilege. Later writers, who did not share what we think of as the crudity of the author of the Paradise story, still used the metaphor of physical fellowship to express the profoundly spiritual fellowship to which they called men. When Amos asks if two can walk together except they be agreed,[1] it is clear that he not only thinks that men may walk with God, but that it is important for their well-being that they should do so. 'Seek Yahweh and ye shall live'[2] he cries elsewhere. God's fellowship was given to Joseph in a prison. 'Yahweh was with Joseph, and shewed kindness unto him.'[3] Familiar is the great word 'Thus saith the high and lofty one who inhabits eternity, whose name is Holy: I dwell in the high and holy place, with him also who is of a contrite and humble spirit.'[4] So, too, with Jeremiah's call in the name of God 'Let him that glories glory in this, that he understands and knows me.'[5] In none of these passages is the thought really of men's physical association with God, but of a spiritual experience which is open to them. Some are thought of as knowing this experience in a special degree. The prophet is described as the man who has stood in the council of God,[6] and who has there learned the counsel of God,[7] entering into his thought and purpose. But the knowledge of the Lord was not reserved for prophets alone. When we read God's primary demands upon men in the memorable passage in the book of Micah,[8] we find them expressed in terms of the reflection of the

---

[1] Amos 3.3.   [2] Amos 5.6.   [3] Gen. 39.21.   [4] Isa. 57.15.   [5] Jer. 9.24 (Heb. 23).
[6] Jer. 23.18, 23. Cf. H. Wheeler Robinson, *J.T.S.*, xlv, 1944, pp. 151 ff.
[7] Cf. Amos 3.7.
[8] Micah 6.8. Many scholars deny this passage to Micah, and assign it to an unknown prophet of the period of Manasseh's reign (so T. H. Robinson, *Die zwölf Kleinen Propheten* (H.A.T.), 2nd ed., 1954, p. 147). For our present purpose it is immaterial whether Micah himself is the author, or another a few decades later. There is, however, today greater caution in labelling the last three chapters of this book as secondary. Cf. A. George, *Michée, Sophonie, Nahum* (Jerusalem Bible), 1952, p. 12: 'Une nouvelle période a commencé, où l'on ne refuse plus de lui (i.e., to Micah) attribuer des fragments importants en v.8–vii.17'. D. Deden (*De Kleine Profeten* (B.O.T.), i, 1953, p. 201) regards the whole book as probably from Micah himself, but compiled by an editor from two collections of his oracles. Cf. A. Weiser, *Die zwölf Kleinen Propheten* (A.T.D.), i, 1949, pp. 203 f., and *Einleitung in das Alte Testament*, 2nd ed., 1949, p. 190; and my *Growth of the Old Testament*, 1950, p. 116. On this verse George observes (op. cit., p. 39): 'Cette triple exigence, d'ordre tout spirituel, correspond précisément aux revendications fondamentales des trois grands prophètes antérieurs à Michée'.

will of God, based on humble fellowship with him. Without fellowship there can be no obedience; without the obedience there can be no fellowship. Yet this is no deadlock from which there can be no release. This fellowship with the God in whose image he was created is open to the man of submissive spirit, the desire of whose heart is to obey.

This does not mean that man may have an easy familiarity with God, and know an equal fellowship with him. A vast gulf separates man from God, and in his presence he must ever be filled with awe. If that gulf is bridged in fellowship, it is of God's grace that it is so bridged, and man is filled with the sense of unspeakable privilege in its enjoyment. The dignity that man has is his because God conferred it on him, and the highest dignity is not something inalienably conferred on him in his manhood, and now inherent in him, but something that is his only so long as he accepts the conditions it entails. For while he is often represented as superior to the animal creation, and charged with the rule of the lower creatures, it is rather in his potential relation to God that his real dignity lies. He may have fellowship with God, but only so long as his heart is right with God, and so long as he bows himself before God in worship and reflects the will of God in his life.

It is this spiritual kinship with God, making possible a real fellowship with his Maker, which lies behind the thought that man was created in the image of God. It also makes possible the divine inspiration of man. That man is other than God is never lost sight of in the Bible, which could never be guilty of speaking of the divinity of man; that man is *wholly* other than God is equally alien to biblical thought, and could hardly be accepted by any believer in the Incarnation. It is important to remember that though men are frequently held to be the vehicle of the divine self-revelation this is never conceived of in physical terms. In the Maccabaean age the persecuting Seleucid monarch, Antiochus IV, was styled Theos Epiphanes, God Manifest, because of some fancied likeness between himself and the traditional representation of Zeus. Such an idea is utterly alien to the thought of the Bible. Wherever man stands as the vehicle of divine revelation it is always a spiritual revelation, and never a physical revelation, such as might have been expected if its thought of man's likeness to God were primarily in physical terms. This is the more remarkable since, as we are often reminded, Hebrew thinking was characteristically concrete. The essence of the divine revelation was always in the intangible realm of the spirit. Even in the early source which pictures God as coming to the patriarchs in human form, the real point of the revelation is never in the physical form of God, but in his message. Similarly when men became the vehicle of revelation, it was not in themselves but in their message. So again, when in the New Testament Christ is spoken of as the image of God,[1] or when Paul speaks of 'the light of the knowledge of the glory of God in the face of Jesus Christ',[2] none could suppose that the thought is of the perfect revelation of the form of God in the body of Christ. The image of God is spiritually conceived. This is so manifestly true of the Old Testament as a whole, as well as of the New, that it is highly improbable that the latest source of the Pentateuch, in which the transcendence of God is particularly emphasized, fell to the level of thinking of him in essentially physical terms, and virtually certain that Gen. 1.26 f. is to be interpreted spiritually.[3]

Man's body is perceived to be inhabited by something more than breath. He has also a spirit.[4] It is true that the word which

---

[1] II Cor. 4.4, Col. 1.15; cf. Heb. 1.3.　　[2] II Cor. 4.6.

[3] Cf. G. E. Wright, *The Interpreter's Bible,* i, 1952, p. 368 a; F. Ceuppens, op. cit., pp. 46 f. Cf. also H. Holzinger, in *H.S.A.T.*, 4th ed., i, 1922, p. 11: 'Der Gedanke an eine Nachahmung der Liebesgestalt Gottes ist für den Gottesbegriff von P völlig ausgeschlossen. Der Besitz des göttlichen "Ebenbildes" besteht für den Menschen in der Zugehörigkeit zu der Gattung der geistig-sittlichen Wesen, deren oberste Spitze Gott selbst ist, sowie in der Ordnung, dass er über der gesamten übrigen Kreatur steht.'

[4] R. Dussaud (*Les Origines cananéennes du sacrifice israélite*, 2nd ed., 1941, pp. 83 f.; cf. also *Syria*, xv, 1935, pp. 267 ff.) holds that man was conceived of as having two souls, the one spiritual (*rûaḥ*) and the other vegetative (*nephesh*), the latter being located in the fat parts of the body. Oehler (op. cit., § 70—Zondervan reprint, pp. 150 f.) argues that the *rûaḥ* is the source of the *nephesh*, which exists and lives only by the power of the *rûaḥ*. He finds that the impulse to act proceeds from the *rûaḥ*, but the seat of the personality is the *nephesh*. Hence 'the Old Testament does not teach a trichotomy of the human being in the sense of body, soul, and spirit, as being originally three co-ordinate elements of man; rather the whole man is included in the *basar* and *nephesh* (body and soul) which spring from the union of the *rûaḥ* with matter' (p. 151). It is notoriously difficult to define the relations between the terms *rûaḥ* and *nephesh*. Often they are interchangeable; e.g., 'Impatience' is 'shortness of spirit' (Ex. 6.9, Job 21.4) or 'shortness of soul' (Num. 21.4, Judg. 16.16); 'patience' may be 'length of spirit' (Eccl. 7.8) or 'length of soul' (Job 6.11); 'bitterness' may be 'of spirit'. (Gen. 26.35) or 'of soul' (I Sam. 1.10, 22.2, 30.6; Job 3.20, 27.2, and often). Even of God either term can be used; cf. Judg. 10.16 (*nephesh*) and Micah 2.7 (*rûaḥ*). Yet they cannot be simply identified, since in other usages they are not interchangeable. Thus, for 'myself' the Hebrew said 'my soul', but not 'my spirit'.

is rendered *spirit* can also mean *breath* or *wind*, but it is equally clear that in many of its usages it denotes a quality of personality.[1] When we read, in the already cited text, that God dwells with him that is of a contrite and humble *rûaḥ*,[2] it is clear that the thought is of character and personality. Similarly, when the psalmist cries 'Create in me a clean heart, O God, And renew a right spirit within me',[3] his real thought is not of the heart and the breath, but of character. Frequently we find a moral judgement passed upon this *rûaḥ* of men. The psalmist can speak of a man 'in whose spirit there is no deceit.'[4] There are passages which speak of a change of spirit within the one body. Saul was told that he should find the spirit of God come upon him, so that he should become another man,[5] and elsewhere we read that an evil spirit rushed upon him and transformed him again.[6] Ezekiel can speak of men's heart of stone being changed for a heart of flesh, and a new spirit being put within them.[7]

God also is thought of in terms of *rûaḥ*, or spirit, and as being able to communicate of his own spirit to men. We read that the spirit of God clothed itself with Gideon,[8] and a prophetic passage opens with the words 'The spirit of the Lord Yahweh is upon me'.[9] This is a great and important element in the Old Testament thought of man, that he may become the vehicle of the divine purpose. He not merely has the command of God laid upon him. He may be lifted in some measure into the very personality of God. This is especially so in relation to the prophets. Without ceasing to be themselves, and while still reflecting in style and metaphor their own individuality, outlook, and experience, they were yet conscious that they were the mouthpiece of God, the vehicle of his message, and hence they could address men in the first person, as though they were themselves impersonating God. For the purpose of their message they were God, an extension of his personality.[10] They never forgot that they were not God, and they could pass from speaking God's message in the first person to speaking of him

---

[1] On the meaning and usage of the word *rûaḥ* cf. C. A. Briggs, *J.B.L.*, xix, 1900, pp. 132 ff., W. R. Schoemaker, ibid., xxiii, 1904, pp. 13 ff., E. D. Burton, *A.J.Th.*, xviii, 1914, pp. 59 ff., A. R. Johnson, *The Vitality of the Individual*, pp. 26 ff.; C. Ryder Smith, *The Bible Doctrine of Man*, 1951, pp. 9 ff.; and A. Neher, *L'Essence du Prophétisme*, 1955, pp. 85 ff.
[2] Isa. 57.15. [3] Psa. 51.10 (Heb. 12). [4] Ps. 32.2. [5] I Sam. 10.6.
[6] I Sam. 18.10, 19.9. [7] Ezek. 11.19. [8] Judg. 6.34. [9] Isa. 61.1.
[10]Cf. A. R. Johnson, *The One and the Many*, pp. 36 ff.

in the third person. It was not that the prophet was in himself
identified with God, but that in so far as he was God's messenger
he was an extension of the personality of God while he was delivering his message. Yet it is clear from the study of their
prophecies that if their oracles were the oracles of God, they
bore the mark of the personalities of the men through whom
they were spoken. Hence, just as we found subjective and
objective factors in revelation, the human and the superhuman
entwined together, so here in inspiration, which is the organ of
one of the forms of revelation, we find divine and human
factors inextricably interwoven in a way that testifies to the
Old Testament experience of the kinship of man with God, and
of God's otherness than man.

Nor can it be thought that this relationship with God was
reserved for prophets. The prophet could be filled with the
spirit of God to speak his word; but others could be filled with
the spirit to do his work, or to lead his people. Yet again, men
could be filled with his spirit to live in accord with his will. The
psalmist could cry 'Take not thy holy spirit from me'.[1] There are
passages which think of the universal possession of the spirit of
God. When Moses said 'Would God that all Yahweh's people
were prophets'[2] such a thought is implicit in his word, though a
remote possibility, while Joel could express it as a future certainty: 'I will pour out my spirit upon all flesh.'[3]

Again, in the thought of the Old Testament man is endowed
with moral freedom, and can therefore use that freedom to
resist the will of God. It is often said that later Judaism was
obsessed by the thought of sin, and especially of unconscious
sin. It is true that sin comes before us most in the latest strands of
the Law, but it has long been recognized that many of the ritual
usages preserved in that strand are of ancient origin,[4] and this
is recognized today more fully than ever.[5] But the fact of sin

---

[1] Ps. 51.11 (Heb. 13).   [2] Num. 11.29.   [3] Joel 2.28 (Heb. 3.1).
[4] Cf. A. Kuenen, *The Religion of Israel to the Fall of the Jewish State*, E.Tr. by A. H.
May, ii, 1875, p. 252: 'The priestly lawgiver neither could nor would create a
new state of affairs, but closely annexed himself to what he found in existence
. . . The sacrifices and feasts to Jahveh were of much older date.' Cf. also
D. C. Simpson, *Pentateuchal Criticism*, 1914, pp. 126 ff.
[5] Cf. S. H. Hooke, *The Origins of Early Semitic Ritual*, 1938, p. 45: 'It is now generally recognized that even the late parts of the Pentateuch preserve much early
material, and it is legitimate to use evidence from the Deuteronomic and Priestly
legislation relating to the ritual, with due precaution, as some indication of the
forms of ritual which existed in the pre-prophetic period.'

figures in the Bible from the beginning. The story of Paradise stands in the earliest strand of the Pentateuch, and it presents to us the fact of sin. It was sin that came between man and God, to break the intimate fellowship of the garden days, and thus to bring calamity upon man. Various terms for sin are used in the Bible,[1] but common to every form of sin is its disharmony with the will of God.

Many of the specific sins which are mentioned, and especially in the Levitical and Priestly Law, are ritual offences, such as contact with death or various forms of uncleanness, or the breach of food *tabus*, and rites for their removal are presented. Although these are found in what are believed to be the later strands of the Law, they are undoubtedly of very ancient origin, and there is none who would regard them as the climax of the development of Old Testament thought or religion. The Christian no longer observes them, and the passages that deal with them are amongst the least read by him in the Bible. Nevertheless, they cannot be ignored in a study of the faith of Israel, since they are not amongst the primitive things that were outgrown and shed in the course of Israel's history, but amongst those that persisted throughout the whole Old Testament period and beyond. In New Testament times many Jews made these provisions an end in themselves, and observed them with a precision they did not bring to the observance of the more ethical and spiritual requirements of the Law, and we find them scathingly denounced in the Gospels.[2]

Here we must not forget that the Law concerned itself also with moral offences, and while it provided ritual acts for the cleansing of moral sin, it required those acts to be accompanied by penitence of spirit and by restitution so far as restitution could be made.[3] The Law did not encourage the easy thought that moral sin was a light matter, to be conveniently disposed of by a formal act that was no more than a formal act. The book of Proverbs is often thought of as the repository of a somewhat worldly wisdom and not very profoundly spiritual. Yet

[1] Cf. C. Ryder Smith, *The Bible Doctrine of Sin*, 1953, pp. 15 ff.; and G. Quell, in *Th.W.B.*, i, 1932, pp. 267 ff. (E.Tr. by J. R. Coates, 1951, pp. 1 ff.).

[2] Cf. J. Klausner, *Jesus of Nazareth*, E.Tr. by H. Danby, 1925, p. 92: 'Hence he (i.e., Jesus) stood in opposition to the majority of the Pharisees and their followers, who made the external act the main object and the underlying intention only a secondary matter'; cf. also pp. 213 ff.

[3] Cf. Lev. 5.5 f., Num. 5.6 f.

here we read 'The sacrifice of the wicked is an abomination; how much more when he bringeth it with a wicked mind.'[1] Moreover, the Law offered no ritual means of expiating what it calls high-handed sin, by which it probably means sin wilfully and deliberately indulged in.[2] Nor should we forget that for heinous sins no ritual act was prescribed. For David's sin with Bathsheba, or for the murder of Uriah, no ritual act could atone, and none was prescribed in the Law.

It is therefore probable that those who enshrined in the later Law of Judaism the ancient *tabus* and gave so large a place to the expiation of ritual and technical offences were rather concerned to teach that if even these were to be treated with such seriousness the more grievous sins were to be held in the deepest horror.[3] These ritual offences were sins because they were alien to the will of God, and were therefore to be treated seriously, and they desired men to hold the will of the holy God in such awe that they would be filled with deep concern over the most trifling of them. Despite the danger which these provisions brought, they do not testify to a shallow view of sin on the part of the creators of the Law, but rather to a mistaken way of giving expression to their view. All sin is fundamentally the performance of acts of which God disapproves, and if even the Law makes it clear that his deepest disapproval is of man's moral evil and that penitence of spirit is the first requirement of God, and that for the worst sins no ritual act could have any meaning at all, the prophets give to these weightier sins their chief attention.

Turning then from the unwitting and technical offences to the weightier moral and spiritual offences, we may observe that sin is recognized to be man's spontaneous act of disobedience to God. He was made for obedience, but obedience that was not spontaneous would not be obedience. God compels neither obedience nor disobedience. Though he made man in his own image and for his fellowship, it was of the essence of the dignity of his manhood that he should be morally free—and therefore

---

[1] Prov. 21.27. R.V. marg. has here 'to atone for wickedness', and this is favoured by some, and reflected in Moffatt's rendering 'to atone for crime'. Cf. also Prov. 15.8. For similar passages in Ecclesiasticus and in the Talmud and Midrash cf. *The Unity of the Bible*, p. 46 n.

[2] Cf. *B.J.R.L.*, xxxiii, 1950–1, pp. 96 f.

[3] Cf. Pirke Aboth 2.1, where the saying of Rabbi Judah the Prince is recorded: 'Be heedful of a light precept as of a weighty one.' Here the meaning is that even the lightest of sins were serious.

able to repudiate the dignity of character for which he was designed. When man listens to the seductive voices that call him away from God, his act is essentially his own. But the fundamental character of sin is seen in that it comes between a man and God, and isolates him from his Maker. In the profoundly penetrating story of the Garden of Eden this is well brought out. After his act of disobedience Adam hid himself from the face of God.[1] Before God drove him forth from the garden he had thus withdrawn himself from God and was conscious of a barrier which was not of God's creation, but his own.

All sin is sin against God. This is continually brought out in the Bible. When Cain murdered Abel he sinned against God, and his brother's blood cried out unto God.[2] When David committed adultery with Bathsheba and had Uriah removed from his way, he sinned against God. 'And David said unto Nathan, I have sinned against Yahweh.'[3] When men oppressed one another, and cheated and defrauded one another, and perverted judgement in the courts, they sinned against God, as Amos and other prophets declared with insistence. Equally it is true that all sin is sin against man. It is sin against one's fellows. Clearly Cain sinned against Abel, and David against Uriah. But it is not only a sin against the victim of the act. It is also a sin against society, of which the sinner forms a part. By his sin he lowers its level of goodness, and in various ways involves others besides himself in the consequences of his act. When Gideon made an ephod 'all Israel went a whoring after it'.[4] Yet again, all sin is sin against oneself. 'He who sins against me injures himself.'[5] Its first consequence is just that it breaks that fellowship with God which is the foundation of man's well-being. Hence, instead of being guided and sustained by that fellowship he stumbles in folly to his own hurt. Moreover, it is as a canker in his soul, demeaning and defiling his manhood, until 'every imagination of the thoughts of his heart' becomes 'only evil continually'.[6]

[1] Gen. 3.8.   [2] Gen. 4.10.   [3] II Sam. 12.13.   [4] Judg. 8.27.
[5] Prov. 8.36. R.V. marg. and R.S.V. understand the verse to mean 'he who misses me injures himself', and note the contrast with the preceding verse, 'he who finds me'. This is probably correct; but he who misses God misses him because he sins, and the verb is used for 'to sin' just because sin was regarded as a missing of the mark. Ben Sira probably reflects this verse when he says: 'He who sins offends against his own soul' (Ecclus. 19.4).
[6] Gen. 6.5.

God's reaction to sin is not merely to punish it. In a sense it is rather the sinner who punishes himself and those around him. By abandoning the way of God he misses the goal of his own well-being, and it is rather he than God who brings about the discipline of sorrow. Yet the recognition that God is not a mere spectator of his world, but active on the plane of history and experience, leads also to the thought that he has not merely put it into the nature of a moral universe to discipline the sinner, but that he himself is active in the discipline.[1] It has already been said that if this is evidence of the wrath of God and of his justice, it is equally evidence of his love. For God's love is not soft sentimentality that is indifferent to moral considerations. It is strong to discipline man for his good, and to awaken him to a sense of his folly, or when there is no hope of his reform to discipline him to awaken others to a sense of the folly of sin.

It is more characteristic of the thought of the Old Testament to regard punishment of sin as disciplinary than as penal, though both figure in its pages. When it is merely penal, it is the indication that discipline can have no effect on the disciplined, since moral decay has gone too far. Nowhere is sin thought of as atoned for by punishment, so that by the mere fact of punishment fellowship is restored.[2] It is when punishment has wrought its work of chastening the spirit that fellowship is restored. This thought is common in the Deuteronomic framework of the book of Judges, where it is the community rather than the individual that is in mind. By religious declension and the decay of the spirit the people called down upon themselves

---

[1] Thus in the story of man's first sin, Adam first isolated himself from God by his sin, and then God is represented as driving him forth from the garden.

[2] Taken by itself, Isa. 40.2 might seem to present such a view, since the prophet is bidden to cry to Jerusalem 'that her time of hard service is ended, and her iniquity pardoned, for she hath received of Yahweh's hand double for all her sins'. But it is clear from the following chapters that Deutero-Isaiah believed that her spirit had been chastened so that she was now ready to return to obedience. Again and again she is described as the servant of Yahweh, and nowhere is the thought found that she is entitled to deliverance and restoration, whether she gives obedience or is indifferent to God (cf. B. W. Helfgott, *The Doctrine of Election in Tannaitic Literature*, 1954, p. 65, where R. Joshua ben Hananiah's view that 'salvation will come to Israel regardless of whether they repent or not' is cited). It is 'they that wait for Yahweh' who renew their strength (Isa. 40.31), and if the men of Israel are promised help (Isa. 41.14) there is the faith that they will rejoice in Yahweh (Isa. 41.16). The whole burden of the message of Deutero-Isaiah is of the grace of God, to be proved anew in the deliverance she will experience, and not the thought that she has earned it by her punishment.

the chastening experience of foreign oppression until they were ready to return to God, when a new leader was raised up to deliver them. In individual experience it is also true that when the heart is softened by sorrow, and the sinner humbles himself before God, fellowship may be restored.[1]

Nor does God rely merely on the entail of sorrow that sin brings to awaken men to the folly of their way. He sends his prophets to warn men of the folly of the way wherein their feet are set. Jeremiah, with that anthropomorphism which has been already noted, speaking of God rising up early to send his prophets, finely expresses the conception of the yearning desire of God to reclaim the sinner, a yearning desire which figures elsewhere in other ways. Certainly the ministry of the prophets, with their emphasis on conformity to the moral will of God, is something unique in the history of the ancient world, and God did not leave himself without witness in Israel, to call men back to himself and his obedience. Sometimes their word was effective and penitence was induced. So when David sinned and the prophet Nathan rebuked him, it was not the death of Bathsheba's child which broke his heart in contrition, but the word of Nathan which led him to say 'I have sinned against Yahweh'[2] The end, whether of the discipline of events or the ministry of the prophets, was submission to God and renewed obedience to his will.

Beyond this the Old Testament has a message of salvation.[3] It does not speak only of discipline and warning to deal with the dark fact of sin which comes between man and God to frustrate the purpose of his creation. It offers power for the cleansing from sin and the renewal of fellowship. To review the whole range of the concept of salvation in the Bible is impossible here. Often it is national salvation from foreign foes who would conquer, or who have oppressed. In the individual sphere it might be salvation from disease, or trouble, or powerful oppressors. In all this there is nothing of unusual significance, however. Men have always looked to their gods to save them from this kind of situation, and have resorted to prayer in the assurance that salvation may be the act of the deity. Nor was Israel unique in

---

[1] Cf. II Sam. 12.13.   [2] II Sam. 12.13.
[3] Cf. A. Médebielle, 'Expiation dans l'Ancien Testament', in *S.D.B.*, iii, 1938, cols. 48 ff.

seeking salvation from sin. Where sin was ritually conceived, it was held to be capable of ritual removal. The god was believed to be the remover, but he was thought to be open to ritual persuasion to exercise his power. In Israel, too, with its deeper conception of sin there was a ritual of salvation. And here the sacrificial ritual calls first for notice.

The religion of Israel, like that of the surrounding peoples, whose religion formed the background out of which it came and in the setting of which it developed, expressed itself through the ritual of sacrifice. Of the origin of sacrifice and its presumed first meaning, it would not be in place to speak here, save to say that it is improbable that any simple theory does justice to the facts.[1] Certainly within the Old Testament no theory of a single purpose of sacrifice can be satisfactory. For it is clear that whereas some sacrifices were propitiatory, all were not.[2] The thank offering[3] was certainly not. Some sacrifices were conceived of as charged with an effect upon the persons who offered them, or upon others for whom they were offered. The purpose of the sacrifices which Job offered at the conclusion of each of the rounds of his sons' feasts was in part to turn away the anger of God, which might have been aroused by any thoughtless word or deed of theirs, and in part to cleanse his sons.[4] The variety of the sacrifices and of the meaning given to them must always be remembered. Nor can a single sacrifice be adequately interpreted in terms of a single idea. While one element might be especially prominent, others might also be present.

It has been maintained that the sacrificial ritual of Israel was essentially of Canaanite origin.[5] Such a view may claim some support from Amos 5.25 and Jer.7. 22, as these texts are commonly understood. Amos asks 'Did you bring me sacrifices and offerings during the forty years in the wilderness, O house of Israel?', while Jeremiah says 'For I did not speak unto your fathers, or give them commands concerning burnt offerings or sacrifices in the day that I brought them out of the land of

---

[1] Cf. *B.J.R.L.*, xxxiii, 1950–51, pp. 76 ff.
[2] On sacrifice cf. W. P. Paterson, in *D.B.*, iv, 1902, pp. 329 ff., G. F. Moore, in *E.B.*, iv, 1907, cols. 4183 ff., G. B. Gray, *Sacrifice in the Old Testament*, 1925, and W. O. E. Oesterley, *Sacrifices in Ancient Israel*, 1937.
[3] Cf. Lev. 7.11 ff., where the thankoffering is treated as a variety of the peace-offering.
[4] Job 1.5.   [5] Cf. especially R. Dussaud, op. cit.

Egypt.' Both of these texts would seem to deny that Israel had offered sacrifice in the wilderness period. I have more than once offered my reasons for dissenting from the common view.[1] In passages of greater antiquity than the time of Amos we find references to sacrifices in the time of Moses, and if Amos and Jeremiah had wished to challenge this tradition they would have done so more directly than by a rhetorical question and a passing allusion. Moreover, the sacrifice of the Passover is fundamental to the story of the Exodus, and it is difficult to suppose that these two prophets denied that it had been ordained by God or actually offered.

Quite apart from these two texts, however, it may be agreed that much of Israel's ritual was probably of Canaanite origin, or of pre-Mosaic origin.[2] On the testimony of the Old Testament itself there was much intermarriage of Canaanite religious practice with Israelite religion through long periods, and while some things were ultimately eliminated others remained, to be embodied in the practice of Israel and made the vehicle of her faith.

It is, however, unlikely that all of Israel's ritual was taken over from her Canaanite neighbours. Even if it were, we should still have to recognize that the significance attached to the rites is of more importance than the rites themselves, and that in the true faith of Israel that significance may not be the same as in Canaanite religion. The Passover, which was almost certainly not taken over from the Canaanites, but offered before the Israelites entered the land, was probably of very ancient and pre-Mosaic origin.[3] But from the time of Moses its significance was linked with the deliverance of the Exodus, and whatever meaning it may have had before was no longer of importance

[1] Cf. *B.J.R.L.*, xxix, 1945–6, pp. 16 ff., xxxiii, 1950–1, pp. 79 ff., and *The Unity of the Bible*, pp. 30 ff.

[2] Cf. J. Pedersen, *Israel III–IV*, 1940, p. 317: 'Our knowledge of the Phoenician-Canaanite cult is now quite sufficient to warrant the conclusion that the greater part of the Israelitish sacrificial practices had been learnt from the Canaanites'. Cf. J. P. Hyatt, *Prophetic Religion*, 1947, p. 128; S. H. Hooke, *The Origins of Early Semitic Ritual*, 1938, pp. 45 ff.

[3] E. Dhorme, *La Religion des Hébreux Nomades*, 1937, p. 211, says: 'Tel est le rituel de la Pâque dans sa primitive simplicité et je ne trouve point d'exemple plus typique du sacrifice des nomades'. On the Passover cf. *D.B.*, loc. cit., pp. 338 f., and *E.B.*, loc. cit., cols. 4207 ff.; G. B. Gray, *J.T.S.*, xxxvii, 1936, pp. 241 ff.; N. H. Snaith, *The Jewish New Year Festival*, 1947, pp. 13 ff.; T. H. Gaster, *Passover: its History and Tradition*, 1949; and H. Haag, *Luzerner Theologische Studien*, 1954, pp. 17 ff.

for her. Not alone in this connexion, but in relation to all sacrificial and other rites, the meaning attached to the rites is of more significance than a merely antiquarian interest in the origin of the rites themselves.

It has already been said that all Israelite sacrifices cannot be interpreted in terms of a single idea. Not all sacrifices, indeed, were animal sacrifices. Beside these there were the first fruits and tithes.[1] These were believed to belong to God, and were not thought of as man's gift to God. His bounty was their source, and he was therefore entitled to them, so that it would be sacrilege for a man to take them for himself. Again there were meal offerings[2] and freewill offerings of substance[3] to be distinguished from animal sacrifices. Of the animal sacrifices some were thought of as gifts to God, some as means of expiation, and some as means of effecting communion with him. Probably the *minḥāh* was a gift, though its precise purpose is not clear.[4] It was originally an animal sacrifice,[5] but later it became a meal offering,[6] but whether it was the expression of devotion or the plea for some boon is uncertain. Some of the animal sacrifices were wholly consumed on the altar, while others were in part the perquisite of the priest and in part consumed on the altar, and yet others were in part consumed by the offerer himself.

Not all animal sacrifice was therefore related to sin and its expiation, or the securing of some boon. Thankofferings were rather the recognition that some boons had been received from God. So, too, were the sacrifices in fulfilment of vows.[7] The contracting of the vow was as voluntary as the bringing of a thankoffering, but once the vow was made it laid an obligation upon a man, to repudiate which would be a sin. But in itself it was a contractual thankoffering. There were other sacrifices more directly connected with sin. These included peace offerings, sin offerings and guilt offerings, to use the normal English terms in translations. In Lev. 5.1–9 the sin offering and the guilt

[1] Cf. O. Eissfeldt, *Erstlinge und Zehnten im Alten Testament*, 1917.
[2] On the meal offering, or *minḥāh*, and its varieties, cf. G. F. Moore, in *E.B.*, iv, 1907, cols. 4207 f.
[3] Cf. II Kings 12.4 ff., 22.3 ff.
[4] Cf. G. B. Gray, *Sacrifice in the Old Testament*, 1925, pp. 14 ff.
[5] This term is used of Abel's sacrifice, Gen. 4.4.
[6] Cf. Lev. 2.
[7] Cf. J. Pedersen, *Israel III–IV*, pp. 324 ff.

offering appear to be equated, but probably they were originally distinct.[1] Both appear to have been offered for more
specific sins than the peace offering.[2] This, again, is of uncertain
meaning. It may have been offered to ensure the maintenance
of right relations with God or for the restoration of such
relations.

Beyond these individual sacrifices we find in the Law provision for the daily offerings on behalf of the community,[3] so
that right relations might be maintained between it and God.
Further, on the annual Day of Atonement, whose ritual was
certainly of very ancient origin, sacrifice was offered for the sin
of the community during the year.[4] Here, however, the scape-
goat on which the sin of the people was put was driven out into
the wilderness, and not sacrificed in the shrine.[5] All of this
sufficiently indicates without exhausting the variety of sacrificial
rites and the variety of purposes for which they were offered.

More important is it to observe that no sacrifice is represented
in the teaching of the Bible as effecting salvation by the mere
performance of an outer rite. That many people thought of
them in such terms is unquestionable, and that they were so
thought of outside Israel is not to be denied. But the prophets
continually challenged the idea that by the offering of abundant
sacrifices the well-being of individual or community was
assured, and the Law no more than the prophets was content
with a merely formal act. Where sacrifice was offered for sin,
the Law demanded the confession of the sin and humble penitence of spirit, and where the sin was against another man and
restitution could be made, it demanded restitution.[6] On the
Day of Atonement, the High Priest had to make confession for
the sin of the community.[7] He was the representative of the
community in confession as well as in the sacrifice itself, and
unless his confession genuinely represented the spirit of the
people the sacrifice was hollow and meaningless.

[1] Cf. J. H. Kurtz, *Sacrificial Worship in the Old Testament*, E. Tr. by J. Martin, 1863,
pp. 189 ff.; G. B. Gray, op. cit., pp. 57 ff.
[2] In post-exilic times the peace offering included the thank offering, the vow, and
the freewill offering; cf. Lev. 7.11 ff.
[3] Cf. Ex. 29.38 ff., Lev. 6.8 ff. (Heb. 1 ff.), Num. 28.3 ff.
[4] Cf. Lev. 16. Cf. Gray, op. cit., pp. 306 ff., Oesterley, op. cit., pp. 226 ff.; also
S. Landersdorfer, *Studien zum biblischen Versöhnungstag* (A.A., x, 1), 1924.
[5] Cf. Gray, op. cit., pp. 306 ff., and Oesterley, op. cit., pp. 226 ff.
[6] Cf. Lev. 5.5 f.; Num. 5.6 f.
[7] Lev. 16.21.

At the same time, it must be clearly recognized that sacrifice rightly offered was believed to be charged with power. It was not merely the symbol of the plea of the offerer, but charged with power which derived from God and not from the offerer. The latter laid his hands on the head of the animal, and so in some way identified himself with it.[1] It was not merely that the animal was a substitute for him, dying in his stead. In its death he was conceived of as dying—not physically, indeed, but spiritually. The death of the animal vividly symbolized his death to whatever stood between him and God, in the case of a sacrifice for sin, or his surrender of himself to God in thankfulness and humility in other cases. But beyond that it was believed to be the medium of cleansing for him, or of the fellowship with God which was opened up to him, or the assurance of blessing with which he went away. Sacrifice thus both expressed the spirit of the worshipper and did something for him; it bore his spirit to God and bore to him from God that which he sought and needed.

This means that while sacrifice was believed to be charged with power, it was only when it was offered in genuine penitence and submission. The prophetic denunciations were of those who offered sacrifices which were in no sense the organ of their spirit, and whose proud indifference to the will of God was proclaimed in their lives. On the other hand, it should not be forgotten that where sacrifice was prescribed, penitence and submission of spirit alone were not enough. That obedience is better than sacrifice, and that obedience is expressed in life and not alone in worship, was always recognized in the true stream of the faith of Israel.[2] But it was not thought that a man could save himself from his sin by his penitence and obedience. It was God alone who could save him, and sacrifice was thought to be the means of that divine salvation, when a man presented himself with his sacrifice.

Nevertheless, sacrifice was not the sole organ of the divine power or of man's approach to God. For many sins no sacrifice was prescribed, but the door to the divine forgiveness was not necessarily closed. Reference has already been made to David's response in penitence to Nathan's rebuke. Thereafter we read

---

[1] Lev. 1.4, 3.2, 8, 13, 4.4, 15, 24, 29, 33, 8.14, 18, 22, 16.21; cf. Ex. 29.10, 15, 19.
[2] Cf. I Sam. 15.22; Hos. 6.6, Prov. 15.8, Eccl. 5.1.

that Nathan said: 'Yahweh also hath put away thy sin.'[1] No sacrifice could be offered, for none was prescribed in the Law; yet the sin was cleansed. It was not cleansed by the king's penitence, but by the act of God in response to his penitence. Nor did the forgiveness of David's sin dispense with the punishment. In the faith of Israel forgiveness is the cleansing from the sin, not the avoidance of punishment. In the case of David the punishment took the form of the death of Bathsheba's child,[2] but this was thought of as the punishment of the king. So again, when Ahab humbled himself before God after Elijah had rebuked him for the death of Naboth, his repentance was accepted by God but punishment was not avoided.[3] In this case the penalty for the sin was reaped in the days of his son. With our more individualistic outlook we are inclined to see some injustice here, though experience shows that children today may pay the price for the sins of their parents. But in Israel there was a stronger feeling of the solidarity of the family and the nation, and no thought of injustice would arise. More important is the recognition that even the divine forgiveness does not cancel all the effects of the sin, and that the only true penitence is a genuine horror of the sin, and not a selfish desire to avoid its consequences.

It is therefore clear that salvation from sin in the thought of the Old Testament is something more inclusive than sacrifice, though that belongs to it. Salvation is always the act of God, and it restores the relation between man and God which the sin has broken. It may be effected through sacrifices or without sacrifice. On the other hand all sacrifice is not designed to effect salvation from sin. Neither term is tied exclusively to the other. Moreover, the most significant word on sacrifice found in the Old Testament does not stand in the Law, and does not speak of a victim offered on the altar. It is in the prophetic canon that we read of the death of the Suffering Servant,[4] whose death was a sin offering for many, and wider in efficacy than any sacrifice offered in the Temple. This was not the death of an animal without blemish, offered involuntarily, but the willing sacrifice of one who was without moral stain.[5] The Temple sacrifices could be effective for the individual, or for the community of Israel, but the death of the Servant was described

[1] II Sam. 12.13.   [2] II Sam. 12.14.   [3] I Kings 21.29.   [4] Isa. 53.8 f.   [5] Isa. 53.9.

as effective for the nations. It was the people of the nations who were depicted as confessing their sins as they looked upon him, and acknowledging that the chastisement that should have been theirs was borne by him.[1] Moreover, his death was not effective for them until they brought to it that spirit of humble confession which the Law demanded with its sacrifices. Again it was not their penitence and surrender which effected their salvation. It was the Lord who laid on the Servant the iniquity of men in the moment of their confession, and who made his death a sin offering for their salvation.[2]

There are many levels in the Old Testament, but certain constants are found at all levels. Salvation from the Egyptian bondage or from neighbouring foes is not on the same level as salvation from sin, and salvation from unwitting sin is not on the same level as salvation from sins of the spirit. Yet at all levels salvation was perceived to be God's act. Its condition is always presented as humble surrender and faith, with repentance where there had been sin. Throughout the Old Testament man is thought of as the creature of God, made for his fellowship and service, and able to enjoy the fellowship only so long as he continues in the service. Throughout the Old Testament man's exercise of his freedom to sin is brought before us. Moreover sin is everywhere something which not alone offends God but injures man and robs him of the resources in God's fellowship which God designed for him. Throughout the Old Testament the love of God is presented. For though human sin is an offence to him, his eager yearning for the restoration of fellowship is seen in his discipline and his warning, and in his ready response to man's desire for the restoration of fellowship by the exercise of his divine power to remove the barrier which man had erected. What the fruit of fellowship means in the life that is conformed to the will of God we shall consider in a later lecture.

[1] Isa. 53.4 f.   [2] Isa. 53.6, 10.

IV

INDIVIDUAL AND COMMUNITY[1]

In all that has so far been said about man in the thought of Israel, one important question has been left without mention. This is the relation of the individual to society.[2] Is man conceived of merely as a fragment of the community, borne along in its life and involved in the vicissitudes of its fortunes, or is he conceived of as an individual, responsible to God for his own life? It is sometimes suggested that Jeremiah and Ezekiel discovered the individual, and that before their time man was thought of in terms of the society to which he belonged.[3] This is a gross exaggeration. It is true that these prophets stressed individual responsibility, but they were not the first to recognize the importance and the worth of the individual. It is also true that there was a much more vivid sense of the solidarity of a

[1] This lecture has already appeared, by permission of Union Theological Seminary, Richmond, and the publishers of the present book, in *Theology Today*, xii, 1955-6, pp. 491 ff. Some modifications have been made in the text, and fuller references to other literature are given here.

[2] On the subject of this lecture cf. F. Spadafora, *Collettivismo e individualismo nel Vecchio Testamento*, 1953; also M. Löhr, *Sozialismus und Individualismus im Alten Testament* (B.Z.A.W., No. 10), 1906, H. Gunkel, in *R.G.G.*, 1st ed., iii, 1912, pp. 493 ff., A Causse, *Du Groupe ethnique à la communauté religieuse*, 1937, J. Hempel, *Das Ethos des Alten Testaments* (B.Z.A.W., No. 67), 1938, pp. 32 ff., J. de Fraine, *Biblica*, xxxiii, 1952, pp. 324 ff., 445 ff., and G. E. Wright, *The Biblical Doctrine of Man in Society*, 1954.

[3] Cf. C. H. Patterson, *The Philosophy of the Old Testament*, 1953, p. 239, where it is roundly stated that in the mind of the prophets before Jeremiah the idea did not occur 'that Yahweh held individuals responsible for their own deeds'. With this cf. B. M. Pickering, in Gore's *New Commentary on Holy Scripture*, 1928, pp. 487 f. Oesterley and Robinson, while saying (*Hebrew Religion*, 2nd ed., p. 264) that Jeremiah 'is in a very real sense the father of individualism in religion' (cf. pp. 292 f., where it is said that Jeremiah 'was the first to teach that man, the individual, not the nation, was the unit') were careful to recognize that before Jeremiah the individual had standing in the political and religious life of ancient Israel (p. 263). Cf. A. Causse, op. cit., p. 111, where it is said that with Jeremiah 'l'individu a trouvé sa place et sa dignité, et c'est l'homme en tant qu'homme qui est le sujet de la religion'. A. Lods put the beginning of individualism back to the time of Isaiah, and maintained that in gathering round him his disciples to form the nucleus of the 'converted remnant' he 'initiated the religious emancipation of the individual' (*The Prophets and the Rise of Judaism*, E. Tr. by S. H. Hooke, 1937, p. 102). Cf. also J. R. Slater, *The Biblical World*, xiv, 1899, pp. 172 ff.

man with his fellows than has been common in the modern
world until the last generation, when in some societies the
individual has been completely submerged in society. But in no
period of the life of Israel do we find extreme collectivism or
extreme individualism, but a combination of both.[1] Some
writers or some passages emphasize the one side of this dual
nature of man more than the other, but both sides belong to
the wholeness of biblical thought in all periods.[2]

There was individual piety and sin, and individual reward
and punishment, long before the days of Jeremiah.[3] The story
of Achan is the stock illustration of the sense of the solidarity of
the community, and is often given an undue prominence in the
study of Israelite thought. When Achan sinned by retaining for
his own use some of the enemy treasure that should have been
destroyed in accordance with the sacred ban that had been put
on everything that belonged to the enemy,[4] the whole community suffered until Achan and his family had been completely wiped out.[5] His sin was not his private affair alone. It
came not alone between him and God, but between the entire
community and God. In a special sense it involved his whole
family, since the family was conceived of as an extension of the
personality of its head,[6] and so not alone Achan but his family
with him had to be destroyed to rid the community of the taint
that was upon it. Interwoven in this story are many ideas and
practices which we should not share. For the moment this does
not concern us, since all that we are concerned with is the faith
of Israel, and the idea inherent in this story that individual and

---

[1] Cf. J. Hempel, op. cit., pp. 41 ff., and *Gott und Mensch im Alten Testament*
B.W.A.N.T., iii, 2), 2nd ed., 1936, p. 192; O. S. Rankin, *Israel's Wisdom Literature*, 1936, pp. 53 ff. A. Weiser (*Jeremia* (A.T.D.), ii, 1955, p. 293 n.), says:
'Dass der Gedanke der persönlichen Verantwortung schon immer im altesta-
mentlichen Ethos neben dem der solidarischen Vergeltung seine Bedeutung
gehabt hat, braucht wohl kaum betont zu werden'.

[2] Cf. I. G. Matthews, *The Religious Pilgrimage of Israel*, 1947, p. 14: 'Individualism
to a marked degree, paradoxical though it seems, went hand in hand with
solidarity.' On p. 164, however, he speaks of the gradual emergence of the
individual 'under military achievement, the development of industry, and the
growth of society and government', and says it is fitting that Jeremiah should be
called the father of individualism.

[3] Cf. J. de Fraine, loc. cit., pp. 334 ff.

[4] On the ban cf. above, p. 19.

[5] Josh. 7.1 ff.

[6] Cf. J. Pedersen, *Israel I–II*, pp. 46 ff., esp. p. 63: 'Round the man the house groups
itself, forming a psychic community, which is stamped by him. Wives, children,
slaves, property are entirely merged in this unity.'

community formed a single unit. The same idea may be seen in the story of David's sin in numbering the people, which led to a plague upon the whole nation, with great loss of life.[1]

A moment's reflection will show that this was not the whole of the teaching found in the Old Testament before the time of Jeremiah and Ezekiel.[2] In a sinful world Enoch walked with God in individual piety, until God took him.[3] When human sin cried out and God sent the waters of the flood, Noah was saved from the general disaster.[4] Abraham stands out for the nobility of his individual character. If it be said that these all belong to the legendary past, they none the less testify to the recognition of the importance of the worth of individuals, and of the reality of an individual relationship to God. Moreover, humble individuals like Hannah, who scarcely belongs to the legendary past, could bring their pleas to God and find them answered.[5] For he was not a god who had regard to men only in the mass.[6] Every true prophet was an individual who felt that the hand of God was upon him and that he was called to an individuality of service. The God who could speak to Moses in the burning bush,[7] to Samuel as he kept watch by the Ark,[8] to Amos as he pursued his humble avocation,[9] and to Isaiah amid all the Temple throng,[10] was not a God who was indifferent to the individual. Further, none of the prophets could be accused of forgetting the individual in their concern for society. When David sinned with Bathsheba and against Uriah, it was to David as an individual sinner that Nathan went.[11] He did not wait until divine sanctions against the community, as in the affair of Achan, involved society in the effects of David's sin. When Jezebel invaded the private rights of Naboth and had him judicially murdered, Elijah took up the cause of Naboth in the name of the Lord.[12] When the eighth and seventh century

---

[1] II Sam. 24.1 ff.
[2] Cf. H. Gunkel, in *R.G.G.*, loc. cit., col. 495: 'Trotzdem würde die Annahme, dass das Individuum in der Religion des Alten Israel überhaupt keine Beziehung gehabt hat, ein starker Irrtum sein'; similarly W. Eichrodt, in *Festschrift Otto Procksch*, 1934, p. 47: 'Es war freilich ein starkes Missverstehen der israelitischen Anschauung vom Bundesgott, wenn man bisweilen gemeint hat, von einem persönlichen Vertrauen auf Jahve könne beim einzelnen Israeliten bis auf die Zeit des Prophetismus herab keine Rede sein.'
[3] Gen. 5.24.   [4] Gen. 6 ff.   [5] I Sam. 1.10 ff.
[6] A. Lods (op. cit., p. 169) recognizes that there had been individualism in prayer long before the time of Jeremiah.
[7] Ex. 3.4 ff.   [8] I Sam. 3.4 ff.   [9] Amos 7.15.
[10] Isa. 6.7 ff.   [11] II Sam. 12.1 ff.   [12] I Kings 21.17 ff.

prophets saw individual men and women under the harrow, suffering from the selfish greed and the unscrupulous exercise of power on the part of the mighty, it was as individuals that they saw them, and with hot indignation they denounced the wrong-doers. It is true that all these things were in their eyes not simply individual matters, but matters that concerned the whole community and its relations with God. They were not doctrinaire individualists; but neither were they doctrinaire collectivists, who were indifferent to the individual save as a fragment of the community. They believed that the life of every individual concerned the whole community, but they nevertheless saw the individual as an individual, and denounced the sins of individuals as well as of society, and proclaimed the wrongs suffered by individuals.

That they were also concerned for the collective sins of society and for the collective well-being of society should be remembered. There was a balance and a wholeness in their thought that is often lacking in ours. Too often in our thought sin is wholly an individual thing, and we forget that the community has a life and a character and a will, and that it may defy the will of God and therefore sin, to its own grave hurt and the hurt of all its members. The religious leaders of Israel never forgot that. They recognized that man has sociality as well as individuality, and that the community as well as the individual may have relations with God. The Old Testament knows nothing of the idea that you cannot indict a nation. Frequently a whole people is indicted. The opening chapters of the book of Amos contain a series of national indictments, in which the neighbouring peoples are successively denounced because they have been guilty of sinning against the principles of humanity, and therefore against the law of God. In the prophetic collections associated with the names of Isaiah, Jeremiah and Ezekiel, there are many oracles directed against foreign peoples.[1] Moreover, all the great pre-exilic prophets pronounce judgement on their own people as a whole, and not merely on the rulers or on guilty individuals. Similarly we find that in the sacrificial law, provision is made for daily sacrifices on behalf of the community, and for the annual sacrifice of the Day of Atonement for the sins of the community during the preceding

[1] Cf. Isa. 13 ff.; Jer. 46 ff.; Ezek. 25 ff.

year. Neither the Law nor the prophets regarded religion as merely a man's private traffic with God, but something which was of social and of individual concern. It should not, however, be forgotten that in no period of Israel's history was sacrifice conceived of simply as a social rite. There were always individual offerings as well as corporate, and individual thanksgivings and pleas could always be brought to God.[1]

It is to be noted that the biblical teaching of the grace of God is such that when a nation is indicted, something more is meant than that the balance of the life of the community is alienated from God. The Bible teaches that for the sake of a small minority, which is as the salt of society, the whole community may be spared. Sodom might have been spared for but a handful of righteous men,[2] and in the thought of the Remnant, which runs through so much of the Old Testament, we have further illustration of the same principle.[3] A society that is rotten through and through may bring disaster upon itself, lest its corrupting influence spread more widely. But where there is hope of reform the divine mercy persists, and even where there is no hope for the society as a whole, a Remnant may be spared, either for its own sake[4] or for the sake of those who will come after.[5] Yet, as will be seen, there is no biblical doctrine of the rigid equation of desert and fortune, and it is recognized that frequently the righteous are involved in the disasters the unrighteous bring upon the community to which they belong. Righteous and unrighteous are members of a common society, and are alike involved in its experience. For the sin of society, like the sin of individuals, is sin against God and against its

---

[1] Cf. *The Rediscovery of the Old Testament*, pp. 151 f. (American edition, pp. 214 f.).
[2] Gen. 18.16 ff.
[3] On the Remnant cf. S. Garofalo, *La Nozione profetica del 'Resto d'Israele'*, 1942, H. Dittmann, *T.S.K.*, lxxvii, 1914, pp. 603 ff., R. de Vaux, *R.B.*, xlii, 1933, pp. 526 ff., W. E. Müller, *Die Vorstellung vom Rest im Alten Testament*, 1939, V. Herntrich, in *Th.W.B.*, iv, 1942, pp. 200 ff., E. W. Heaton, *J.T.S.*, N.S. iii, 1952, pp. 27 ff.; also S. Mowinckel, *Profeten Jesaja*, 1925, pp. 66 ff., and H. Gressmann, *Der Ursprung der israelitisch-jüdischen Eschatologie*, 1905, pp. 229 ff.
[4] Cf. Noah in the time of the flood, or the seven thousand who had not bowed the kneel to Baal in the time of Elijah (I Kings 19.18). Cf. also Amos. 5.15; Zeph. 2.3. Frequently the Remnant is thought of as justifying its survival by its loyalty after it has been spared; cf. Isa. 4.3, 10.20 ff., 28.5.
[5] Cf. Amos 3.12, 4.1, and perhaps Isa. 1.9. In none of these passages is there any suggestion that the Remnant was spared because it deserved to be, and in the second of them it is explicitly stated that it did not. Cf. also N. K. Gottwald, *Studies in the Book of Lamentations*, 1954, p. 99, where the thought of this book is expressed in terms of the divine mercy to an undeserving Remnant.

members as individuals, as well as against its own corporate body.

Frequently men inveigh against the injustice that is in the world and indict God for it, as though he ought to see to it that every man's fortune corresponded precisely to his desert. It is particularly when they see individuals involved in the consequences of national policies, for which they cannot be held responsible, that they raise this cry. But their cry is wrongly directed. God is not responsible for the acts of men or of nations. He has given man freedom and for his exercise of that freedom man is alone responsible. When Cain murdered Abel,[1] the act was his and not God's. It is true that God created man capable of committing murder and other evils. But if he had not been so capable, he would not have been man. Similarly, when a nation pursues a policy which leads to dire disaster, and scenes of horror are witnessed, the responsibility is upon the nation and not upon God. It is vain to cry out against God when the fruits of human sin are reaped. That there is injustice in the world is manifestly true, and is abundantly recognized in the Old Testament. But that is because sin is in the world, and sin ever works injustice. The prophets were tireless in warning men of the fruits of the follies they loved, both the follies in their individual lives and the follies in the life of the state. They called on men to renounce the evil in their hearts, to change their ways, that they might avoid the grievous ills into which they were plunging. They hated injustice, and therefore they hated sin, and instead of sitting idly in judgement on God they rose to fight against the sin, and to warn men of its hateful nature. The Bible is under no illusions as to the character of sin, whether individual or corporate, and it finds it the deadliest foe of God and man.

We may now observe that while it is true that Jeremiah and Ezekiel emphasized some aspects of individualism, and particularly individual responsibility, this is not the whole of their teaching. They lived in days when men blamed their fathers for the misfortunes which came upon the land, and excused themselves from any share of the responsibility by saying 'The fathers have eaten sour grapes and the children's teeth are set on edge.'[2] To them came Jeremiah enunciating the doctrine

[1] Gen. 4.8.   [2] Jer. 31.29, Ezek. 18.2.

'Every one shall die for his own iniquity';[1] and later we find the same teaching on the lips of Ezekiel.[2] To these prophets the responsibility was not to be put on an impersonal community, and still less on the community of a former generation. Every individual had his share of responsibility for the life of the community. He was not merely a fragment of the corporate whole; he was a responsible individual. Yet let it not be forgotten that this emphasis of the teaching of Jeremiah and Ezekiel was a corrective to the false opposite emphasis of their day.[3] Jeremiah did not render obsolete all the thought of man as a member of society, and we should never father on to him a mere individualism, as though he regarded men as a tray of sand, with no cohesion, and simply a collection of units.[4] For Jeremiah warned men of the sorrows their children should know as the fruit of their own policies. It is therefore clear that his doctrine of individualism was but one side of the truth, and not the whole truth.[5] Here, as so commonly, truth is to be found in the tension between two apparently opposed principles. In declaring that while their fathers' sins had not brought their misfortunes, their sins would bring misfortunes upon their children,[6] Jeremiah was certainly not teaching a consistent doctrine of the rigid equation of desert and fortune. Moreover, the New Covenant of which he prophesied, while it was to be written on men's hearts, and thus to be an individual covenant, was at the same time a covenant with the house of Israel, and thus a

[1] Jer. 31.30.

[2] Ezek. 18.4. A. S. Peake (*The Problem of Suffering in the Old Testament*, 1904, p. 24) maintains that this word of Ezekiel's 'created a revolution in religious thought and life'.

[3] Cf. A. Médebielle, in *S.D.B.*, iii, 1938, col. 86: 'L'individu n'est pas dans la société comme une roue dans un engrenage. Il est libre, il peut, il doit par ses bonnes œuvres échapper à la responsabilité du mal. Si le prophète Ézéchiel a prêché cette liberté et ce devoir avec plus de force que ses prédécesseurs, c'est que les circonstances rendaient cet enseignement à la fois plus nécessaire et plus opportun'.

[4] Cf. Spadafora, *Collettivismo e Individualismo*, p. 398: 'In Geremia ed in Ezechiele, come in tutto el Vecchio Testamento, abbiamo soltanto la coesistenza del collettivismo e dell 'individualismo'. J. Skinner (*Prophecy and Religion*, p. 152) says: 'With all this, it is doubtful if Jeremiah's view of sin is strictly individualistic. It makes a long advance in that direction; but it is not so clear that the goal is reached.'

[5] This appears to be forgotten by A. Causse, op. cit., pp. 110 f., where he says that in the teaching of Jeremiah children would no more suffer for the sins of their parents, and that therefore this was the decisive moment in the evolution of religion when the individual found his place.

[6] Jer. 16.3 f.

collective one.[1] An arid individualism can no more satisfy the wholeness of the teaching of the Old Testament than an arid collectivism. Any emphasis on the one to the exclusion of the other in any period is a misrepresentation of the faith of Israel. A single word, or a single incident, may bring out one side of the truth more than the other, but both sides must be remembered in any study of the thought and teaching of the Bible.

Reference has been made to the story of Achan, where the whole people was involved in disaster through the sin of one man. In that story there is a profound spiritual message, though its form embodies the long outgrown idea of wholesale massacre, to which both Israel and her neighbours sometimes resorted as a religious act.[2] Achan had retained some of the material spoil because his selfishness of spirit triumphed over his public duty, and by every standard he was to be condemned, as he doubtless was condemned by his own conscience. But God was so offended by Achan's act that he withdrew his aid from the entire people, until the offender was cut off with his entire family. In this story there is not a little that is offensive to us, and that belongs to the ideas of the time. That Achan's family should be destroyed with him is offensive to us, but would not be so to the men of his time, though it stands condemned within the pages of the Old Testament itself. For in Deut. 24.16 we read 'Fathers shall not be put to death for their children, neither shall children be put to death for their fathers: every man shall be put to death for his own sin.' Nevertheless, this story contains a sound warning that one individual's failure of duty may involve a whole community in disaster and suffering, and that a man's private sin is never simply his own private affair. As an individual he is responsible for his act; yet others are inevitably involved in his act.

That a single individual may involve a whole community in disaster is amply attested by history. It takes but one traitor to betray an army or a nation, and a single careless deed may expose large numbers of people to danger. Yet in all such cases as we recognize there is a direct causal chain between the individual failure and the public consequences, whereas in the

---

[1] Jer. 31.31 ff. On the authenticity of this passage cf. above, p. 36.
[2] See above, p. 19.

case of Achan no causal chain can be demonstrated between his sin and the national impotence that followed it. Often in the world of the spirit causal chains cannot be demonstrated, while yet they exist. The subtle and imperceptible influence of one spirit upon another is real, though hard to assess, and an evil man is a social liability. Even if Achan's sin had not been discovered, he would still have been a social liability, a centre of moral disease within the life of the community. If there is disease in the body at any point, it is as real a menace to the body before its nature and location are discovered by a doctor as it is after diagnosis. So the sinner, even though his sin is concealed, is a menace, in the measure of his sin, to the welfare of the community. When Achan's sin was known he was destroyed, less to punish him than as an act of social hygiene, to cleanse the community of his stain.

Where the individual is a representative and leader of the community, it is less surprising that his act should affect the welfare of the whole society, and that if he is evil he should be a public liability. The action of a leader may determine the policy of the state and involve the people in disaster or blessing. The folly of Rehoboam, while in no sense the only cause of the disruption, was its occasion, by its provocation of the outbreak which effected it.[1] The act of David in numbering the people was followed by the plague,[2] and while here once more there was no direct chain of causal connexion, it was believed that the one was the consequence of the other. Here again there is an element of enduring validity in the story. The private sin of a leader necessarily comes between him and God, and therefore makes him insensitive to the guidance of God, without which there can be no true well-being. If the fundamental teaching of the Bible is true, that there can be no real well-being for men, either as individuals or collectively, save in the will of God, then it is in the highest degree important that the leaders of men should do his will. Yet they who repudiate the fellowship of God cannot know his guidance, and if they repudiate his will in their private lives, they cannot with sincerity seek to know and do his will in their public acts.

The king's act is therefore never without significance for the nation. His private life may affect his public act; and his public

[1] I Kings 12.1 ff.   [2] II Sam. 24.1 ff.

act is not merely his but the community's, since he is its representative.[1] It is frequently said in the Bible that Jeroboam I not only sinned but made Israel to sin, and by this is meant that he not only led them in the way of evil, but that his act as the representative of the nation was itself an act of corporate sin, whose consequences went on after he himself had died. The prophets denounced both the political and the religious leaders of the nation precisely because their acts were always more than their own. Nevertheless, it is not to be supposed that only the leaders are important. Everyone, whether leader or common man, may contribute something to the strength of the life of the community, or may diminish it. Where there runs through a people indifference to the will of God, it will have leaders who will lead it in the way that is alien to his will; for only in such a way will they be content to follow. If they had other leaders, the spirit of the community would nullify their leadership. Jeremiah declared that though Moses or Samuel were to act as intercessor for the people of his day, the intercession would be unavailing, since the nation was so corrupt.[2] Neither of these great men would be really representative of the nation that Jeremiah knew. Wise leaders must be supported by the spirit of the communities they lead. On the other hand, unwise leaders, whose acts may compromise and menace the communities they lead, are not to be endured patiently with a disclaimer of responsibility for their acts. Without any thought of the machinery of modern democracy, the prophets were sure that a people which walked in the way of God would find all its interests watched by God, who would raise up for it leaders attuned to his spirit. Thus Jeremiah said 'Return, apostate children, saith Yahweh . . . And I will give you shepherds after my own heart, who will feed you with knowledge and understanding.'[3] When we view the thought of the Old Testament as a whole, therefore, we see that the corporate spirit of society, and the individual spirit of the leader or the common man, are alike important. They may be a source of strength to

---

[1] Cf. J. Pedersen, *Israel III–IV*, 1940, p. 82: 'The people share in the responsibility of the king and must take the consequences of his action, even if they have not taken part in it.'

[2] Jer. 15.1. On the prophet as intercessor cf. F. Hesse, *Die Fürbitte im Alten Testament*, 1949, pp. 39 ff.; also N. Johansson, *Parakletoi*, 1940, pp. 3 ff.

[3] Jer. 3.14 f.

the community if directed by the spirit of God; they may be a source of weakness if they are marred by sin. For every individual, whether great or small, is a member of the corporate society, carried in the current of its life and bringing his contribution to that current. He cannot live to himself alone. For his life belongs to all, and the life of all around him belongs to him.

It has been said that there is no biblical doctrine of the rigid equation of desert and fortune. The book of Deuteronomy and the writings of the Deuteronomic school are governed by the theory of such an equation in the experience of the nation. Deuteronomy promises that so long as Israel is obedient to the will of God it will prosper in all its life, while when it is disobedient it will suffer natural calamities and grievous ills at the hands of foes.[1] The book of Judges represents history in the form of alternation between foreign oppression as the result of religious disloyalty and deliverance through a God-given leader when repentance brings men back to God. The prophets of the pre-exilic period promised disaster to generations that were not walking in the way of God. All of this presupposes that desert and fortune, at least on the national scale, are linked together. Broadly speaking there is truth in this, though it is not the whole truth. Still less is it the whole truth, when it is individualized and used as a basis for the doctrine that every man gets precisely what he deserves. With Jeremiah, as we have seen, it was not presented as the whole truth, but balanced by other aspects of truth.

There are passages in the Old Testament which, taken by themselves, imply that the good man is assured of good fortune and the wicked man is certain to run into trouble. The opening psalm of the Psalter enunciates this doctrine, and promises that the man who finds his delight in the law of the Lord will discover that 'whatever he does will prosper', while the wicked will be 'like the chaff which the wind drives away' and experience will show that 'the way of the wicked will perish'. Such a thought is found in not a few passages in the Psalter. 'Blessed is the man who fears Yahweh . . . Wealth and riches are in his house . . . He shall never be moved . . . He shall not be afraid of evil tidings . . . His horn shall be exalted with

[1] Deut. 28.1 ff.

honour.'[1] Or again, 'Blessed is every one who fears Yahweh, who walks in his ways. For thou shalt eat what thy hands earn: Happy shalt thou be, and it shall be well with thee. Thy wife shall be as a fruitful vine, within thy house: Thy children like young olive shoots, around thy table.'[2] A more familiar psalm says 'Fear Yahweh, ye his saints: For there is no want to those who fear him. The young lions have need and suffer hunger: But they who seek Yahweh shall not be in need of any good thing.'[3] In the book of Proverbs we find the same sentiments. 'Honour Yahweh with thy wealth, And with the first fruits of all thine increase: So shall thy barns be filled with plenty, And thy vats shall overflow with new wine.'[4] Or again, 'Happy is the man who finds wisdom, And the man who gets understanding . . . Length of days is in her right hand; In her left hand are riches and honour.'[5] When Solomon went to Bethel and saw God in his vision and chose wisdom as the supremely desirable gift, we read that God said to him that riches and honour and long life should also be his.[6] All this, taken by itself, would seem to support the view that prosperity is regarded as the supreme blessing in the Old Testament,[7] and that piety was believed to be the sure way of finding it.

In contrast to this is sometimes set the New Testament,[8] where we read 'Blessed are ye poor: for yours is the kingdom of God. Blessed are ye who hunger now: for ye shall be filled. Blessed are ye who weep now: for ye shall laugh.'[9] Such a contrast is quite unfair, as is the one-sided representation of the teaching of the Old Testament that singles out such passages as have just been quoted to the ignoring of much else. Many examples of undeserved suffering and oppression have already been given. Beyond these we have the frequent complaints of the psalmists that they are in trouble, from which they beseech God to deliver them, and frequent reflections on the prosperity of the wicked. Sometimes the psalmist cheers himself with the thought that that prosperity is insecure, while for him there will

---

[1] Ps. 112.1, 3, 6, 7, 9.   [2] Ps. 128.1 ff.   [3] Ps. 34.9 f. (Heb. 10 f.).

[4] Prov. 3.9 f.   [5] Prov. 3.13, 16.   [6] I Kings 3.13.

[7] On the Old Testament conception of blessing cf. J. Pedersen, *Israel I–II*, pp. 182 ff.

[8] Cf. Francis Bacon, *Essay on Adversity*: 'Prosperity is the blessing of the Old Testament, adversity is the blessing of the New.'

[9] Luke 6.20 f.

be deliverance. But even so there is the clear recognition that there is no simple equation between merit and lot.

That virtue leads to well-being is firmly believed to be one side of the truth, whether on the individual or on the national scale; but it is not the whole of the truth. In a world in which there was no sin and no disobedience to God, it was believed that this would be the whole of the truth, and hence the Golden Age is depicted in terms of perfect righteousness and economic bliss.[1] But because here and now there is sin, and because men and nations are involved in the sin of others, the fruits of virtue may not always be reaped. Only the fool is led to conclude from this that virtue does not matter, since its fruits may not be reaped. The man who plants a fruit tree may not gather the fruit. The frosts may carry off the blossom or the storms the fruit and the tree yield no harvest, since the harvest depends not merely on the nature and quality of the tree but on other factors. But no wise man would conclude that the nature and quality of the tree were of no moment.

The story of Joseph is of high value as showing that in quite early times there was the perception that the real reward of virtue was not in prosperity or in adversity, but was quite other. It is true that Joseph comes ultimately to riches and honour, but whether in his adversity or in his prosperity he has God, and therefore his real well-being is secure. This thought we find expressed in some of the proverbs. 'Better is a little with righteousness Than great revenues with injustice.'[2] 'How much better is it to get wisdom than gold! To get understanding is more to be desired than silver.'[3] 'Better is the poor man who walks in his integrity, Than he who is perverse in his ways, though he be rich.'[4] The author of Ps. 73 begins by envying the wicked, but ends by realizing that in his own misfortune he is far better off than they, because while they have their riches and ease he has God. 'Nevertheless I am continually with thee: Thou dost hold my right hand.'[5] It is this aspect of the teaching of the Old Testament, which is found alongside the other, and that not merely in a single period, which should always be remembered to balance the other, and which makes it quite misleading to suggest that in the faith of Israel a man's lot, or a

[1] See below, pp. 182, 190 f. [2] Prov. 16.8. [3] Prov. 16.16.
[4] Prov. 28.6. [5] Ps. 73.23.

nation's lot, was believed to be strictly proportioned to his or its merit.

Between a doctrine of such an equation of desert and fortune on the national and on the individual scale there must inevitably be a tension. For when the folly of a king or people brings the disaster of war upon a community, its weight falls on good and bad alike, and all are involved in the common suffering. Similarly the sin of an individual may bring suffering on others, sometimes on the victims of his acts, as the sin of Cain brought suffering on Abel,[1] or the sin of David on Uriah,[2] and sometimes on his family, who are involved in the sorrow and shame he may bring upon himself.[3] When either side of the truth is pressed to the exclusion of the other, problems arise. In the days of Jeremiah men were excusing themselves of any share of the responsibility for their misfortunes; in the days when the book of Job was written, there were circles that were obsessed with a hard individualism, and that believed that precise justice was invariably reflected in individual fortune. Neither theory can fit all the facts of experience. Habakkuk is troubled with the problem of the wicked swallowing up one more righteous than himself,[4] and Jeremiah[5] and some of the psalmists were puzzled by the prosperity of the wicked and the adversity of the righteous.

The question of man's sociality is complicated further by the bond which unites him to the generations of the past and of the future. He is not merely a member of contemporary society. He belongs to the past and to the future. While Jeremiah rebuked his fellows for blaming their fathers for their misfortunes, the Bible teaches that there are occasions on which one generation sins and the next generation pays the price. When Ahab repented on hearing the rebuke of Elijah, the word of the Lord came to Elijah, saying 'Seest thou how Ahab has humbled himself before me? because he has humbled himself before me, I will not bring the evil in his days; but in his son's days will I bring this evil upon his house.'[6] When Isaiah came to Hezekiah to predict that because he had opened his treasuries to the messengers of Merodach-baladan, his treasures should one day be carried off to Babylon, and his descendants be eunuchs in the

---

[1] Gen. 4.8.   [2] II Sam. 11.6 ff.
[3] Cf. *The Rediscovery of the Old Testament*, p. 149 (American edition, p. 211).
[4] Hab. 1.13 ff.   [5] Jer. 12.1 ff.   [6] I Kings 21.29.

palace of the Babylonian king, Hezekiah replied 'Good is the word of Yahweh which thou hast spoken . . . Is it not so, if peace and stability[1] shall be in my days?'[2] Here experience tallies with the Bible. It often happens that the evils of one generation take time to bring forth their fruits, and a later generation must pay the price of the mistakes of their fathers. Moreover, the Decalogue, in the expanded form it now has in both Exodus and Deuteronomy, declares that God visits the sins of fathers upon the children to the third and fourth generation.[3] To many modern minds this appears to be unjust, though it is undeniable that in experience children are involved in the fruits of their parents' lives. If we consider man merely as an individual it may seem unjust; but if we realize that he belongs to the continuous stream of the generations and to the society of which he is a member, it is not. He is born into an ever changing society and family, which yet has a continuity within its change that makes it a unity from moment to moment and from generation to generation. He is the heir of the past and a fragment of the society of the present. While he is liable to suffer for the common sins, or for the sins of other individuals, he also receives a rich inheritance from those who have gone before and from his contemporaries, and from both he may receive great blessings. If he shares ills he has done nothing to deserve, he also receives blessings he has not merited. If he wishes to cry out against God because of the debits of this balance, he rarely complains of the far greater credits.[4] An arid individualism can neither justify the vast and beneficent heritage from the past which comes to every man nor begin to understand the richness and complexity of the divine justice. Nevertheless we are individuals, with an individual responsibility. We may raise or lower the spiritual quality of the society of which we form a

---

[1] R.V. here has 'peace and truth', but in Jer. 14.13, where the same terms appear, but in a genitive relation, we find the rendering 'assured peace', instead of 'peace of truth'. The word *'emeth*, which is commonly rendered 'truth' comes from the root *'āman*, which means 'to be faithful', or 'reliable' (see above, pp. 66 f.). It is fundamentally something which can be relied on, and so 'stability' or 'security' (so R.S.V.) is the most suitable rendering here. Similarly in Isa. 42.3, where R.V. has 'judgement in truth', the meaning is more probably 'enduring justice' (where 'justice' means both the principles of true religion and their outcome in perfect righteousness; see below, p. 147 n.4), as is seen by G. W. Wade, *Isaiah* (West. C.), 1911, p. 269. Cf. also R. Asensio, *Misericordia et Veritas*, 1949 pp. 16 f.
[2] II Kings 20.19, Isa. 39.8.
[3] Ex. 20.5, Deut. 5.9; cf. Ex. 34.6 f.
[4] Cf. *The Rediscovery of the Old Testament*, pp. 150 f. (American edition, pp. 213 f.)

part, and contribute something to the enlargement of the heritage which we pass on to our children, and the effect of our character will fall in some measure on others, so that our lives are not wholly ours. At the same time, they are ours, and the effect of our character will fall also on ourselves. Either side of this truth may be appropriately emphasized in different situations. Both have to be held together in the totality of truth, and the faith of Israel, as reflected in the Old Testament, was wisely balanced in combining both.

This means that there is a problem of suffering which cannot be solved. The book of Job was written to deal with that problem, but not to solve it. Rather was its purpose to insist that there is a problem of innocent suffering, which cannot be explained by any process of human reasoning. It is sometimes suggested that until the book of Job was written it was the orthodox Israelite view that there was no such thing as innocent suffering.[1] Such a suggestion is patently false. There is not the slightest suggestion that Uriah deserved his death, or that Abel was justly murdered. Jeremiah was sure that the malice of his kindred was undeserved.[2] And all the prophets who denounced the oppressions of their time were persuaded that the oppressed were not reaping the fruit of their sins. It was only in certain circles, at the time when the book of Job was written, that a hard and rigid equation of desert and fortune, such as is nowhere characteristic of the Old Testament as a whole, was made. If a man's acts may involve others in suffering, clearly the suffering cannot prove the sin of the sufferer; on the other hand, if his acts may involve himself in suffering, that suffering may be the fruit of his sin. Hence there may be innocent suffering, though not all suffering is innocent. The Bible never tries to reduce the facts of experience to the simplicity the theorist seeks. Jeremiah and Ezekiel insisted that not all suffering is innocent; the book of Job insists that some suffering is. It does not attempt to fathom the cause of innocent suffering. It tells the reader the cause in the case of Job;[3] but that is necessary in order to establish to the reader that Job was not suffering for his sin. Here he is told that Job is suffering to vindicate God's

---

[1] Cf. I. G. Matthews, *The Religious Pilgrimage of Israel*, pp. 171 f., where it is said that the friends of Job 'reiterated the time-honoured assumptions of the ancients', while Job 'challenged the sacrosanct conclusions of the centuries'.
[2] Jer. 11.21 ff., 12.6.   [3] Job 1.6 ff., 2.1 ff.

faith in the purity of his motives against the slanders of the
Satan. It thus appears that Job was supremely honoured in his
very sufferings; for God had staked himself upon Job's integrity.
Nor did Job fail him.[1] Nevertheless, all this was concealed from
Job and from the friends, and despite all their discussion none
of them could fathom the reason. The friends were sure there
must be some explanation in Job's own life, while Job maintains
with vigour that he had not been so notable a sinner as to
justify his phenomenal misfortunes. The explanation of Job's
troubles was not given in the divine speech from the whirlwind,
and if it had been the book would have lost its message for men
who have to suffer in the dark. When God spoke from the
heavens, it was not to enlighten Job, but to remind him that
there were things too deep for him to understand, and that it is
idle for man to pass judgement on them in his ignorance. The
intellectual problem is left unsolved, so far as Job and his
friends are concerned, but rather lifted up into the larger
problems of the mysteries of life and of the universe.

Something of more worth than an intellectual solution of the
problem of suffering may be found here, however. If there may
be innocent suffering, then suffering does not of itself prove sin,
as Job's friends were too ready to suppose, and it is therefore
no evidence that a man is cut off from God. It was just here
that the cruelty of the view represented by the friends was
seen. In the hour of his suffering, when a man most needed
God, his suffering was increased by the knowledge that men
held it to be evidence that he was isolated from God, and he
himself was tortured by doubt of himself and of God, and uncertain whether God's fellowship could still be his. But if
suffering does not prove sin, then the sufferer may not be excluded from God's presence, but may enjoy his fellowship.
And in the climax of the book Job rests in this thought. 'I had
heard of thee by the hearing of the ear' he cries; 'But now I see
thee with my eyes.'[2] His suffering had brought him a deeper
knowledge of God than he had hitherto had, and he rests in the

---

[1] It must be remembered that though Job roundly complains of the injustice of his
sufferings, he nowhere expresses the slightest regret for the integrity of his way.
He affirms and clings to his integrity in his suffering, no less than in his prosperity,
and therefore he vindicates God's faith in the purity of his motive, and establishes
the slanderous nature of the Satan's implication that he was only righteous for
what he got out of it.

[2] Job 42.5.

contemplation of God. It is significant that it is to this point
that we are brought. For in the thought of the Old Testament
the intellectual solution of a problem is of less moment than the
fellowship of God, which was of supreme moment to man in all
its teaching. Its nearest approaches to philosophy are always
still theology. Nor can the intellectual problem of suffering yet
be solved by intellect alone. It is sometimes said that the faith in
a worth-while after life has given us an answer to the problem
denied to Job. But that is still the answer of faith and not of
demonstration. Nor does it really touch the problem. For whatever bliss the righteous may enjoy in the afterlife, that can offer
no explanation of suffering they may experience here. We, no
more than Job, can deduce the cause of all human suffering,
and when men experience suffering which they feel to be
innocent, instead of crying out against the injustice of God they
are wise to believe that it has some cause or purpose, though
concealed from them and hidden in the heart of God, and
through trust in him to find fellowship with him.[1] For in God's
fellowship is the spring of man's truest life and health.

All this may be found in germ in the ancient story of Joseph,
and men did not have to wait till the author of the book of Job
should write before they were given any glimpse of this profound
truth. Joseph was treated with a malice he did not deserve, and
was carried down to Egypt and set menial tasks in a prison. In
the development of the story both Joseph and the reader come
to see that there was a divine purpose behind all this; but when
Joseph was in the prison he had no more means than Job of
understanding his misfortune in being swiftly taken from being
the favourite son of his father to be a slave in a foreign land.
Yet Joseph does not torture himself with doubts, but reaches
quite simply the point that Job attains with so much difficulty.
'Yahweh was with Joseph.'[2] He accepts ill fortune as he had
accepted good, without complaint and without question, and is
content to find in the presence and fellowship of God that which
transfigures the experience for him.

[1] In *Submission in Suffering and other Essays*, 1951, pp. 1 ff., I have examined the
varying basis of the attitude of patient acceptance of suffering inculcated by a
number of eastern religious teachers, and have argued that more important than
patience is the spring of power offered for its attainment. Cf. now E. F. Sutcliffe,
Providence and Suffering in the Old and New Testaments, 1955 (issued while the present
work was in the press).
[2] Gen. 39.21.

Reference has been made to the thought of the Remnant, in relation to the Israelite idea of man's individual and social character. The community could be narrowed down to a part, which could represent it and continue its inheritance. This idea of the Remnant is found throughout the Bible, and is not confined to the teaching of the prophets.[1] In the story of the flood Noah and his family constitute the Remnant, in whom the divine creative purpose is concentrated. The blessing promised to Abraham and his seed was limited to one of the sons of Isaac. In the time of Elijah we read of a righteous Remnant of seven thousand, who had not bowed the knee to Baal, but remained loyal to God.[2] Amos speaks of a Remnant who were saved as a brand plucked from the burning,[3] or as a few scraps of a sheep saved from the lion's mouth.[4] Especially characteristic is the thought of the Remnant in Isaiah,[5] but it is also found in Micah,[6] in Jeremiah[7] and in Ezekiel.[8] Sometimes the Remnant

---

[1] It is partly for this reason that I am not able to subscribe to the view of Gressmann (*Die Ursprung der israelitisch-jüdischen Eschatologie*, 1905, pp. 229 ff., 242 f.) that the concept of the Remnant belongs to the terminology of eschatology. Cf. J. Skinner, *Isaiah* (Camb. B.), i, 1915 ed., p. lxiv, and S. Mowinckel, *Psalmenstudien*, ii, 1922, pp. 276 ff. R. de Vaux (*R.B.*, xlii, 1933, p. 539) well says: 'À chaque époque le Reste, c'est d'abord ce qui échappera du danger présent. Mais, derrière ce premier plan où les événements contemporains se dessinent plus nets dans la conscience du prophète, on en discerne un second, dominé par la personne du Messie: le Reste y est identifié à l'Israël nouveau; établi en Terre promise, il y forme une communauté sainte qui vit dans l'amour et la crainte de Jahvé et recueille ses bénédictions. Ce n'est pas tout, car on devine un plan plus lointain et plus vaste encore; il se déploie à l'horizon des temps, lorsque le Reste, non seulement Israël nouveau, mais l'Israël spirituel, ayant recueilli à la fois tous les dispersés du peuple et tous les convertis des nations, subsistera seul devant Jahvé dans l'anéantissement définitif des méchants'.
[2] I Kings 19.18.
[3] Amos 4.11. On the Remnant in Isaiah cf. K. Cramer, *Amos* (B.W.A.N.T., iii, 15), 1930, pp. 130 ff.
[4] Amos 3.12.
[5] Cf. Isa. 1.9, 4.3, 7.3, 8.18, 10.20 ff., 17.4 ff., 28.5, 37.31 f. On the Remnant in Isaiah cf. Garofalo, *La Nozione profetica del 'Resto d'Israele'*, pp. 70 ff.; also G. A. Danell, *Studies in the Name Israel in the Old Testament*, 1946, pp. 162 f.
[6] Micah 2.12 f. and Micah 5.7 f. (Heb. 6 f.). This latter passage is attributed to Micah by E. Sellin, *Das Zwölfprophetenbuch* (K.A.T.), 1929, p. 308, while O. Eissfeldt (*Einleitung in das Alte Testament*, 1934, p. 457) is doubtful if it should be so attributed. Others with more confidence deny it to Micah; so K. Marti, *Dodekapropheton* (K.H.C.), 1904, p. 285, J. M. P. Smith, *Micah, Zephaniah and Nahum* (I.C.C.), 1912, pp. 110 f., H. Guthe, in *H.S.A.T.*, ii, 1923, p. 61, G. W. Wade, *Micah, Obadiah, Joel and Jonah* (West. C.), 1925, pp. 38 f., T. H. Robinson, *Die zwölf Kleinen Propheten* (H.A.T.), 2nd ed., 1954, p. 144, R. H. Pfeiffer. *Introduction to the Old Testament*, p. 593, and A. Weiser, *Die zwölf Kleinen Propheten* (A.T.D.), i, 1949, p. 246. These differ widely as to the probable date of the oracle. For our present purpose neither date nor authorship is of moment.
[7] Jer. 23.3 f. On the Remnant in Jeremiah cf. Garofalo, op. cit., pp. 117 ff.
[8] Ezek. 11.19 f., 36.22 ff. On the Remnant in Ezekiel, cf. Garofalo, op. cit., pp. 138 ff.

is thought of as bringing about the sparing of the community, as a Remnant might have saved Sodom,[1] and sometimes as being itself spared to convey to a future generation the promise of God and the knowledge of his will. Always the Remnant concentrates in itself the life and the promise of the community. It is not always a righteous Remnant. Sometimes it is spared in the mercy of God,[2] not because it deserves to be spared,[3] but in order that it may carry down to another day the revelation it does not value itself. It is never thought of as a company of individuals, but as a corporate whole. Wherever it appears, the Remnant is for the moment the people of God, heirs of the promises and of the revelation and purpose of God.

This narrowing down of the community is found in the Old Testament in other forms. Attention is frequently called to the Hebrew conception of corporate personality.[4] The term occurs nowhere in the Bible, but is a modern creation to express a view which is common in the Old Testament. It is a particular form of the concentration of the life of the community for the moment, often in a single individual, and much wider in its reference than the thought of the Remnant. For any purpose the Hebrew could think of an individual who was the representative of the community, or whose experience was typical of that of the community, as identified with the community.[5] For the time being he was the community, and he could use the first person singular when he was speaking in the name of the community. He could equally speak of the community in the third person. For there was in his thought a fundamental fluidity, whereby he could pass back and forth from the thought of himself to the thought of the community, and from the thought of the community to himself, in whom for the moment its experience or its life is concentrated or represented.

It is probable that the Suffering Servant of Deutero-Isaiah is to be understood in this way, the Servant standing both for

---

[1] Gen. 18.16 ff.   [2] Cf. Amos 3.12, Isa. 1.9.   [3] Cf. Amos 4.11.

[4] This term is associated especially with the name of H. Wheeler Robinson, though others have also recognized the phenomenon the term denotes. Cf. *The People and the Book*, ed. by A. S. Peake, 1925, pp. 353 ff., *The Psalmists*, ed. by D. C. Simpson, 1926, pp. 67 ff., *Werden und Wesen des Alten Testaments* (B.Z.A.W., No. 66), ed. by J. Hempel, 1936, pp. 49 ff.

[5] Cf. H. W. Robinson, *Werden und Wesen*, p. 49: 'The whole group including its past, present and future members, might function as a single individual through any one of those members conceived as representative of it.'

the personified community and for an individual who should perfectly represent it and fulfil in himself the mission of the community. To review the endless discussion which has been devoted to the question of the identification of the Servant is both unnecessary and impossible here.[1] In the nineteenth century many scholars adopted the view which had long been current in Jewish circles, that the Servant was the whole people Israel.[2] This left some problems unsolved, since in one of the songs the Servant has a mission to Israel,[3] and would seem to be distinct from Israel. Hence the view was put forward that the Servant was the ideal Israel,[4] or else the Israel within Israel,[5] the faithful Remnant,[6] in whom the mission of the entire community was concentrated. Yet the fourth song, the song that tells of the death and resurrection of the Servant, gives so strong a feeling of the individuality of the Servant, that scholars returned to an individual interpretation of this figure. Instead of returning to the traditional Christian messianic view, however, they looked for some figure contemporary with the prophet, or of the preceding ages, who might seem to fit the part, and a whole series of unlikely candidates were brought forward. A

[1] This has been admirably done by C. R. North in *The Suffering Servant in Deutero-Isaiah*, 1948, and, more briefly, with reference to a much shorter period, by the present writer in *The Servant of the Lord*, pp. 3 ff. Much additional literature is cited by W. Zimmerli and J. Jeremias, in *Th.W.B.*, v, 1954, pp. 653 ff. (E.Tr. *The Servant of God* (S.B.T.), to appear in 1957).

[2] This view was still maintained by A. S. Peake, *The Servant of Yahweh*, 1931, pp. 1 ff., and A. Lods, *The Prophets of Israel*, E. Tr., pp. 244 ff.

[3] Isa. 49.5 f.

[4] This view was maintained by H. Ewald, *Commentary on the Prophets of the Old Testament*, E. Tr. by J. F. Smith, iv, 1880, pp. 248 ff., 292 ff., S. Davidson, *Introduction to the Old Testament*, iii, 1863, pp. 62 ff., A. B. Davidson, *Old Testament Prophecy*, 4th imp., 1912, pp. 408 ff., and J. Skinner, *Isaiah xl-lxvi* (Camb. B.), rev. ed., 1917, pp. 263 ff. Cf. J. Lindblom, *The Servant Songs in Deutero-Isaiah*, 1951, where it is argued that the Servant is an allegorical figure, symbolizing Israel in its call, present situation, and mission (cf. p. 102).

[5] This view is represented by O. C. Whitehouse, *Isaiah* (Cent. B.), ii, pp. 18 ff., E. König, *Das Buch Jesaja*, 1926, pp. 444 ff., and *Z.A.W.*, xlvii (N.F. vi), 1929, pp. 255 f., and I. G. Matthews, *The Religious Pilgrimage of Israel*, pp. 174 f.; cf. also P. A. H. de Boer, *O.T.S.*, iii, 1943, p. 196, and O. J. Baab, *The Theology of the Old Testament*, p. 197.

[6] Miss A. E. Skemp (*E.T.*, xliv, 1932-3, pp. 94 f.) advances the theory that the Servant is a personification of the Remnant, and couples this with the suggestion that in Isa. 7.14 Immanuel is a similar personification. On this view the one passage tells of the birth of 'Immanuel', and the others of 'his' reaching his full stature.

nameless contemporary leprous rabbi,[1] or Jeremiah,[2] or Zerubbabel,[3] or Jehoiachin,[4] or Uzziah,[5] or Moses,[6] was suggested. More recently Deutero-Isaiah himself has been proposed.[7] It seems very unlikely that any of these can really have been thought of in the terms in which the Servant is portrayed,[8] and the fact that in one verse the Servant is identified with Israel[9] provides a difficulty for all these individual views. It is common to resort to surgery to cut out the difficult word but there is no serious evidence in support of this excision, save the

[1] Cf. B. Duhm, *Jesaia* (H.K.), 2nd ed., 1902, p. 359, A. Marmorstein, *Z.A.W.*, xliv (N.F. iii), 1926, pp. 260 ff., M. Buber, *The Prophetic Faith*, E.Tr. by C. Witton-Davies, 1949, pp. 237 f.; cf. also J. Monteith, *E.T.*, xxxvi, 1924–5, pp. 449 f.

[2] Cf. F. A. Farley, *E.T.*, xxxviii, 1926–7, pp. 521 ff., where it is argued that the writer began with the thought of Jeremiah as the personification of Israel's mission, and on his career bases his representation of the fulfilment of that mission by the prophetic element in Israel. Cf. also S. H. Blank, *H.U.C.A.*, xv, 1940, pp. 18 ff. The identification of the Servant with Jeremiah was proposed long ago by Saadia Gaon (cf. P. Volz, *Jesaia II* (K.A.T.), 1932, p. 188, and C. R. North, op. cit., pp. 20 f.).

[3] Cf. E. Sellin, *Serubbabel*, 1898, pp. 148 ff. (this view was later abandoned by Sellin).

[4] Cf. E. Sellin, *Der Knecht Gottes bei Deuterojesaja* (Studien zur Entstehungsgeschichte der jüdischen Gemeinde nach dem babylonischen Exil, i), 1901, pp. 284 ff., and *Das Rätsel des deuterojesajanischen Buches*, 1908, pp. 131 ff., J. W. Rothstein, *T.S.K.*, lxxv, 1902, pp. 282 ff., esp. 319 ff., A. van Hoonacker, *Expositor*, 8th series, xi, 1906, p. 210 (where Jehoiachin is regarded as the model for the description of the future Messiah), W. Staerk, *Die Ebed Jahwe-Lieder in Jesaja 40 ff.* 1913, pp. 137 f. (in the fourth song; in the first three songs (p. 129) Jeremiah is found), E. Burrows, *The Gospel of the Infancy*, 1940, pp. 59 ff. (where the Servant is identified with the house of David, past, present, and future, Jehoiachin being its present representative), J. Coppens, *Pro regno pro sanctuario* (Festschrift for G. van der Leeuw), 1950, pp. 118 ff. (where Jehoiachin is held to be the model for the portrayal of the Messiah in the first three songs, and Zechariah in the fourth), F. M. Th. Böhl, *Ned.T.T.*, iv, 1949–50, pp. 161 ff. (where it is suggested that Jehoiachin was put to death the year after his release as the royal substitute).

[5] Cf. K. Dietze, *Ussia, der Knecht Gottes*, 1929, and *Nachwort zu 'Ussia'*, 1930. This view was presented a century and a quarter earlier by J. C. W. Augusti (cf. North, op. cit., p. 41).

[6] Cf. E. Sellin, *Mose und seine Bedeutung für die israelitisch-jüdische Religionsgeschichte*, 1922, pp. 81 ff. For some writers who have held the Servant to be a second Moses, cf. *The Servant of the Lord*, p. 46 n.

[7] Cf. S. Mowinckel, *Der Knecht Jahwäs*, 1921 (but cf. his later view, modifying this, in *Z.A.W.*, xlix (N.F. viii), 1931, pp. 242 ff., *Acta Orientalia*, xvi, 1938, pp. 1 ff., and *Han som kommer*, 1951, pp. 129 ff.), E. Sellin, *N.K.Z.*, xli, 1930, pp. 73 ff., 145 ff., and *Z.A.W.*, lv (N.F. xiv), 1937, pp. 177 ff., J. Begrich, *Studien zu Deuterojesaja* (B.W.A.N.T., iv, 25), 1938, pp. 131 ff., and P. Volz, *Jesaia II* (K.A.T.), 1932, pp. 149 ff.

[8] In addition there are the views of the Swedish school, for some account of which cf. *The Servant of the Lord*, pp. 42 ff., and C. R. North, *S.J.T.*, iii, 1950, pp. 363 ff. The view of A. Bentzen, and his critical survey of the views of some of his Scandinavian colleagues, are now available in English in *King and Messiah*, 1955, pp. 48 ff.

[9] Isa. 49.3.

theory it is intended to serve. A single Hebrew manuscript omits the word, but it is a very poor manuscript, which is taken no account of anywhere save here.[1] Metrical considerations are invoked in favour of the excision, but metrically a better case can be made out for the retention than for the excision.[2] It is often stated that the Septuagint offers evidence for its excision, but the standard editions of the Septuagint show no such evidence,[3] and the scholars who most insist that the Septuagint does offer evidence do not say in what manuscripts they find it.

All this means that unless we adopt a fluid view of the identification of the Servant we can find no satisfactory answer to the problem. One form of the fluid view has been in terms of corporate personality, as just outlined. Here it is held that there is a transition between the thought of Israel and the prophet himself.[4] In some of the songs we find the first person singular, and in others the Servant is spoken of in the third person. This view does not seem to do justice to the problems of the fourth song, and it seems more satisfactory to adopt a view which is not new, indeed, but which sees in the Servant Israel, called to be the light of the nations and charged with a mission to the world, narrowing down to the Remnant and then to a single individual, in whom the mission is concentrated.[5] The Servant is at once Israel and an individual, who both represents the

---

[1] Cf. J. A. Bewer, *Jewish Studies in Memory of George A. Kohut*, 1935, pp. 86 ff. B. Kennicott (*Vetus Testamentum Hebraicum cum variis lectionibus*, ii, 1780, p. 79) notes that this MS shows many variants. It is curious that this one, and this one alone, should be given exaggerated significance by scholars to whose theories it happens to be convenient. Cf. R. Kittel, *Geschichte des Volkes Israel*, iii, p, 228, J. van der Ploeg, *Les Chants du Serviteur de Jahvé*, 1936, pp. 36 ff., L. Dennefeld, *Les grands Prophètes* (Pirot-Clamer's Sainte Bible), 1947, p. 179.

[2] Cf. F. Prätorius, *Z.A.W.*, xxxvi, 1916, pp. 9 f., P. Humbert, *La Bible du Centenaire*, ii, 1947, p. 407.

[3] Holmes and Parsons (*Vetus Testamentum graecum cum variis lectionibus*, iv, 1827, ad loc.) do not record any MS which lacks this word; neither do H. B. Swete (*The Old Testament in Greek*, iii, 3rd ed., 1905, ad loc.) and J. Ziegler (*Isaias* (Septuaginta xiv), 1939, ad loc.). It is clear that the 'many MSS' which are often stated to omit this word (cf. S. Mowinckel, *De senere profeter*, 1944, p. 233 n., and *Han som kommer*, p. 334; L. Koehler, *Deuterojesaja stilkritisch untersucht*, 1923, p. 37) are either non-existent or completely unimportant. It is much to be desired that the scholars who invoke them should disclose which MSS they are.

[4] Cf. H. Wheeler Robinson, *The Cross in the Old Testament*, 1955, pp. 78–9.

[5] Cf. *The Servant of the Lord*, pp. 49 ff., for my presentation of this view; cf. also A. Causse, *Israël et la vision de l'humanité*, 1924, p. 54. For the 'pyramid' view of Delitzsch and of his followers, which is in some respects similar to this view, cf. C. R. North, *The Suffering Servant in Deutero-Isaiah*, 1948, pp. 44 ff.

whole community and carries to its supreme point the mission of the nation, while calling the whole people to enter into that mission, so that it shall be its mission and not merely his. That this is a future individual in the thought of the prophet seems to me beyond question.

If this view is correct, we have here a particular illustration of the Old Testament conception of the solidarity of the community of all generations, and of the relation of the individual to the community. The Servant is Israel today and tomorrow; but Israel may be all or a few or one of its members. All this springs readily out of the full recognition of man's sociality and individuality, and is unintelligible without that twofold recognition. The nation was never thought of as an association of individuals, but as an organic whole, in which the parts were knit together as parts of one another, without losing their individuality. On the other hand, there was never any lack of recognition of the due rights of the individual. No social contract theory of the state, and no absolutism of the state or of the king, could be tolerated in the view of Israel's religious teachers. The judicial murder of Naboth was an invasion of the rights of the individual, and an incident that would provoke no comment amongst many peoples not alone aroused deep resentment in Israel, but stirred a prophet to vigorous denunciation of the king face to face. The rights and duties of the state and of the individual rested on no agreement or on human power, but on the will of God. They are therefore essentially an element of the faith of Israel.

There are corollaries of importance arising from the Old Testament view of the individuality and the sociality of man. If the well-being of the individual lies in his harmony with the will of God, and if that well-being is bound up with the well-being of the society of which he forms a part, it is of importance to him that the whole society should be in harmony with the divine will. By the same token, it is of importance to society that all its individuals should be in harmony with God's will, since an individual could involve the community in dishonour or suffering. No man could be indifferent whether his neighbour walked in God's way or not, and there could be no delusion that a man's religion was merely his own affair. Just as a modern community recognizes that disease is not an exclusively individual concern, so in the Old Testament sin, which consists in disharmony with the will of God, is not simply an individual concern. Nor can any individual be wisely indifferent to the sin of those around him. That was why the prophets were tireless in calling men to walk in the way of God. It was because this was their truest service to themselves, to their fellows and to God. And since the nation was but a part of the wider society of the world, Israel could not be indifferent to foreign peoples. Amos was concerned about the neighbouring peoples, and not merely about their attitude towards his own people. Their inhumanity to one another stirred him.[1] Deutero-Isaiah proclaimed the mission of Israel to spread the light of her faith through all the world.[2] The book of Jonah presents that mission not in abstract terms, but in the concrete setting of a personal mission to Nineveh. It is important that we should not think of all this as something wholly new that came into the religion of Israel at a particular date, but should recognize that it developed from a seed which was already there, and that it grew from the fundamental thought of the Old Testament on the nature of man as created in God's image, for his fellowship and service, but as a member of a corporate society and not merely as an individual, bearing his own measure of responsibility both for himself and for that society, and involved in the corporate life of society and in the life of the individuals that comprised it, and ultimately concerned with the life of nations other than his own. In the biblical conception of man there is a grandeur and a wholeness that excites ever new wonder. It is the murderer, Cain, who asks 'Am I my brother's keeper?'[3] In the true faith of Israel every man was his brother's keeper, and his brother was every man.

[1] Amos 1.3, 6, 9, 11, 13, 2.1.   [2] Isa. 42.6.   [3] Gen. 4.9.

V

THE GOOD LIFE

In the faith of Israel the good life consists in doing the will of God. But this is of little significance until the will of God has been defined. Islam demands implicit obedience to the will of God no less than the Old Testament. In one of the papers read to the twenty-third International Congress of Orientalists at Cambridge the speaker said 'Allah is represented in the Qur'an as a slave-owner whom the people who are Allah's slaves must obey implicitly.'[1] In the Bible the term '*Ebedh Yahweh*, which could be translated 'slave of Yahweh', is found often enough,[2] and men are exhorted to 'serve' God, where the verb is from the same root as the noun 'slave'. Yet here nothing could be farther from the truth than to suppose that in biblical thought the relation between God and men is that of master to slave. The Suffering Servant of Isa. 53 is '*Ebedh Yahweh*, and both here and elsewhere it is a title of honour rather than of dishonour. The Suffering Servant was dishonoured and maltreated by men, but honoured by God. For in biblical thought the service of God is always perfect freedom.

While there are passages in the Old Testament which understand the will of God in ritual terms, it is of the essence of the faith of Israel that his will is conceived in moral and spiritual terms. Those who framed the Law, with all its insistence on the minutiae of the ritual, were not indifferent to the spirit. In the book of Exodus we read 'If ye will truly obey my voice, and keep my covenant, ye shall be my own special treasure',[3] where

[1] E. A. Belaiev, *Formation of the Arab State and the Origin of Islam in the VII Century* (Papers presented by the Soviet Delegation at the XXIII International Congress of Orientalists, Islamic Studies), 1954, p. 23.

[2] Cf. C. Lindhagen, *The Servant Motif in the Old Testament*, 1950, pp. 152 ff., and V. de Leeuw, in *L'Attente du Messie*, 1954, pp. 51 f.n., where full references are given. The term is used of prophets, of Moses, of individual Israelite kings (David, Solomon, Hezekiah), and of Nebuchadnezzar, as well as of the figure depicted in the Servant Songs of Deutero-Isaiah.

[3] Ex. 19.5.

there is no suggestion that ritual acts were in mind. In Deuteronomy we read 'Thou shalt love Yahweh thy God with all thy heart',[1] and this is more fundamental than any of the detailed regulations that follow. In Leviticus we find the great word 'Thou shalt love thy neighbour as thyself'[2]—a word which would have graced any prophet. In the unpromising context of a chapter which abounds in ideas and practices which were not specifically Israelite but shared with her neighbours—the un-provoked attack on neighbouring peoples when opportunity offered, the fierce and inhuman massacre of whole communities, and the cold-blooded slaughter of conquered foes—in such an unpromising context we find the classic word 'Has Yahweh as much delight in burnt offerings and sacrifices as in obedience to his voice? Behold, to obey is better than sacrifice, and to hearken than the fat of rams.'[3] In Proverbs we have 'To do righteousness and justice is more acceptable to Yahweh than sacrifice',[4] and in the Psalter 'The sacrifices of God are a broken spirit: a broken and a contrite heart, O God, thou wilt not despise'.[5] The thought that obedience is more important than sacrifice is therefore one which is found in various forms widely expressed in the Bible, and it is clear that in such a context obedience must mean something other than obedience to ritual ordinances.

What is believed to be the oldest Decalogue in the Bible is found in Ex. 34.[6] This is commonly referred to as the Ritual Decalogue, because it is concerned only with such things as the observance of feasts, and the offering of sacrifices and first-fruits. Three provisions it has in common with the more familiar Decalogue of Ex. 20. It demands the exclusive worship of Yahweh,[7] it prohibits the making of images,[8] and it requires the observance of the sabbath.[9] I have elsewhere argued that this was a pre-Mosaic Decalogue which was taken over by Israel, and which prescribed some of the forms of the religion which Moses established.[10] But Moses gave the people a new Decalogue to epitomize the basic demands of their faith. This

---

[1] Deut. 6.6. [2] Lev. 19.18. [3] I Sam. 15.22.
[4] Prov. 21.3. [5] Ps. 51.17 (Heb. 19).
[6] Ex. 34.14 ff. In its present form it contains more than ten commands, but it is commonly believed that there were originally ten, though there is less agreement as to which they were. On this Decalogue cf. *B.J.R.L.*, xxxiv, 1951–2, pp. 88 ff., and the literature I there cite.
[7] Ex. 34.14. [8] Ex. 34.17. [9] Ex. 34.21. [10] *B.J.R.L.*, loc. cit.

is the Decalogue contained in Ex. 20. Apart from the provisions which it has in common with the other Decalogue it is concerned with such things as the honouring of parents, and the avoidance of murder, theft, adultery and false witness. These are ethical and not ritual matters. Moreover, the last command penetrates beneath conduct to the spring of conduct,[1] and calls for a watch on the heart, that evil desire may be avoided before it leads to evil acts. Here, then, we see something of what obedience to the will of God meant for Israel from the days of Moses. It meant the bringing of ordinary life under God's control, and beyond that the bringing of the spirit into harmony with his.

The common notion that ethical religion took its rise with the eighth century prophets will scarcely bear examination. The prophets were filled with indignation when they saw men oppressing and exploiting one another. But long before their day Moses was filled with indignation when he saw Egyptians oppressing Israelites. His response was to kill an Egyptian taskmaster,[2] and while that led him but to the wilderness it clearly showed his attitude towards oppression. Moreover, in his call he found that his hatred of oppression was but a reflection of the divine hatred,[3] though God's way of dealing with it was other than his had been. It may be said that in all ages men have found it easy to wax indignant against foreign oppressors. But Moses, like the prophets, was just as ready to rebuke his fellow-Israelites as foreigners. When he saw an Israelite maltreating another he said to the one who wronged his fellow 'Wherefore smitest thou thy fellow?'[4] The story of Sodom and Gomorrah was recorded long before the time of the eighth century prophets, and it proclaims the divine condemnation of moral iniquity. The city might have been spared had it contained but a handful of righteous men,[5] and it is clear that righteous men were thought of as men who were virtuous in life. It was by their life that they were judged by God, and not by their observance of any form of religion. Even Solomon, who erected the Jerusalem Temple, which was so highly esteemed by the Deuteronomic editor of the book of Kings, is not exempt from

---

[1] On this command cf. J. Herrmann, in *Beiträge zur Religionsgeschichte und Archäologie Palästinas* (Sellin Festschrift), 1927, pp. 69 ff.; B. Jacob, *J.Q.R.*, N.S. xiv, 1923-4, pp. 166 ff.; W. J. Coates, *Z.A.W.*, lii (N.F. xi), 1934, pp. 238 f.
[2] Ex. 2.12.   [3] Ex. 3.7.   [4] Ex. 2.13.   [5] Gen. 18.32.

criticism, and the same Deuteronomic editor records how the prophet Ahijah instigated Jeroboam to head a revolt.[1] Though the revolt was nipped in the bud and Jeroboam was forced to flee to Egypt,[2] he returned later to carry through the disruption of the kingdom.[3] Long before the eighth century prophets there was a hatred of oppression, injustice and unrighteousness manifest in the religious leaders and writers of Israel.

In the earliest Israelite law-book which has come down to us we read 'Thou shalt not pervert the judgement of thy poor in his cause . . . The innocent and righteous slay thou not: for I will not acquit the guilty.'[4] In Deuteronomy, again, the strict administration of justice is enjoined. 'Thou shalt not pervert judgement; thou shalt not respect persons: neither shalt thou take a bribe . . . That which is altogether just shalt thou follow.'[5] In the Holiness Code we find the same thing. 'Ye shall do no unrighteousness in judgement; thou shalt not be partial to the poor, nor honour the person of the mighty: but with justice shalt thou judge thy neighbour.'[6] In all periods Israelite law forbade the perversion of justice. When the eighth century prophets so vigorously denounced the bribery that went on in the courts, and the miscarriage of justice that went on around them, and called for righteousness to flow through the life of the nation as a never-failing stream,[7] they were calling men to obedience to what they ought to have known to be the will of God.

Similarly righteousness in commercial transactions was seen to be the corollary of this justice which should flow through all the nation, and not merely be a quality of judges. 'Thou shalt not have in thy bag different weights . . . A perfect and just weight shalt thou have' is the demand of Deuteronomy,[8] and a similar law stands in the Holiness Code.[9] While these codes in their present form are later than the denunciations of some of the prophets, they are not presenting new principles, which were first formulated by the prophets. The whole weight of the prophets' word lies just in the fact that men who used unjust measures ought to have known, and indeed, did know, that they were doing wrong. In our desire to recognize the greatness of the prophets, we should not attribute to them originality

[1] I Kings 11.26 ff.   [2] I Kings 11.40.   [3] I Kings 12.2.   [4] Ex. 23.6.
[5] Deut. 16.19.   [6] Lev. 19.15.   [7] Cf., e.g., Amos 5.12, 15, 24.
[8] Deut. 25.13, 15; cf. Amos 8.4 ff.   [9] Lev. 19.35 f.

where they were calling men to obedience to the known principles of Israel's faith. Amos denounced those who lay down in the shrines on pledged clothes,[1] when the older law of the Book of the Covenant had demanded that such garments should be handed back to the borrower every night.[2] When Isaiah castigated those who added lands to lands,[3] and used their power to dispossess their weaker neighbours, or when Micah similarly lashed those who coveted their neighbours' fields and took them away,[4] they were condemning men who forgot the tenth commandment.

It should never be forgotten that the prophetic demand was religious, and that it sprang from the conception of God. If God demanded righteousness, it was because he was himself righteous. In the ancient story of Abraham's pleading with God before the destruction of Sodom, a story which in its literary form is older than the eighth century prophets, the patriarch asks 'Shall not the Judge of all the earth do right?'[5] This appeal to the justice of God is an implicit recognition of that justice. Elsewhere, it is stated explicitly. It is declared by Jeremiah;[6] it is declared in the Song of Moses in Deut. 32;[7] it is declared by psalmists.[8] Moreover, in the pictures of the messianic age a righteousness which is the reflection of the righteousness of God is an integral element. The shoot out of the stock of Jesse, of whom Isaiah speaks,[9] was to have the spirit of the Lord upon him, and because of that it was said 'with justice shall he judge the needy, and give decision with equity for the meek[10] of the earth.'[11] There is no part of the Old Testament which does not recognize that justice belongs essentially to the good life. It is not merely prescribed for rulers and judges, but for all classes and in all relations of life.

Some of the evils which the prophets denounced were denials of mercy as well as of justice. And mercy also is an element of the good life. Not all the appropriations of land were carried

---

[1] Amos 2.8.   [2] Ex. 22.26 (Heb 25).   [3] Isa. 5.8.   [4] Micah 2.2.

[5] Gen. 18.25.   [6] Jer. 12.1.   [7] Deut. 32.3.   [8] Psa. 116.5, 119.137, 145.17.

[9] On the authorship of this passage cf. below, p. 188, n.7.

[10] There has been much discussion of the word used here and another closely similar form, and of the whole question of the poor in the Old Testament. Cf. H. Birkeland, '*Anî und 'Anāw in den Psalmen*, German Tr. by L. Rapp, 1933; A. Causse, *Les 'Pauvres' d'Israël*, 1922; J. van der Ploeg, *O.T.S.*, vii, 1950, pp. 236 ff.; A. Gelin, *Les Pauvres de Yahvé* (Témoins de Dieu, No. 14), 1953; C. van Leeuwen, *Le Développement du sens social en Israël*, 1954.

[11] Isa. 11.4.

through by bribery and by the perversion of justice in the courts. The poor were sometimes compelled to borrow from the rich to tide them over till the harvest, and so the rich obtained power over them which they were ready to exploit. The appeal here was not to justice but to mercy. For if justice forbade a man to seize from another more than was his due, mercy might lead him to demand less than he might claim. The appeals on behalf of the widow and the fatherless were probably not all appeals to justice against men who were illegally crushing them. Some were almost certainly appeals to men who might legally crush them to have mercy on their pitiful state. The justice to which the prophets summoned men was no hard and unfeeling inflexibility, but a justice which was tempered with compassion, and which reflected the divine compassion for Israel. Just as God had had mercy on the people who were suffering the Egyptian bondage, so the hearts of his people should be moved with compassion for those who were suffering, whether from injustice or from circumstances.

The book of Deuteronomy is commonly held to reflect the teachings of the eighth century prophets. While this is probably true, it should not be forgotten that those prophets reflected the spirit of Israel's faith as it was known before their time. They were not the first to perceive the mercy of God; and the mercy of God was itself the demand for mercy amongst men. But these prophets gave fuller expression to the spirit of compassion, and brought this corollary of their faith into clearer focus, and the book of Deuteronomy nobly embodied that corollary in its legislation. 'If there be with thee a poor man, one of thy brethren . . . thou shalt not harden thy heart, nor shut thy hand from thy poor brother.'[1] The widow, the fatherless and the Levite are commended to charity.[2] Further, when Job maintains the integrity of his way, he shows clearly some of the elements that were believed to belong to the good life. He says 'If I have withheld the poor from their desire, Or have caused the eyes of the widow to fail; Or have eaten my morsel alone, And the fatherless has not eaten thereof . . . If I have seen any perish for want of clothing, Or the needy lack covering . . . Then let my shoulder-blade fall from the shoulder, And mine arm be broken from the joint.'[3]

[1] Deut. 15.8.   [2] Deut. 16.11, 14, 24.19, 20, 26.13.   [3] Job. 31.16 f., 19, 22.

This mercy could be a form of the expression of *ḥesedh*, which was, however, much more than compassion. It was a quality of loyalty and devotion which a man should show towards God in response to all that God had done for him as a member of the covenant community of Israel.[1] It was also a quality which he should show towards those who stood with him within the covenant. It involved more than mere loyalty to one another, important though that was. It also involved a devotion, or loving-kindness, as the word is often rendered in the English version, that would lead to the initiative in service comparable with the divine initiative towards Israel. It was a reflection of the spirit of God, and not merely a response to that spirit. Hosea declares that it is this quality which God looks for more than sacrifice,[2] and Micah defines the demand of God in terms of justice and of this rich quality of mutual service, springing from the humble walk with God.[3]

Jeremiah found that men were neighing after one another's wives in Jerusalem,[4] and before him Hosea had declared that in northern Israel adultery was rampant.[5] Here was a breach of one of the Ten Commandments and a denial of that mutual loyalty to one another that was involved in *ḥesedh*. There is much evidence in the Old Testament that sexual vice of various kinds was common in Israel, but it stands everywhere con-

---

[1] This statement was challenged by one of my audience, who denied that man can show *ḥesedh* towards God. It is true that the word does not often occur in this sense. In Jer. 2.2 and Hos. 6.4 it would seem to have it, though less probably in Hos. 6.6, where it may better be taken to refer to behaviour towards fellow-men. But the word *ḥāsīdh*, which means 'one who practises *ḥesedh*' is frequently used for the 'pious', or the one who is dutiful towards God. By its form it could be active or passive, one who shows *ḥesedh*, or one who is treated with *ḥesedh*; but many passages allow only of the former meaning. This is made quite clear in many passages in the Targum. Thus the word is rendered by 'righteous' in I Sam. 2.9 and Prov. 2.8, by 'innocent' in Ps. 4.3 (Heb. 4), 16.10, 43.1, by 'good' in Ps. 12.1 (Heb. 2). Since the word itself was also an Aramaic word, and is usually represented in the Targum by the same word as in the Hebrew, it may be presumed that the translator understood it. In Deut. 33.8, where the Targum employs the same word, instead of 'thy *ḥāsīdh*', it has 'the one who is found to be *ḥāsīdh* before thee'. Clearly, therefore, it did not understand it to mean 'the one who receives *ḥesedh* from thee'. Moreover, decisive for the active sense is the fact that this word is used of God in Jer. 3.12, Ps. 145.17. It is quite impossible to suppose that when God says in the former of these verses 'I am *ḥāsīdh*' he means that he has been treated with *ḥesedh*, since the whole burden of the verse is that he has not. Cf. L. Gulkowitsch, *Die Entwicklung des Begriffes ḥāsid im Alten Testament* (Acta Seminarii Universitatis Tartuensis Judaici, No. 1), 1934. S. T. Byington (*J.B.L.*, lx, 1941, p. 283) defines a *ḥāsīdh* as 'one who is in friendly relations with God'.

[2] Hos. 6.6.   [3] Micah 6.8.   [4] Jer. 5.8.   [5] Hos. 4.2.

demned. In the fertility cult of Canaan ritual prostitution was
one of the forms of religion,[1] and too often under the influence
of this cult we find its presence in Israel.[2] Amos[3] and Hosea[4]
condemned it, though it is a common view that Hosea's wife
was a sacred prostitute before he married her.[5] On this view
he was impelled by what he felt to be a divine urge to take from
what was to him the most loathsome of lives the woman who so
unworthily requited his love. Be that as it may, there can be no
doubt that sexual purity belonged to the good life in the eyes of
the prophets,[6] who refused to distinguish between sacred and
secular prostitution. To them all extra-marital relations were
an abomination. The same is true of the sages whose words are
preserved in the book of Proverbs. Again and again the disciples
are warned against the strange woman,[7] and the intention is to
warn against every sort of illicit relation.

Nevertheless, there was nothing ascetic about the faith of
Israel, and the family virtues were inculcated. The first command of God is said to have been 'Be fruitful and multiply',[8]
and marriage and the raising of a family were held to be a part
of the good life. 'Enjoy life with the wife whom thou lovest all
the days of the life of thy vanity' said the preacher.[9] It is true

[1] Cf. J. Pedersen, *Israel III–IV*, pp. 469 ff. Similar practices were current in
Babylonia (cf. Driver and Miles, *The Babylonian Laws*, i, 1952, pp. 369 ff.).
There was also a class of votaries, distinct from the hierodules, but also dedicated
to the service of the temple (ibid., p. 371). That these were also sacred prostitutes,
though of a different class, under vow never to marry, is maintained by D. D.
Luckenbill (*A.J.S.L.*, xxxiv, 1917–18, pp. 1 ff.). According to the Code of
Hammurabi death was the penalty if they entered a tavern (§ 110), which was
synonymous with a house of ill fame (cf. S. A. Cook, *The Laws of Moses and the
Code of Hammurabi*, 1903, pp. 149 f.), and any false accusation of them was treated
as on the same level as a false accusation against the chastity of a married
woman (§ 127). Their profession was therefore treated as an honourable one,
and they were distinguished from secular prostitutes.
[2] Pedersen (op. cit., p. 470) says: 'We receive the impression that sexual rites
dominated the Israelite cultus throughout the monarchical period.'
[3] Amos 2.7 f.   [4] Hos. 4.13 f.
[5] Cf. H. Schmidt, *Z.A.W.*, xlii (N.F. i), 1924, pp. 245 ff.; T. H. Robinson, *T.S.K.*,
cvi, 1934–5, pp. 301 ff.; O. R. Sellers, *A.J.S.L.*, xli, 1924–5, p. 245; H. G. May,
J.B.L., lv, 1936, p. 287; W. A. Irwin, in J. M. P. Smith, *The Prophets and their
Times*, 2nd ed., 1941, pp. 71 f.; G. Fohrer, *Die Symbolischen Handlungen der
Propheten*, 1953, p. 21; A. Gelin, in *Initiation Biblique* (ed. by A. Robert and
A. Tricot), 3rd ed., 1954, p. 169.
[6] Other prophets also, of course, condemn sacred prostitution, which appears to be
referred to in the following, amongst other, passages: Micah 1.7; Jer. 2.20,5. 7.
It is prohibited in Deut. 23.17 f. (Heb. 18 f.) and Lev. 19.29.
[7] Cf. Prov. 2.16, 5.3, 20, 6.24, 7.5, 22.14, 23.27. On the 'strange woman' in Proverbs cf. P. Humbert, in *Mélanges Syriens offerts à M. René Dussaud*, i, 1939, pp.
259 ff., L. A. Snijders, *O.T.S.*, x, 1954, pp. 1 ff., 88 ff.
[8] Gen. 1.28.   [9] Eccl. 9.9.

that polygamy was not forbidden, but there are warnings
against its attendant evils through the dissension and bitterness
it could bring into the home.[1] Moreover, monogamy must
always have been far more common than polygamy, and in the
later period there is little evidence of polygamy.[2] The ideal set
before men is never couched in terms of this, but always in
terms of mutual loyalty between husband and wife and of the
purity of the life of the home.[3]

It is not without significance that the Song of Songs is included in the Bible. The interpretation of this collection of
poems has been very varied and has been marked by many
fantastic improbabilities.[4] It is most probable that the book
is no more than it purports to be, a collection of love songs,
expressing with much freedom the spiritual and physical
emotions on which matrimony rests, and the delight of a man
and a woman in one another. That such a book should be in
the Bible should occasion no surprise. The first command of
God, as has been said, was 'Be fruitful and multiply', and there
may be, and ought to be, something profoundly sacred in pure
human love. The Church has always encouraged men and
women to seal their union by an act of consecration before God,
and has taught them to think of it as Holy Matrimony. It is
therefore fitting that these poems should be found in the sacred
Canon, thus symbolically reminding men that their love should
be under the control of God and the life of their home be not
remote from their faith.

It will be observed that this aspect of the good life is not a
reflection of the life of God, since he is nowhere presented as
having sex. Many in Israel appear to have worshipped the
fertility goddess, and the book of Jeremiah gives us a glimpse of
rites whereby the Queen of Heaven was honoured.[5] In the
Jewish temple at Elephantine there appear to have been other

[1] Cf. Gen. 29.30 f., 31.1, I Sam. 1.6; also Deut. 21.15 ff.
[2] E. Neufeld (*Ancient Hebrew Marriage Laws*, 1944, pp. 118 f.) notes that though it
was uncommon in post-exilic times, it continued to be practised in some Jewish
communities down to the Middle Ages. Cf. L. M. Epstein, *Marriage Laws in
the Bible and Talmud*, 1942, pp. 16 ff.
[3] Cf. W. P. Paterson, in *D.B.*, iii, 1900, p. 265 a: 'Of still greater importance . . .
is the circumstance that monogamous marriage was extensively used in the
prophetic teaching as the symbol of the union of God with Israel, while polygyny
had its counterpart in idolatry.'
[4] On this subject cf. my essay in *The Servant of the Lord*, pp. 187 ff.
[5] Jer. 7.18, 44.17 ff.

deities[1] beside Yahweh,[2] and it is possible that he was provided with a consort in the impure worship that prevailed there.[3] But in the true faith of Israel there is no evidence that Yahweh was ever thought of as having a consort or as a being of sex. It is true that God is thought of as sharing in all human procreation. Children were received as his gift, and men could speak of God as forming them in the womb.[4] But that was because he was thought of as the author of all creation, and not because he was thought of in sexual terms.

In a previous lecture it was said that God was believed to be holy, with a holiness that consisted in moral loftiness and not merely separateness from man. It was because he was conceived in such terms that men were called to show moral purity in their lives. The qualities of God were called for from men, in so far as they could be translated into the terms of human life and experience, and the family virtues were one of the forms of that translation. Yet they were far from being the only form.

When Isaiah cried 'Woe to me! I am ruined; for I am a man of unclean lips, and I dwell in the midst of a people of unclean lips',[5] he was thinking of something much wider than sexual impurity. In the light of the divine holiness he was conscious of all that marred his spirit, and of every moral blemish that marked him. When the coal touched his lips it consumed all the evil of his being,[6] so that he could now reflect the loftiness of God's spirit in his life. Long before the time of Isaiah

---

[1] In a subscription list from Elephantine (AP 22) we find that the donations were divided as follows: 126 shekels for Yahweh, 120 shekels for Anath-bethel, and 70 shekels for Ishum-bethel (cf. A. Cowley, *Aramaic Papyri of the Fifth Century B.C.*, 1925, pp. 65 ff.). Here Ishum-bethel is perhaps to be connected with Ashimah (II Kings 17.30 and Amos 8.14, where 'Ashimah of Samaria' should be read instead of 'the sin of Samaria') while Anath-bethel is to be connected with Anath, whose name survives in some biblical place names, and who figures in the Ras Shamra texts. In another Elephantine text one swears by Anath-yahu (AP 44.3; ibid., p. 147) and in yet another one is challenged to swear by Ḥerem-bethel (AP 7:7; ibid., p. 20). U. Cassuto held that these were all foreign gods, not worshipped by the Jews, but only by the Gentile colonists (cf. *Kedem*, i, 1942, pp. 47 ff.), while W. F. Albright thinks they were hypostatized aspects of Yahweh (*From the Stone Age to Christianity*, 2nd ed., pp. 286 f.; cf. *Archaeology and the Religion of Israel*, 3rd ed., 1953, pp. 168 ff.). Cf. E. G. Kraeling, *The Brooklyn Museum Aramaic Papyri*, 1953, pp. 87 ff. Kraeling says it is indubitable that we have to do with deities here (p. 88). Cf. also A. Dupont-Sommer, *R.H.R.*, cxxx, 1945, pp. 17 ff., where evidence of the worship of some other god beside Yahweh, possibly Chnub, is given from an ostracon from Elephantine.
[2] The name stands here in a triliteral form, and is commonly transliterated Yahu.
[3] It is possible that Anath, to whom the second largest gifts in the subscription list go, was regarded as the consort of Yahweh (cf. Cowley, op. cit., p. xix).
[4] Cf. Job 10.10 ff., 31.15.   [5] Isa. 6.5.   [6] Isa. 6.7.

we find examples of the loftiness of spirit that belonged to the good life. In the story of Abraham we find depicted real nobility of character. It is true that the patriarch was not monogamous and that his passing his wife off as his sister to avoid trouble for himself[1] cannot be commended. Yet when we judge him in the light of the times in which he lived we are bound to recognize true loftiness of character. His generosity to Lot[2] and his concern for him after he had chosen to dwell in Sodom,[3] and even his concern for that wicked city itself, impresses the reader with his quality of personality. Even if this is only a story, it reveals the writer's ideals, which were set before his readers. But I may be permitted to add that I am persuaded there is some genuine tradition concerning the character of Abraham embodied in this story. If the stories of the patriarchs were mere fiction, it would be hard to see why Abraham should be so much nobler a character than Jacob, since Jacob was the ancestor of the Israelite tribes while Abraham was the ancestor of other tribes also. Israelite pride would have tended to exalt Jacob rather than Abraham. The fact that it does not do so, and that Isaac, who stands between them, is so largely colourless a creature, would seem to imply that fidelity to an ancient tradition was observed.

Again, Joseph is presented as a man of real integrity of character. In adversity or in prosperity he is unwilling to turn aside from the path of rectitude, and he knows no bitterness of spirit. His magnanimity towards the brothers who had envied and wronged him is one of the most moving stories of the Bible,[4] and it testifies to the integrity and grandeur of character that was felt in Israel to belong to the good life.

Such character was no mere human achievement. Its source was the fellowship of God. 'Yahweh was with Joseph',[5] as he is said to have been with many others, and it is only they who know the humble walk with God who can conform to his high demands upon their lives.[6] When the finger of God has written his law on the heart, and when his spirit is given to man, then, and then only, can he reflect the character of God and show the qualities denoted by holiness and righteousness and mercy and loyalty.

---

[1] Gen. 13.10 ff., 20.1 ff. [2] Gen. 13.8 f. [3] Gen. 18.20 ff.
[4] Gen. 45.1 ff. [5] Gen. 39.2, 21. [6] Micah 6.8.

This, however, brings us to another aspect of the good life, without which his fellowship cannot continue to be enjoyed. When Isaiah experienced the cleansing and renewal of his personality he immediately consecrated himself to the service of God.[1] Without that consecration he could not have known the fellowship of God. It is true that there were some persons who were especially consecrated to God, such as kings and priests and prophets and Nazirites. But that should not blind us to the fact that every member of the Covenant people was called to consecrate himself in a real sense to God. Just as Isaiah's consecration was the response he made to his cleansing, so at Sinai the whole people consecrated itself to God in response to its deliverance. The call for universal consecration is implicit in the statement that Israel was called to be a kingdom of priests,[2] devoted to God's service and the medium of his service to the world. Moreover, the great Deuteronomic word which Judaism has always cherished, which calls on every Israelite to love the Lord with every fibre of his being,[3] demands the spirit of consecration from all men. Whoso loves God with all his heart must consecrate himself to manifest his love. The good life consists not alone in living uprightly, but in loving God; for love leads to fellowship and fellowship to service. 'Teach me thy way, O Yahweh' cried the psalmist; 'I will walk in thy truth:[4] Let my heart rejoice[5] to fear thy name. I will praise thee, Yahweh my God, with my whole heart; And I will glorify thy name for ever.'[6]

It is to be noted that the Wisdom writers are in fundamental agreement here. It is often thought that the sages inculcated a spirit of worldly wisdom that was not profoundly religious. This is to do them an injustice. For all their teachings are rooted and grounded in religion. 'The fear of Yahweh is the beginning of wisdom' was their first principle,[7] and by the fear of the Lord they did not mean terror before him, but reverence. Where we read of love for God, as in the Deuteronomic word just quoted, and in some passages in the Psalms, we are not to think of an

---

[1] Isa. 6.8. [2] Ex. 19.6. [3] Deut. 6.5.

[4] J. M. P. Smith (*The Old Testament: an American Translation*) here well renders 'in fidelity to thee'. Cf. above, p.113, n.i, on the meaning of the word *'emeth*.

[5] R.V. has 'Unite my heart'. The rendering above follows the LXX and Syriac renderings, which involve no change of the consonantal Hebrew text, and which are followed by many editors.

[6] Ps. 86.11 f. [7] Prov. 9.10.

easy familiarity, but a love which is penetrated with reverence. When the Wisdom writers speak of the fear of the Lord, they are not thinking of something quite other than that love of God. They recognize that God is the source of the good life, and that his will is the foundation of human well-being. 'Behold, the fear of the Lord is wisdom; And to depart from evil is understanding.'[1]

From all this it follows that worship is integral to the good life. Not seldom the prophets are presented as men who were opposed to the entire worship of the Temple, and who taught that God wanted only obedience in daily life. It may suffice to quote one writer of the present generation: 'These men had denounced ritual as of no avail, but now, if possible, they went farther, and made social ethics the essential, even the sole, requirement of Yahweh.'[2] I have more than once offered reasons for dissenting from this view,[3] and for maintaining that while they did indeed demand that every aspect of daily life must be brought under the control of God's will and purpose, and held that without this any worship or offering was hollow and meaningless, they were not indifferent to the value of worship rightly offered. But even if it were true that the pre-exilic prophets despised worship and demanded only conduct, we should still need to remember that they were not the only exponents of the faith of Israel, and that the importance of worship is clearly recognized in much of the Old Testament.

The prophets resorted to the temple to find their audiences. Amos went to the shrine of Bethel,[4] and Jeremiah to the Temple in Jerusalem.[5] It was in the Temple that Isaiah received his call,[6] and it is not surprising that it had a peculiar place in his thought. In dark days, when he foresaw grave disasters before the state, he promised that the Temple should be spared, and for its sake Jerusalem.[7] When Jeremiah wrote down some of his oracles through the pen of Baruch, he sent the scribe into the Temple to read them publicly.[8] Whatever their attitude to the sacrificial cultus may have been, they were clearly not opposed to the existence of a centre of worship. It is true that

---

[1] Job. 28.28.
[2] I. G. Matthews, *The Religious Pilgrimage of Israel*, 1947, p. 128.
[3] Cf. *B.J.R.L.*, xxix, 1945–6, pp. 326 ff., xxxiii, 1950–1, pp. 74 ff., and *The Unity of the Bible*, pp. 30 ff.
[4] Amos 7.10 ff.   [5] Jer. 7.2, 26.2.   [6] Isa. 6.1 ff.   [7] Isa. 31.4 f., 37.33.   [8] Jer. 36.6 ff.

Jeremiah,[1] like Micah,[2] predicted the destruction of the Temple, but this was as a punishment and not because a centre of worship was in itself evil. Moreover, Jeremiah made it plain that by genuine repentance this destruction might be averted.[3] In the well-known oracle which is attributed to both Isaiah[4] and Micah[5] there is a prophecy of the day when men of all nations should go up to the house of the Lord in Zion. While we can never know with security what prophet uttered this oracle, there is no need to transfer it to the post-exilic age, as some scholars have done.[6] In the book of Jeremiah there is an oracle, which is often denied to that prophet, and which can scarcely be in its original place,[7] which similarly promises the day when Jerusalem shall be called the throne of the Lord, and when all nations shall be gathered unto it.[8] That Ezekiel valued the Temple and its worship is manifest from the thought that he gave to its rebuilding and the detailed plan for its reconstruction which he sketches.[9] Haggai and Zechariah rebuked men because they had not rebuilt it, and under their inspiration the second Temple was erected.[10] Trito-Isaiah echoes the thought of some of the other passages just mentioned when he says 'My house shall be called a house of prayer for all peoples.'[11] There is nothing to suggest that pre-exilic or post-exilic prophets thought that a centre of public worship was in itself something objectionable or meaningless.

[1] Jer. 7.14, 26.6.   [2] Micah 3.12.   [3] Jer. 7.3, 26.3.   [4] Isa. 2.2 ff.   [5] Micah 4.1 ff.
[6] Scholars who assign this passage either to Isaiah or to Micah, or to an even earlier prophet, include B. Duhm, C. Cornill, A. van Hoonacker, G. H. Box, E. Sellin, H. Schmidt, J. Fischer, J. Lippl and J. Theis, E. J. Kissane, A. H. Edelkoort, L. Dennefeld, and J. Steinmann (for references cf. *The Unity of the Bible*, p. 87 n.).
[7] Cf. F. Giesebrecht, *Jeremia* (H.K.), 1894, pp. 16 f., B. Duhm, *Jeremia* (K.H.C.), 1901, pp. 39 f., A. S. Peake, *Jeremiah* (Cent. B.), i, pp. 108 f., A. W. Streane, *Jeremiah and Lamentations* (Camb. B.), 1913, pp. 24 f., L. E. Binns, *Jeremiah* (West. C.), 1919, pp. 30 f., J. Skinner, *Prophecy and Religion*, 1922, p. 80, G. A. Smith, *Jeremiah*, 3rd ed., 1924, p. 18, 99, P. Volz, *Jeremia* (K.A.T.), 2nd ed., 1928, p. 48, F. Nötscher, *Jeremias* (H.S.A.T.), 1934, p. 50, W. Rudolph, *Jeremia* (H.A.T.), 1947, pp. 22 ff., A. Weiser, *Jeremia* (A.T.D.), i, 1952, pp. 35 ff. Weiser would allow the possibility that the passage is genuinely Jeremianic; he says (p. 36): 'Es scheint mir deshalb nicht angebracht, diese als unjeremianisch dem Propheten absprechen zu wollen'. Similarly G. A. Smith, op. cit., p. 99 n., says that it contains genuine fragments from Jeremiah.
[8] Jer. 3.17.
[9] Ezek. 40 ff. These chapters are denied to Ezekiel altogether by some writers, while others are prepared to allow that they contain a substantial Ezekielian element; cf. *B.J.R.L.*, xxxvi, 1953–4, pp. 146 ff., where I discuss with references to other writers the modern theories on the book of Ezekiel.
[10] Hag. 1.4; Zech. 1.16, 8.9.   [11] Isa. 56.7.

In recent years much attention has been drawn to the fact that the prophets whose oracles have been preserved for us in the prophetic canon were not the only prophets in Israel, and that prophets and priests are often mentioned together in intimate connexion, and not seldom brought under the same condemnation. There were prophets closely associated with the priests in the cultus of the Temple. These are frequently referred to as cultic prophets.[1] It has even been argued that all the prophets were cultic officials and that they belonged to various orders of diviners.[2] While this goes much too far, it should be remembered that there were many kinds of prophets, and that they functioned in a great variety of ways. Sometimes they functioned singly and sometimes in groups, sometimes in home or palace, sometimes by the wayside and sometimes in the shrine. There were inner divisions amongst them, divisions which concerned the content of their message. Some clearly stood in closer relation swith the Temple authorities of their day than did the great pre-exilic prophets whose names are familiar to us, and they may have had a defined place in the service of the Temple, though we cannot now define it with precision.

It is believed by many writers that they composed liturgies for use in the Temple services. Such liturgies have been found by some scholars in the books of Nahum and Habakkuk and Joel,[3]

---

[1] Cf. G. Hölscher, *Die Profeten*, 1914, p. 143, S. Mowinckel, *Psalmenstudien*, iii, 1923, A. Causse, *R.H.P.R.*, vi, 1926, pp. 1 ff., O. Eissfeldt, *Einleitung in das Alte Testament*, pp. 115 ff., and *The Old Testament and Modern Study*, ed. by H. H. Rowley, 1951, pp. 119 ff., A. Jepsen, *Nabi*, 1934, pp. 143 ff., A. R. Johnson, *E.T.*, xlvii, 1935–6, pp. 312 ff., and *The Cultic Prophet in Ancient Israel*, 1944, E. Würthwein, *Z.A.W.*, lxii (N.F. xxi), 1950, pp. 10 ff., and *Z.Th.K.*, xlix, 1952, pp. 1 ff., A. S. Kapelrud, *Studia Theologica*, iv, 1950–1, pp. 5 ff., F. Hesse, *Z.A.W.*, lxv (N.F. xxiv), 1953, pp. 45 ff. Cf. also *The Servant of the Lord*, pp. 104 ff., and N. W. Porteous, *E.T.*, lxii, 1950–1, pp. 4 ff. A. Robert (*Miscellanea Biblica B. Ubach* (Scripta et Documenta, i), 1953, p. 12) declares that 'l'hypothèse des prophètes cultuels est absolument gratuite'. Cf. also now K. Roubos, *Profetie en Cultus in Israël*, 1956 (issued while the present work was in the press).

[2] See above, p. 30.

[3] Cf. P. Humbert, *Z.A.W.*, xliv (N.F. iii), 1926, pp. 266 ff., *A.f.O.*, v, 1928–9, pp. 14 ff., *R.H.P.R.*, xii, 1932, pp. 1 ff.; A. Haldar, *Studies in the Book of Nahum*, 1947, and *S.B.U.*, ii, 1952, cols. 417 ff.; E. Balla, in *R.G.G.*, 2nd ed., ii, 1928, cols. 1556 f.; S. Mowinckel, *Psalmenstudien*, iii, 1923, p. 27; P. Humbert, *Problèmes du livre d'Habacuc*, 1944, pp. 296 ff.; I. Engnell, *S.B.U.*, i, 1948, cols. 769 ff., 1075 ff.; Mowinckel, loc. cit., p. 65; A. S. Kapelrud, *Joel Studies*, 1948 (where the book is held to be composed in part in the style of a liturgy, though it is not stated that it was actually employed in the cult); J. Steinmann, in *Études sur les Prophètes d'Israël* (Lectio Divina, No. 14), 1954, pp. 171 f. Cf. also P. Haupt, *J.B.L.*, xxvi, 1907, pp. 1 ff., where the first two chapters of Nahum were already said to be a liturgy, composed to celebrate the victory over Nicanor in 161 B.C.

and even more widely.[1] To them has been attributed the composition of psalms to accompany ritual acts.[2] All this means that we should beware of any simple antithesis between prophetic religion and the religion of the Temple, and still more should we beware of suggesting that prophetic religion could dispense with the element of worship.

It is true that for Jew and Christian the sacrificial system of the Temple has come to an end. For the Jew it ceased when the Temple was destroyed and when it was no longer possible to offer sacrifices in the one legitimate sanctuary which the Law allowed. For the Christian it was not abolished by the teaching of the pre-exilic prophets, but by the death of Christ, which gathered into itself the significance of all sacrifice by fulfilling the Old Testament prophecy of the sacrifice of the Servant of the Lord, where the highest point of Old Testament sacrifice is found. There is nothing to indicate that Jesus regarded sacrifices as in itself alien to the will of God. He would not have told cleansed lepers to go and offer sacrifice[3] if he had believed it to be displeasing to God. Paul certainly did not regard sacrifice as evil, and as a Jew he continued to observe the sacrificial law.[4] Yet he did not seek to impose the law of sacrifice on Gentile Christians, because he realized that for the Church sacrifice was abrogated in the death of Christ.

Moreover, Judaism had developed another centre of worship long before the Temple was destroyed. It had developed the Synagogue. It is a surprising fact that we do not know how or when the Synagogue came into being, and the institution which has meant so much to both Judaism and Christianity, since its worship formed the basis of Christian worship as well as Jewish, came unheralded into the world. It is commonly believed that it was during the period of the exile that it had its

---

[1] Cf. H. Gunkel, *Z.A.W.*, xlii (N.F. i), 1924, pp. 177 ff. (Isa.33), and *What Remains of the Old Testament*, E. Tr. by A. K. Dallas, 1928, pp. 115 ff. (the end of Micah; cf. Kapelrud, *S.B.U.*, ii, 1952, cols. 278 f.); G. Gerleman, *Zephanja textkritisch und literarisch untersucht*, 1942 (Zephaniah); I. Engnell, *B.J.R.L.*, xxxi, 1948, p. 64, and *S.B.U.*, i, col. 1032 (Deutero-Isaiah a prophetic imitation of a cult liturgy). In *S.B.U.*, ii, cols. 763 ff., Engnell classifies prophecy as either *diwan*-type or liturgy-type.

[2] Cf. J. P. Peters, *The Psalms as Liturgies*, 1922; C. C. Keet, *A Liturgical Study of the Psalter*, 1928; S. Mowinckel, *Psalmenstudien*, ii, 1922, iii, 1923 and *Religion und Kultus*, German Tr. by A. Schauer, 1953, pp. 115 ff.; H. Gunkel, *Einleitung in den Psalmen* (H.K.), 1933, pp. 10 ff.; A. Causse, *Les plus vieux Chants de la Bible*, 1926, pp. 79 ff.; A. C. Welch, *Prophet and Priest in Old Israel*, 1936, pp. 131 ff.

[3] Luke 17.14.   [4] Cf. Acts 21.26, 25.8, 28.17.

first beginnings, and that it was in Babylonia that the exiles
first began to gather together for mutual comfort and exhortation and to cherish the faith they had so imperfectly cherished
in their own land.[1] Of this there can be no certainty. It is believed that the earliest known evidence of the existence of a
synagogue comes from the end of the fifth century B.C., and
from outside Palestine, though not from Babylonia.[2] It may
well be that it began in some simple way in a private home,
and that when it was found to minister to a need it grew, and
that later the exiles brought back this institution to Palestine
when they returned. Certain it is that in the post-exilic days the
synagogue would be found to minister to a need which could
hardly have been felt in the same way in pre-exilic days. In
those days there was a multiplicity of shrines throughout the
land, to which men commonly resorted. In the days of Hezekiah's reform all were closed throughout Judah, save the
Jerusalem Temple,[3] but that reform could not have lasted long.
It was the political side of the revolt against Assyria which
proved disastrous, even though Jerusalem was spared, and it
is certain that in the reign of Manasseh the old position was
restored. Again in the time of Josiah there was a new bid for
independence, with a religious reform associated with it.[4] This

[1] Cf. A. Menes, *Z.A.W.*, l (N.F. ix), 1932, pp. 268 ff.; also E. Schürer, *History of the Jewish People*, II ii, 1890, pp. 53 ff. (4th German ed., ii, 1907, pp. 498 ff.), W. Bacher, *J.E.*, xi, 1905, p. 619, G. F. Moore, *Judaism*, i, 1927, p. 283. Bousset-Gressmann, *Die Religion des Judentums in späthellenistischen Zeitalter*, 3rd ed., 1926, p. 172, put its origin much later, in the Hellenistic period, and claim that it was not known in Palestine in the time of the Chronicler. So also Oesterley and Box, *The Religion and Worship of the Synagogue*, 1911, p. 337.
[2] Cf. *B.A.S.O.R.*, No. 84, December 1941, pp. 4 f., where C. C. Torrey reads *bêth kenîshāh* = 'synagogue' on an ostracon from Elath, which W. F. Albright (ibid., No. 82, April 1941, pp. 11 ff.) dates at the end of the sixth century B.C.
[3] II Kings 18.4 ff. Many scholars deny the historicity of this reform; so J. Well-hausen, *Prolegomena*, E. Tr., p. 25, B. Stade, *Geschichte des Volkes Israel*, 2nd ed., i, 1889, p. 607, G. Hölscher, *Geschichte des israelitischen und jüdischen Religion*, 1922, p. 99, H. Schmidt, in *S.A.T.*, II ii, 2nd ed., 1923, pp. 9 f. Others find no reason to deny it; so C. Steuernagel, *Deuteronomium* (H.K.), 1898, p. xiv, R. Kittel, *Geschichte des Volkes Israel*, ii, 7th ed., 1925, pp. 375 f., A.-R. Siebens, *L'Origine du Code deutéronomique*, 1929, pp. 156 ff., Oesterley and Robinson, *History of Israel*, i, 1932, pp. 392 f., G. Ricciotti, *Storia d'Israele*, i, 2nd ed., 1934, pp. 443 f. (E. Tr. by C. della Penta and R.T.A. Murphy, 1955, pp. 372 f.), W. F. Albright, *The Biblical Period*, 1950, p. 42. With these latter I stand; cf. *The Relevance of Apocalyptic*, 2nd ed., p. 15.
[4] II Kings 22 f. Again some scholars have denied the historical value of the story of Josiah's centralization of the worship in Jerusalem; so L. Horst, *R.H.R.*, xvii, 1888, pp. 11 ff., M. Vernes, *Précis d'histoire juive*, 1889, p. 795 n. G. Hölscher, while allowing a measure of reform to Josiah (cf. *Eucharisterion* (Gunkel Fest-schrift), i, 1923, pp. 206 ff.) thinks the account in II Kings has been much em-

time it spread beyond the bounds of Judah.[1] But again independence was not achieved, and the reform was not lasting. It was therefore only for brief periods in the pre-exilic days that there was only one legitimate place of worship acknowledged. In post-exilic days, however, we hear little of the country shrines, though we do not know when they faded out or were abolished. Whenever it was that they ceased to function, the need for some local centre of worship would be felt. It has been maintained that the synagogue began as a secular meeting place before it was used as a centre of worship.[2] But however that may be, it is certain that in the post-exilic age it became established as a centre of local worship, without sacrificial cultus, and that by New Testament times it was found not alone in Palestine, but wherever there were Jewish communities. That its worship included the reading of Scripture and exhortation we know from the Gospels,[3] and similarly that it was a place of prayer.[4] Through its worship the faith of men was nourished, and through its reading of the Scriptures men were reminded of the demand of the faith of Israel for the expression of devotion in life as well as in worship. We know that our Lord valued its worship, and that he was found in the synagogue[5] as well as in the Temple, and that it became the model which was adapted for the worship of the Church.

Nor should we forget the institution of the Sabbath. It has already been said that the Sabbath figures in the Ritual Decalogue of Ex. 34 as well as in the familiar Decalogue of

---

bellished (*Z.A.W.*, xl, 1922, pp. 227 ff.); cf. E. Havet, *Le Christianisme et ses Origines*, iii, 1878, pp. 32 ff., R. H. Kennett, *The Church of Israel*, 1938, pp. 83 ff. (first published in 1920), F. Horst, *Z.D.M.G.*, lxxvii, 1923, pp. 220 ff., A. Loisy, *La Religion d'Israël*, 3rd ed., 1933, pp. 200 f. On this view cf. L. B. Paton, *J.B.L.*, xlvii, 1928, pp. 326 ff. Most scholars, however, accept the historicity of the account in II Kings, and I share that view; cf. *Studies in Old Testament Prophecy*, ed. by H. H. Rowley, 1950, pp. 161 ff.

[1] I find no reason to doubt that Josiah carried his reform to the north, at least as far as Bethel, which is mentioned in II Kings 23.15 ff. Cf. ibid., pp. 165 f.

[2] So S. Zeitlin, *P.A.A.J.R.*, ii, 1931, pp. 69 ff.

[3] Luke 4.16⁵.

[4] Matt. 6.5; cf. Acts 16.13, where, however, the 'place of prayer' does not seem to have been a synagogue (cf. F. F. Bruce, *The Acts of the Apostles*, 1951, p. 314), though the term is often used for synagogue (cf. ibid., p. 155). Cf. Strack-Billerbeck, *Kommentar zum Neuen Testament aus Talmud und Midrasch*, i, 1922, p. 397: 'Ausserhalb Jerusalems kamen als Gebetsstätten in ersten Linie die Synagogen in Betracht'; cf. also ibid., pp. 398 f.

[5] Luke 4.16—'as his custom was'.

Ex. 20. I have also said that I believe the Ritual Decalogue was a pre-Mosaic formula, which belonged to the worship of Yahweh before the time of Moses. I therefore accept the Sabbath as a very ancient institution.[1] That it was a religious institution is clear from its inclusion in the Decalogue, but the only provision given is that it was to be a day of rest from work. Its holiness consisted in the *tabu* against any sort of work which belonged to it. Yet it must quite early have developed into a day of religious worship. The Ritual Decalogue does not call upon men to worship on that day. It demands that all males should appear before the Lord three times a year,[2] and says nothing about a weekly summons to worship. But we know from the story of the murder of Athaliah and the enthronement of Joash[3] that it was a day on which large numbers resorted to the Temple. For we find that the royal guard was divided into three companies, of which two appear to have guarded the palace and one the Temple on ordinary days, but on Sabbath days to have changed over, so that the two companies were in the Temple. Quite early, therefore, the Sabbath was associated with the worship of the Temple, and hence it was natural that when the synagogue came into being as a local centre of worship, it should be resorted to especially on the Sabbath.

The worship of the Temple consisted of more than sacrifice. It consisted, indeed, of more than organized worship. In the fellowship of its courts there was opportunity for religious address, such as the prophets sometimes gave, or such as Jesus gave. But the organized worship included more than sacrifice. From the work of the Chronicler we learn that in the post-exilic age there was a carefully regulated musical element in its worship, and it is probable that this already held in the pre-

---

[1] Cf. *B.J.R.L.*, xxxiv, 1951–2, pp. 109 ff., where references to some of the considerable literature on this question may be found. Some scholars hold the Sabbath to be a post-Mosaic institution, and on that account argue that the Decalogue is post-Mosaic; so J. C. Matthes, *Z.A.W.*, xxiv, 1904, pp. 31 ff., S. Mowinckel, *Le Décalogue*, 1927, pp. 75 ff. The fact that the Sabbath law is found in Ex. 34.21, which is assigned to J, and in Ex. 23.12, which is assigned to E, as well as in the Decalogue of Ex. 20 and Deut. 5, where the different expansions are evidence that the present texts rest on an older form, seems to me to witness to the antiquity of the Sabbath as an institution. Ex. 16.29 f. also offers evidence of a weekly sabbath, and this is commonly assigned to the oldest strand of the Pentateuch. Other scholars who hold that the Sabbath was pre-Mosaic include B. D. Eerdmans, in *Vom Alten Testament* (Marti Festschrift, B.Z.A.W., No. 41), 1925, pp. 69 f., and K. Budde, *J.T.S.*, xxx, 1928–9, pp. 11 ff.
[2] Ex. 34.23.   [3] II Kings 11.4 ff.

exilic age. Indeed, it is clear from Amos's denunciation of the noise of songs and the melody of viols[1] that there was music in the pre-exilic worship of the shrines. Much recent study of the Psalter leads to the view that the psalms were composed to accompany ritual acts, both to interpret the significance of the ritual to those present, and to call forth from them the spirit that would make the ritual act the expression of their thought and will.[2] While it is hard to define the precise age of any particular psalm, it is believed that there is a substantial pre-exilic element in the Psalter. The prophets denounced those who came with proud hearts to the Temple from their harsh and selfish ways, who offered splendid sacrifices that were not the organ of their spirit, and who really cared little for the will of God in their daily lives. Their worship was a hollow pretence and offensive in the eyes of God. But there was that in its worship which could nurture the spirit of the sincere and the humble, and could lift into the spirit of God those who truly desired to walk in his way. Had there not been it is hard to understand why Jesus should have resorted to its courts. Moreover, Simeon, who is said to have been 'righteous and devout, looking for the consolation of Israel', and on whom the Holy Spirit rested,[3] seems to have found within its precincts that which enriched and fed his spirit, as also did Anna.[4] Nowhere in the Bible is the good life presented as the life that despises the true worship of God's house. Certainly the psalmists did not despise it, and their hymns have been able to inspire devotion of spirit down to our own day. 'O Yahweh, I love the habitation of thy house,' cried one, 'And the place where thy glory dwells,'[5] while another sang 'A day in thy courts is better than a thousand elsewhere.'[6] The same psalm says 'My soul longs, yea, faints for the courts of Yahweh,'[7] and another psalmist voices the desire that he might dwell in the house of Yahweh all the days of his life.[8] Such texts might be multiplied, and they testify to the place that the corporate worship was perceived to be

---

[1] Amos 5.23.
[2] Cf. especially A. C. Welch, op. cit., pp. 103 ff. For a good account of the various sides of modern study of the Psalter cf. A. R. Johnson, in *The Old Testament and Modern Study*, ed. by H. H. Rowley, pp. 162 ff., and J. J. Stamm, *Th.R.*, N.F. xxiii, 1955, pp. 1 ff.
[3] Luke 2.25.   [4] Luke 2.37.   [5] Ps. 26.8.
[6] Ps. 84.10 (Heb. 11).   [7] Ps. 84.2 (Heb. 3).   [8] Ps. 27.4.

capable of playing in the life of those who really cherished the
faith of Israel and who desired to live the good life.

That the Temple, as well as the synagogue, was a place of
prayer is clear from both Testaments. Within the precincts of
the Shiloh shrine Hannah offered her private prayer,[1] and the
New Testament presents us with the parable of the two men
who went up into the Temple to pray.[2] The text 'My house shall
be called a house of prayer for all peoples'[3] has already been
cited. How far corporate prayer entered into the worship of the
Temple is not very clear. The Code of Deuteronomy prescribes
a form of prayer to be used in the Temple on a particular
occasion,[4] but does not indicate whether it was to be individu-
ally used or used together. This does not prove that prayer was
a regular feature of the daily or weekly worship. From the New
Testament, however, we learn that 'Peter and John were going
up into the Temple at the hour of prayer, being the ninth
hour'.[5] This makes it quite clear that by New Testament times
there was an hour when men gathered together in the Temple
for prayer, and this would appear to be for corporate prayer.
But if the view already mentioned is correct, and the psalms
were used in the ordered worship of the Temple, then prayer
had no little part in that worship. For many of the psalms are
prayers. Some of them appear to be individual prayers, while
others appear to be for corporate use, and sometimes we find
swift transitions from one to the other. This is not an isolated
phenomenon in the Old Testament. In the book of
Deuteronomy we find swift transitions from the second person
singular to the second person plural, so that some scholars
have supposed that it rested on separate sources,[6] each marked
by its own usage. This is a needless hypothesis. Once we have
entered into the Hebrew spirit we are not troubled by these
transitions, either in Deuteronomy or in the prophets, where
similar transitions are found, or in the Psalter. Certain it is that
in the psalms we find a great variety of human aspirations and
desires voiced, and they could well be the vehicle of the expression of men's needs as they approached God, whether associated

---

[1] I Sam. 1.11.   [2] Luke 18.10.   [3] Isa. 56.7.
[4] Deut. 26.1–11. On this passage cf. A. C. Welch, op. cit., pp. 112 ff.
[5] Acts 3.1.
[6] So C. Steuernagel, *Das Deuteronomium* (H.K.), 1898, pp. i ff.; cf. G. A. Smith,
Deuteronomy (Camb. B.), 1918, pp. lxxiii ff.

with a sacrifice which symbolized the plea or borne on the spirit alone.[1]

Worship is not all prayer,[2] and prayer is not all petition for boons. Every side of worship is expressed in the Psalter and elsewhere in the Old Testament. The sense of awe in God's presence and of adoration of his majesty is expressed in many passages. 'Remove thy shoes from thy feet, for the place whereon thou standest is holy ground.'[3] 'Holy, holy, holy is Yahweh of hosts: the whole earth is full of his glory.'[4] 'Come let us worship and bow down; Let us kneel before Yahweh our Maker.'[5] 'When I look at thy heavens, the work of thy fingers, The moon and the stars, which thou hast ordered;[6] What is man that thou shouldst think of him? And the son of man that thou shouldst care for him?'[7] 'Let all the earth fear Yahweh: Let all the inhabitants of the world stand in awe of him.'[8]

The feeling of awe in God's presence begets the sense of unworthiness and sin, as it did in Isaiah in the moment of his call. For God is of purer eyes than to behold iniquity,[9] and the sinner who is really conscious of the presence of God must ever be conscious of his sin. He knows that he cannot conceal from the eye of God his inmost heart. 'Thou hast set our iniquities before thee, Our hidden faults in the light of thy countenance.'[10] That consciousness of sin calls forth confession, and confession is followed by the cry for cleansing,[11] that the miracle wrought in Isaiah may be repeated in others. 'Against thee, thee only, have I sinned, And done that which is evil in thy sight.'[12] 'Have mercy on me, O God, according to thy lovingkindness: According to the multitude of thy tender mercies blot out my transgressions . . . Create in me a clean heart, O God; And

---

[1] Cf. H. Gunkel, *What Remains of the Old Testament*, E. Tr., p. 114: 'Whoever earnestly studies these poems will not fail to find many passages which give perfect expression to true religion, and generations still to come will humbly bend the knee on this holy ground and learn from the Hebrew psalmists how to pray.'

[2] On prayer in the Bible cf. O. Piper, *Interpretation*, viii, 1954, pp. 3 ff., and F. V. Filson, ibid., pp. 21 ff.

[3] Ex. 3.5.   [4] Isa. 6.3.   [5] Ps. 95.6.

[6] The Hebrew word here means 'established according to a fixed order'.

[7] Ps. 8.3 f. (Heb. 4 f.).

[8] Ps. 33.8.   [9] Hab. 1.13.   [10] Ps. 90.8.

[11] On the penitential psalms cf. G. Bernini, *Le Preghiere penitenziali del Salterio* (Analecta Gregoriana, lxii, Ser. Fac. Theol., A 9), 1953.

[12] Ps. 51.4 (Heb. 6).

renew a right[1] spirit within me.'[2] 'For thy name's sake, O Yahweh, Pardon mine iniquity, though it is great.'[3]

Here men are fortified with the assurance that such prayers have found their answer. 'The Lord is near to the broken hearted, And saves those who are of contrite spirit.'[4] They may continue to stand in his presence, and find in it fullness of joy. 'With thee is the fountain of life: in thy light we see light.'[5] 'Yahweh is the fortress of my life.'[6] 'He who dwells in the secret place of the Most High shall abide under the shadow of the Almighty.'[7]

Richly does the element of praise enter into the spirit of worship as it is reflected in the Bible. 'I will bless Yahweh at all times: His praise shall continually be in my mouth.'[8] 'Bless Yahweh, O my soul; And all that is within me, bless his holy name.'[9] 'It is a good thing to give thanks to Yahweh, And to sing praises to thy name, O Most High.'[10] 'Come, let us sing unto Yahweh: Let us make a joyful noise to the rock of our salvation.'[11] 'Sing to Yahweh a new song: Sing to Yahweh, all the earth.'[12] This praise is often shot with thanksgiving. For when blessing is received from the hand of God, it should be acknowledged with thankfulness. 'I sought Yahweh, and he answered me, And delivered me from all that I dreaded.'[13] 'O that men would praise Yahweh for his goodness, And for his wonderful works to the children of men.'[14] 'Enter his gates with thanksgiving, And his courts with praise.'[15]

Again and again we find holy aspiration fostered by the words of the psalms. 'Shew me thy ways, O Yahweh; teach me thy paths.'[16] 'Teach me to do thy will; for thou art my God.'[17] 'Teach me thy way, O Yahweh; And lead me in the right[18] path.'[19] 'With my whole heart have I sought thee: Let me not

---

[1] The Hebrew word here is from the same root as the word used above in Ps. 8.3; it therefore means a spirit which is steadfast in its loyalty here.
[2] Ps. 51.1, 10 (Heb. 3, 12).
[3] Ps. 25.11. [4] Ps. 34.18 (Heb. 19). [5] Ps. 36.9 (Heb. 10).
[6] Ps. 27.1. [7] Ps. 91.1. [8] Ps. 34.1 (Heb. 2). [9] Ps. 103.1.
[10] Ps. 92.1 (Heb. 2). [11] Ps. 95.1. [12] Ps. 96.1. [13] Ps. 34.4 (Heb. 5).
[14] Ps. 107.8. [15] Ps. 100.4. [16] Ps. 25.4. [17] Ps. 143.10.
[18] The meaning here may be 'in a path which is free from obstacles or unevenness' (cf. R.S.V. 'on a level path') or 'in the way of uprightness'. For the latter sense cf. Isa. 11.4, Ps. 45.6 (Heb. 7), 67.4 (Heb. 5), where the same word occurs and is rendered by 'equity'. In those passages the word clearly carries some ethical content, and since it stands here parallel to the way of Yahweh, it seems likely that it does here.
[19] Ps. 27.11.

wander from thy commandments.'[1] 'Incline my heart to thy testimonies, And not to unjust gain.'[2]

All these and yet other elements of worship are repeatedly expressed in the words of the Bible, and it would be possible to multiply many times the few examples that have been given. For worship is an integral element of the good life in the thought of the Bible. It is only they who maintain right relationship with God who can do his will. It is only they who go in the strength of the Lord God, and not they who walk in the strength of their own resolve, who can fulfil the law of God. When prophets declaimed against the evils of their time, and stigmatized the worship of men as vain, it was because they perceived that the spirit must give meaning to the act, and not because they advocated a religion without worship. Nor should we forget, when we are inclined to think of post-exilic Judaism as hard and legal and unspiritual, that it was in the post-exilic days that the rich treasury of the Psalter was gathered together, and that it was employed in the worship of Judaism. Worship and life must belong together, the one as leading to the other and the other as expressing the one. It is but a distortion of the teaching of the Bible which concentrates on certain elements of the teaching of the Prophets and ignores all else, which forgets all the rich heritage of the Psalter while cherishing the social message of the Prophets.

Much that is in the Psalter can be used privately to direct and nurture our spirit. It is probable that it was collected primarily for the public worship. But the Bible never thinks of worship as limited to the sanctuary, or God's fellowship as something to be enjoyed only in the corporate fellowship of his house. Private worship and prayer, a fellowship with God that can be enjoyed anywhere, are everywhere recognized. Joseph could know the presence of the Lord in a prison,[3] and Jeremiah in a cistern.[4] It was not limited to fellowship in formulated prayer, though it could express itself in prayer. For private prayer, whether in the sanctuary or elsewhere, is throughout the Bible an expression of religion. Nehemiah could pray in the king's palace[5] and Daniel in his own home;[6] Hezekiah could pray on what he believed to be his death-bed,[7] and Jonah in

---

[1] Ps. 119.10.   [2] Ps. 119.36.   [3] Gen. 39.21.   [4] Jer. 38.6 ff.; cf. 1.8.
[5] Neh. 2.4.   [6] Dan. 6.10.   [7] II Kings 20.3; Isa. 38.3.

the belly of the great fish.[1] Similarly our Lord could pray on the mountain top,[2] or in the Garden of Gethsemane.[3] Prayer is not limited to this place or that. And by the same token, the communion of the spirit with God, whereby the riches of his grace and the strength of his spirit might be received, was not believed to be limited to particular spots, however sacred they might be.

That the prophets knew the riches of God's fellowship in their private life can scarcely be gainsaid. Amos's intimacy with God is represented in the form of conversations which he had with God,[4] and the same is true of Jeremiah. Especially intimate was the fellowship of Jeremiah with God, and some of his prayers are preserved. These passages, sometimes referred to as the 'Confessions of Jeremiah',[5] are described by Skinner as 'the outpouring of his heart to One who seeth in secret and can reward openly.'[6] Of them Skinner observes that if they had perished, 'the devotion of the Jewish Church would have been immeasurably poorer in that strain of personal piety which saves its religion from degenerating into a soulless legalism.'[7] There is no evidence that any of these passages had anything to do with the Temple. They belonged to the private religious life of the prophet.

Even where we have no record of any such experience, we may still be sure that the prophets valued and knew an inner experience of fellowship with God. They would not have urged men to seek God, and to walk humbly with him, if they had not conceived of religion in terms of fellowship as well as ethics. They would not have represented their message as given to them by God, and themselves as men who were privileged to sit in to hear the secrets of God, if they had not known a rich intimacy with him. This intimacy was something deeper than any forms of worship, and that it was more fundamental than any forms cannot be doubted. It could be enjoyed anywhere, since God was everywhere.

[1] Jonah 2.1.
[2] Mark 6.46, Luke 6.12, 9.28.
[3] Mark 14.32 ff., Matt. 26.36 ff.; Luke 22.40 ff.
[4] Amos 7.1 ff., 8.1 ff.
[5] Cf. J. Skinner, *Prophecy and Religion*, pp. 201 ff., E. A. Leslie, *The Intimate Papers of Jeremiah*, 1953, and J. Leclercq, 'Les "Confessions" de Jérémie', in *Études sur les Prophètes d'Israël* (Lectio Divina 14), 1954, pp. 111 ff.
[6] Op. cit., p. 213.   [7] Ibid., pp. 201 f.

The good life, then, as it is presented to us in the Old Testament is the life that is lived in harmony with God's will and that expresses itself in daily life in the reflection of the character of God translated into the terms of human experience, that draws its inspiration and its strength from communion with God in the fellowship of his people and in private experience, and that knows how to worship and praise him both in public and in the solitude of the heart.

VI

DEATH AND BEYOND[1]

In an earlier lecture it has been said that man is conceived of
in the Bible as having an animated body, and as created for the
fellowship and obedience of God. He is like the animals in
having an animated body; yet he has something denied to the
animals in that he alone is in the image of God. It has not yet
been noted that he is also mortal, appointed for death. In the
story of the Garden of Eden he is turned out of Paradise 'lest he
stretch out his hand, and take also of the tree of life, and eat,
and live for ever.'[2] To him God says 'Dust thou art, and to dust
thou shalt return.'[3] This is true also of the animal creation.
Concerning the lower creatures the psalmist says 'When Thou
takest away their breath, they die, and return to their dust.'[4]
Man and animals alike are born and die. 'Who is the man who
will live and not see death?'[5] cries another psalmist, while a
more familiar psalm says 'We bring our years to an end as a
sigh.[6] The days of our years are threescore years and ten, Or if
we are especially strong fourscore years; Yet their greater part[7]

---

[1] The substance of this chapter was given as the Drew Lecture on Immortality
for New College, London, in 1954, and published in *C.Q.*, xxxiii, 1955, pp. 116 ff.
The passages in the present lecture which are in verbal agreement with the
Drew Lecture are repeated by permission of the Trustees of the Drew Lectureship.
[2] Gen. 3.22.   [3] Gen. 3.19.   [4] Ps. 104.29.
[5] Ps. 89.48 (Heb. 49). Cf. Ecclus. 17.30: 'The son of man is not immortal'. Some
MSS have a contradiction of this in 19.19: 'They who do the things pleasing to
him will gather the fruit of the tree of immortality'. But they are not important
MSS and the verse is omitted from R.V., and not even cited in the margin. The
text is given in A. Rahlfs, *Septuaginta*, ii, 1935, p. 409 n.
[6] R.V. 'as a tale that is told'; cf. Jerome, *quasi sermonem loquens* (H. de Sainte-
Marie, *Sancti Hieronymi Psalterium iuxta Hebraeos*, 1954, p. 131). The Syriac has
'as a spider', and LXX has a double rendering 'as a spider have meditated' (cf.
Vulgate, *sicut aranea meditabuntur*). Kissane (*The Book of Psalms*, ii, 1954, pp. 102,
104) offers a conjectural emendation, which yields the sense 'in sorrow'.
[7] The Hebrew has here a word found nowhere else, which R.V. renders by 'their
pride'. But most editors prefer the reading which seems to lie behind LXX,
Syriac and Targum, and which lacks one letter of the Massoretic text and yields
the above rendering. Kissane (op. cit., p. 102) prefers a conjectural expansion of
the Massoretic text, to yield 'much in them'. Other emendations have been proposed, but they are neither convincing nor necessary.

is but toil and sorrow; For it is soon gone, and we fly away.'[1]
This is all but a matter of experience, rather than of the faith
of Israel. The melancholy fact of death must be recognized by
men everywhere, and its shadow lies over all. The breath of
man's nostrils must one day cease, and his body lie cold and still.

It is in the interpretation of the significance of death that
faith figures, and in the thought of what follows death. Is it the
end of man's existence, a terminus beyond which nothing lies?
In Indian thought it is followed by rebirth to life in some form
on earth, the inexorable law of *karma* determining the nature of
that reincarnation, and in Buddhism men are offered the hope
of breaking the weary round of *samsara* in the endless peace of
Nirvana. In biblical thought we find none of this. For here life
is held to be a blessing and not a curse, and its possession is
wistfully desired so long as may be. Yet though long life is
counted an element in the desirable lot of the blessed, it must
have a limit and the grave claim all men. But beyond the grave
—what?

In the New Testament we find a rich, though not clearly
defined, faith. 'If in this life only we have hoped in Christ, we
are of all men most pitiable.'[2] 'I looked, and behold, a great
multitude, which no man could number, out of every nation,
and of all tribes and peoples and tongues, standing before the
throne and before the Lamb, clothed in white robes . . .
These are they who have come out of the great tribulation, and
have washed their robes, and made them white in the blood of
the Lamb. Therefore are they before the throne of God; and
they serve him day and night in his Temple.'[3] Here and in
many other passages we find expressed the faith that beyond
the grave lies an existence that far surpasses anything we know
in this life, so that death becomes not an enemy, but the gate to
a larger life. That faith is expressed in diverse forms.[4] It may be

---

[1] Ps. 90.9 f.
[2] I Cor. 15.19. R.S.V. has: 'If in this life we who are in Christ have only hope',
and similarly J. Moffatt: 'If in this life we have nothing but a mere hope in
Christ'. So G. G. Findlay, *The Expositor's Greek Testament*, ii, p. 925 a. J. Héring
(*La Première Épitre de S. Paul aux Corinthiens* (C.N.T.), 1949, pp. 137 f.) defends the
rendering: 'si c'est seulement dans les limites de cette vie que nous eussions placé
notre espérance en Christ'. Cf. H. D. Wendland, *Die Briefe an die Korinther*
(N.T.D.), 6th ed., 1954, p. 125.
[3] Rev. 7.9, 14 f.
[4] On the diversity of view found in the New Testament, cf. R. H. Charles, *A
Critical History of the Doctrine of a Future Life*, 2nd ed., 1913, pp. 401 ff.

thought of as a resurrection of the body, or as immortal bliss in another state. 'If the dead are not raised,' says Paul, 'neither hath Christ been raised: and if Christ hath not been raised, your faith is vain.'[1] That this is to life on earth is clearly indicated in some passages. In the Apocalypse the first resurrection is to share the millennial reign of Christ on earth,[2] and the second resurrection is to life in the New Jerusalem, which is represented as coming down out of heaven, and therefore to earth.[3] 'Since we believe that Jesus died and rose again,' says Paul in another passage, 'even so them also who are fallen asleep in Jesus will God bring with him . . . We who are alive, who are left until the coming of the Lord, will in no wise take precedence of those who are fallen asleep. For the Lord himself will descend from heaven . . . and the dead in Christ will rise first: then we who are alive, who are left, will be caught up together with them in the clouds, to meet the Lord in the air: and so shall we ever be with the Lord.'[4] Here it is not clear whether the unending fellowship with the Lord is thought of as on earth or elsewhere.[5] In other passages the latter is clearly indicated.[6] 'Let not your heart be troubled: ye believe in God, believe also in me. In my Father's house are many dwelling places; if it were not so, I would have told you; for I go to prepare a place for you.'[7] In writing to the Philippians Paul could say that he had a desire to depart and be with Christ, but it was more expedient for the Philippians that he should continue here.[8] Clearly Paul did not contemplate any waiting till the day of Judgement and Resurrection when he wrote this, but thought of an immediate translation into the presence of Christ, and therefore to the presence of God, since Christ is elsewhere said to be seated at the right hand of God.[9]

---

[1] I Cor. 15.16 f. [2] Rev. 20.4. [3] Rev. 21.1 f. [4] I Thess. 4.14 ff.
[5] J. Moffatt (*The Expositor's Greek Testament*, iv, p. 38 b) says: 'Plainly, however, the saints do not rise at once to heaven, but return with the Lord to the scene of his final manifestation on earth'. Charles (op. cit., p. 444) thinks the scene of their blessedness is a transformed heaven and earth.
[6] R. H. Charles (op. cit., pp. 437 ff.) distinguishes four separate stages in the thought of Paul.
[7] John 14.1. R.S.V., following Moffatt and others, has: 'If it were not so, would I have told you that I go to prepare a place for you?' So H. Strathmann, *Das Evangelium nach Johannes* (N.T.D.), 6th ed., 1951, p. 203. M.-J. Lagrange (*Évangile selon S. Jean* (E. Bib.), 7th ed., 1948, p. 373), retains and defends the interpretation of R.V. given above.
[8] Phil. 1.23 f.; cf. II Cor. 5.8.
[9] Rom. 8.34; Eph. 1.20; Col. 3.1; Heb. 1.3, 8.1, 10.12, 12.2; I Peter 3.22; Rev. 3.21.

In the Old Testament, on the other hand, we find a less sure embrace of the hope of any satisfying life after death, either here or elsewhere. The beginnings of the belief in the resurrection are to be found here, to provide the source of the New Testament thought along this line. But those beginnings appear quite late in the development of Old Testament thought, and we know from the New Testament that the Sadducees rejected any doctrine of resurrection. During the inter-testamental period the hope of a resurrection had grown in certain circles,[1] and it became an accepted element of the faith of the Pharisees.[2] Apart from these first expressions of a faith in the resurrection, it is sometimes maintained that no inklings of a worth-while afterlife are to be found in the Old Testament, and the contrast between the Old Testament and the New is found to be marked. While the differences between the two Testaments are not to be ignored or minimized, it will be seen that the contrast is not quite so strong as is supposed, and the seeds of every side of New Testament thought are to be found here.[3]

We must beware, however, of going to the opposite extreme. A recent writer[4] has read back a sure faith in the resurrection to the beginnings of the Old Testament story. He maintains that 'nothing less than resurrection was in the mind of Abraham and of all the faithful after him'.[5] This is a bold proposition, which rests on the argument that the promise of the land to

---

[1] Cf. II Mac. 7.9, 11, 14, 14.46. In the works commonly subsumed under the term Pseudepigrapha there are many more references to this belief. Some are dealt with in E. F. Sutcliffe, *The Old Testament and the Future Life*, 1946, pp. 167 ff., and a number of additional passages are referred to in my *Relevance of Apocalyptic*, 2nd ed., pp. 55, 60, 67 f., 73, 79, 99, 101, 105, 106 f., 108. R. H. Charles (*The Apocrypha and Pseudepigrapha of the Old Testament*, ii, 1913, p. 218) observes that there are three Jewish doctrines of the resurrection: 1. All Israelites are to rise; 2. All righteous Israelites are to rise; 3. All mankind are to rise.

[2] Cf. Strack-Billerbeck, op. cit., i, 1922, pp. 893 ff.

[3] J. N. Schofield, *Archaeology and the Afterlife*, 1951, emphasizes the variety of view found in the Old Testament, and relates the Old Testament evidence to that provided by archaeology, arguing that funeral and mourning customs point to a belief in survival after death.

[4] Cf. N. A. Logan, *S.J.T.*, vi, 1953, pp. 165 ff.

[5] Ibid., p. 169. E. F. Sutcliffe (*Scripture*, ii, 1947, p. 94) with more justification says: 'There has been a tendency to take it for granted that, like ourselves, Abraham, Moses, David and the other great men of God of the Old Testament looked forward to a judgment of their lives by God after death with a consequent apportionment of reward or punishment. But an attentive reading of the Old Testament shows that this is a mistaken notion and that for many centuries the religious life of the patriarchs and of the people of Israel was based exclusively on God's government of the world during the course of men's pilgrimage on this earth.'

Abraham and his seed implies the belief that he should be raised to share in the inheritance. 'To interpret God's pledge of the promised land to Abraham and his seed as being anything else than a pledge of ultimate and everlasting possession to each and all of them is to rob it of all substance and makes sheer nonsense of the patriarchal faith,' says this writer.[1] It surely makes greater nonsense of it to suppose that Abraham and all his seed have yet to be raised to live in Palestine under conditions of serious over-crowding, and it would be simpler to spiritualize the promise with the author of the Epistle to the Hebrews 'But now they desire a better country, that is, a heavenly'.[2] It is a common-place of Hebrew thought that a man was conceived of as living in his descendants, who were an extension of his personality, so that in the giving of the land to the descendants of Abraham it could be said to be given to him, and there is no occasion to read back a faith in the resurrection by this forced interpreta-tion. Within the Old Testament there is much variety, and even inconsistency, of view on what follows death, and it is impossible to attribute every statement directly to God, let alone to press it in forced and fantastic ways. That divine revelation is mediated through the Old Testament I am profoundly assured, as I said in my first lecture. But that revelation was mediated through human and fallible personality, and it is perilous to ascribe every statement directly to God. To do so would mean to equate God's revelation of himself with man's apprehension of that revelation, and to bring God down to the level of men's understanding of his nature and his will. All the variety of view of the afterlife contained in the Old Testament does not reveal the vacillating and uncertain mind of God, but the imperfect apprehension by men of the truth which is hidden in God's heart.

It has already been said that there is no trace of a belief in reincarnation in the Old Testament, but that there is in the later period a belief in the resurrection. There is also some trace of a belief in immortal bliss in another existence. It is

---

[1] Loc. cit., p. 170. This argument is not new, indeed. As its rabbinic character suggests, it was already found among the Rabbis, where it stands in TB San-hedrin 90 b. D. S. Margoliouth cited it with approval in *The Expositor*, 8th series, x, 1920, p. 105. It is a little surprising to find rabbinic principles of exegesis seriously revived in the twentieth century.

[2] Heb. 11.16.

sometimes maintained that a belief in the immortality of the soul reflects Greek thought, and that it is alien to the thought of the Hebrews.[1] While there are important differences between Greek and Hebrew thought, a belief in immortality is to be found in the Old Testament.

In the earliest of the main sources of the Pentateuch we have the story of Adam's ejection from the Garden of Eden, lest he should put forth his hand and partake of the fruit of the tree of life.[2] Here the thought is of immortality in his physical form. He is assured that he is appointed for death, and that his body must return to the dust whence it was taken. This does not necessarily mean the complete dissolution of his being, and there is no evidence that it was ever part of the faith of Israel that a man wholly ceased to be when his body was laid in the grave.[3] Had it been so there would not have been the concern as to the fate of the body after death which we find in many passages. For a man's body to lie unburied was regarded as a dire misfortune which concerned him, and equally so for his body to be dishonoured after his death. After the battle of Gilboa the Philistines exposed the bodies of Saul and his sons to dishonour on the walls of Beth-shan until the men of Jabesh-gilead, mindful of Saul's first exploit on their behalf,[4] took the bodies down and buried them in Jabesh.[5] Amos condemns the Moabites because they burned the bones of the king of Edom into lime.[6] Behind such an act and behind its condemnation lies the belief that the act was more than something that concerned the king of Edom's memory; it was something that injured him. He was conceived of as still knowing some sort of conscious experience.

That this was so is clear from the references to necromancy in

[1] Cf. M. Burrows, *An Outline of Biblical Theology*, 1946, p. 193; N. H. Snaith, *The Distinctive Ideas of the Old Testament*, 1944, p. 89 n.
[2] Gen. 3.22.
[3] H. Wheeler Robinson would seem to imply that it was believed that a man entirely ceased to be at death. He says (*Redemption and Revelation*, 1942, p. 141): 'The *nephesh* is simply an animating principle, which ceases to be anything when it ceases to function.' On this view there was no distinction between man and animal in Hebrew thought, save in the shape of man's body. This seems to me to do less than justice to the Old Testament. In *The Religious Ideas of the Old Testament*, 1913, p. 83, Wheeler Robinson was a little more cautious: 'Man's nature is the product of the two factors—the breath-soul which is his principle of life, and the complex of physical organs which this animates. Separate them, and the man ceases to be, *in any real sense of personality*' (italics mine).
[4] I Sam. 11.1 ff.   [5] I Sam. 31.10 ff.   [6] Amos 2.1.

the Old Testament. For necromancy implies a belief that the
dead still exist. It is true that necromancy is condemned in the
teaching of the Old Testament,[1] though it is beyond doubt that
it was quite widely practised. Moreover, its condemnation was
not based on the thought that the dead no longer exist.[2] In the
story of the witch of Endor[3] we find reflected the condemnation
of necromancy, and at the same time a clear belief in its
possibility. The witch called up the form of Samuel and
described it to Saul, so that he was able to recognize it to be
Samuel. It is therefore clear that the dead were believed still to
have a body which was like that which had been theirs before
death. Something different from the Greek belief in the immortality of the soul is therefore to be found here, since there is
no idea of a disembodied existence here.[4] We cannot suppose
that it was the lifeless body of Samuel which the witch had
called up from the grave, to be momentarily reinvested with his
vanished spirit. It was to ask him about things subsequent to his
death that he was summoned, so that he was clearly credited
with a consciousness which outlived his body. More probable is
it that he was believed still to have in some other world a body
which was a replica of the body he had had amongst men, though
of thinner substance. Such a belief had a wider significance than
is to be found in necromancy.[5] It explains the concern for the
fate of the body after death. In one of the inter-testamental
books, the *Apocalypse of Moses*, we find that Adam is buried in
the paradise on earth, after which God says to the archangel
Michael 'Go away to Paradise in the third heaven, and strew
linen clothes and cover the body of Adam.'[6] From this it would
appear that there was believed to be a counterpart of the body

[1] Cf. Lev. 19.26, Deut. 18.10; I Sam. 15.23, 28.3; II Kings 17.17, 21.6.
[2] On the traces of the cult of the dead and the protest against this in the Old
Testament cf. A. Bertholet, *Die israelitischen Vorstellungen vom Zustand nach dem
Tode*, 1914.
[3] I Sam. 28.3 ff.
[4] It is, however, not dissimilar to the Homeric conception of the dead. Cf. *Odyssey*,
xi.24 ff., where Odysseus is represented as visiting the underworld and finding
the shades of the dead each in the form they had at death, and eager to drink the
blood of his sacrifice in order to be restored to life.
[5] On the wider, non-Israelite, connexions of such a concept cf. J. H. Moulton
Early Zoroastrianism, 1913, pp. 254 ff., and E. Rohde, *Psyche*, E. Tr. by W. B.
Hillis, 1925, pp. 4 ff., 514 f.
[6] *Apoc. Mos.* 40. 1 (translation of L.S.A. Wells, in Charles's *Apocrypha and Pseudepigrapha*, ii, 1913, p. 151). The *Apocalypse of Moses* is the Greek form of *The Life of
Adam and Eve*.

that is buried on earth in the heavenly paradise. While this stands in a text later than any part of the Old Testament, it probably reflects an old Israelite belief. Such a belief would explain the already noted concern for what might happen to the body after death. If the experience of the replica of that body was conceived of as being in some way bound up with the discarded body, it would be clear how the maltreatment of the one might be thought of as an injury to the other.

In all this we are not carried very far, however, and there is no suggestion of any rich or full existence in the beyond. In the passage that opens the Iliad, Homer says that the fury of Achilles sent the souls of many valiant warriors to Hades, while they themselves were made the prey of dogs and birds. Here what survives death is thought of as a mere shade.[1] It is not merely the bodies of men that are given as prey, but they themselves. The body was the real man. Moreover, there is here no suggestion that the surviving self is in any sense embodied in a replica of the mortal body. The thought must not be equated with any side of Old Testament thought, therefore, though it is not widely different. Oesterley observes that 'the belief in immortality, or at least in life of some kind hereafter, seems to be ingrained in human consciousness; it is doubtful whether any race of men, even the most backward, are without some ideas of an after-life, which is taken for granted.'[2] What really matters, however, is the nature of the afterlife that is expected, and many religions have not advanced very far towards a satisfying faith. In the Old Testament we find variety of view and the seeds of the most satisfying faith which can be found anywhere.

The dead are represented as being in Sheol. In the Authorized Version this word is often rendered by 'the grave'. That this is an inadequate translation is clear from the fact that the

[1] Cf. M. P. Nilsson, *A History of Greek Religion*, E. Tr. by F. J. Fielden, 1925, p. 138: 'The souls are shades possessing neither strength nor consciousness, and such figures there is no need to propitiate and worship. A continued existence of this kind is of no value to man . . . The life after death becomes so pale and empty that it is not far from non-existent;' J. A. K. Thomson, in *E.R.E.*, vi, 1913, p. 765 b: 'The essential thing about the Homeric ghost is its futility'; and Rohde, op. cit., p. 24: 'Homer consistently assumes the departure of the soul into an inaccessible land of the dead, where it exists in an unconscious half-life.'

[2] Cf. Oesterley and Robinson, *Hebrew Religion*, 2nd ed., 1937, p. 17. Cf. also H. Birkeland, *Studia Theologica*, iii, 1950–1, p. 63: 'The belief in a continuance of life after death is not absent from the religion of any people,' and E. Dhorme, *R.H.R.*, cxxiii, 1941, p. 113: 'L'un des phénomènes les plus frappants de la vie religieuse des sociétés, est certainement l'universalité de la croyance à la survie.'

dead are sometimes pictured as being together.[1] In Isa. 14 the king of Babylon is greeted by the assembled shades with a taunt song, in which he is scornfully reminded that he who had once shaken the world was now as powerless as the weakest.[2] Clearly neither he nor his fellow shades are represented as lying in their several graves. It would be unwise to press this, however, if this passage stood alone, since it might be no more than the expression in vivid imaginative poetry of the fact that death lays all men low. Since it does not stand alone, it may be more naturally understood to reflect the belief that the dead were conscious and were gathered together in some common place. It is probable, indeed, that behind the conception of Sheol lay the Babylonian Arallû, which Jastrow describes as 'the great cave underneath the earth in which the dead were supposed to dwell.'[3]

There are passages in the Bible which present Sheol in unattractive terms. It is the place from which there can be no return. 'I shall go to him,' said David, 'but he will not return to me.'[4] Again Job cries 'He who goes down to Sheol shall come up no more.'[5] It is sometimes presented as a place of ignorance, where the dead know nothing of what transpires on earth after their death. 'His sons come to honour,' says Job, 'and he knows it not; they are brought low, but he perceives it not of them.'[6] Similarly in Ecclesiastes we read 'The dead know nothing, neither have they any more a reward.'[7] Or again, 'There is no work or thought or knowledge or wisdom in Sheol, whither thou goest.'[8] There are other passages, however, where, in disagreement with this, the dead are credited with knowledge after death, even of the future. Such a passage is the story of the witch of Endor, where such knowledge is attributed to Samuel. In the taunt song in Isa. 14 the deeds of the king of Babylon would appear to be known to his fellow shades, even though they had followed their own death. In some passages the existence in Sheol is described in terms of unrelieved misery.

---

[1] On the relation between the grave and Sheol cf. J. Pedersen, *Israel I–II*, E. Tr., pp. 460 ff.
[2] Isa. 14.10 ff.
[3] Cf. *The Religion of Babylon and Assyria*, 1895, p. 565. This is not unlike the Homeric conception of the Underworld; cf. J. E. Harrison, in *E.R.E.*, xii, 1921, p. 519 a: 'This underworld is no longer a local grave, but a vast remote kingdom of the dead, separated from the living world by the stream of Okeanos.'
[4] II Sam. 12.23.   [5] Job 7.9.   [6] Job 14.21.   [7] Eccl. 9.5.   [8] Eccl. 9.10.

'His flesh upon him is in pain,' says Job, 'And his soul mourns within him'.[1] Here the thought appears to be that in the decay of the body in the grave the shade is involved in suffering, and we have probably another trace of the belief that the body which lies in the grave is associated with a replica in Sheol, which is involved in its fortunes. In one passage Job pictures Sheol as an abode of peace. 'For now should I have lain down in peace,' he says, ' . . . There the wicked cease from turbulence,[2] and there the weary are at rest. There the prisoners are at ease together; They hear not the voice of the taskmaster.'[3] But this is only to indicate by contrast how miserable his present lot is. For elsewhere he describes Sheol as 'A land of darkness and deep darkness; A land of thick darkness, as dense darkness, Deep darkness and disorder; Where the very light is as dense darkness'.[4] Such a description would well fit the Babylonian thought of the Hereafter. 'The nether world,' says Jastrow, 'is joyless . . . The place is synonymous with inactivity and decay; . . . mortals are doomed to ever-lasting sojourn, or rather imprisonment, in the realm presided over by Allatu and her consort Nergal.[5] It should never be forgotten that many of the lower levels of Old Testament thought are shared with neighbouring people, and represent ideas inherited from the remote past rather than divine revelation to Israel.[6]

In many passages Sheol is conceived of as a place of complete isolation from God. This is reflected in some passages in the Psalter. 'The dead praise not Yahweh, Neither any that go down into silence.'[7] 'What profit is there in my blood, when I

---

[1] Job 14.22.
[2] The root meaning of the Hebrew word here is 'agitation'. A. B. Davidson (*Job* (Camb. B.), 1903 ed., p. 17) comments: 'Even the wicked there are no more agitated by the turbulence of their passions.'
[3] Job 3.13, 17.
[4] Job 10.21 f. In these two verses four different words for darkness are employed. G. R. Driver, in *Wisdom in Israel and in the Ancient Near East*, ed. by M. Noth and D. Winton Thomas, 1955, pp. 76 f., deletes the words 'as dense darkness, Deep darkness' as a repetitious gloss, and for 'disorder' proposes the meaning 'without a ray of light', while for the last line he renders 'gloomy as deep darkness'. For these new meanings of Hebrew words he adduces Accadian evidence in the one case and Arabic in the other.
[5] Op. cit., p. 565. Cf. M.-J. Lagrange, *Études sur les religions sémitiques*, 1903, pp. 291 ff. For a collection of Babylonian texts relating to death and the Underworld cf. E. Ebeling, *Tod und Leben nach den Vorstellungen der Babylonier*, i, 1931.
[6] C. F. Burney (*Israel's Hope of Immortality*, 1909, p. 13) stresses that the Sheol conception was 'entirely unconnected with the religion of Yahwe'.
[7] Ps. 115.17.

go down to the pit? Will the dust praise thee, will it declare thy truth?'[1] 'Wilt thou do wonders for the dead? Will the shades[2] arise and praise thee? Will thy lovingkindness be declared in the grave? Or thy faithfulness in Abaddon?[3] Will thy wonders be made known in the darkness? And thy righteousness in the land of forgetfulness?'[4] It is even suggested that the dead are forgotten by God, even though they have been loyal to him in their lives: 'Like the slain who lie in the grave, Whom thou rememberest no more, For they are cut off from thy hand'.[5] There are some passages which present a less negative view of Sheol, such as the psalmist's cry 'If I ascend unto heaven, thou art there: If I make my bed in Sheol, behold thou art there.'[6] We must always be careful not to use a verse for a purpose for which it was not designed, and to examine it in the light of its context. In this passage there is really only a note of warning, and the thought that neither in life nor in death can a man escape the power of God. The emphasis is not on the fellowship with God, which we shall find in some other passages, but only on the universal range of God's power.

That this is not the whole of the thought of the Old Testament on what lies beyond death has been already stated. For within the course of its development we find the beginnings of the thought of a richer and more worth-while survival in

---

[1] Ps. 30.9 f. (Heb. 10 f.). R.S.V. has 'my faithfulness' for 'thy truth', but offers no authority for the change of pronoun. The noun is the word '*emeth*, commonly rendered 'truth', but cognate with the word '*emûnāh*, which is rendered 'faithfulness'. See above, pp. 66 f.

[2] The Hebrew word used here sometimes denotes an extinct race of giants (e.g., Gen. 14.5, 15.20, Deut. 2.11, 20, 3.11); elsewhere, as here, it denotes the shades of the departed (cf. Isa. 14.9, 26.14, 19; Prov. 2.18, 9.18, 21.16; Job 26.5). Jerome gave the word the former of these meanings here and rendered by *gigantes* (cf. H. de Sainte-Marie, op. cit., p. 126). The LXX and Vulgate rendering rests on a change of vowels (and perhaps a poor esteem for the medical profession; cf. Ecclus. 38.15): 'Will the doctors raise up and will they praise thee?' E. Dhorme (*R.H.R.*, cxxiii, 1941, p. 131), associates the two meanings of the word in Hebrew, and notes the occurrence of the word in Ras Shamra texts. Cf. Ch. Virolleaud, *R.E.S.-B.*, 1940, pp. 77 ff., and *Syria*, xxii, 1941, pp. 1 ff.; R. Dussaud, *Les Découvertes de Ras Shamra et l'Ancien Testament*, 2nd ed., 1941, pp. 185 ff.; J. Gray, *P.E.Q.*, lxxxi, 1949, pp. 127 ff.

[3] This is a poetic synonym for Sheol; cf. Prov. 15.11, Job 26.6, 28.22. In later thought it was used for the part of Sheol to which the wicked go; cf. R. H. Charles, in *D.B.*, i, 1898, p. 3 b. For a developed view of Sheol cf. I Enoch 22. Of this Charles observes: 'This is the earliest statement of the Pharisaic or Chasid doctrine of Sheol, but here it is already fullgrown. The departed have conscious existence, and moral, not social distinctions are observed in Sheol (*Apocrypha and Pseudepigrapha*, ii, 1913, p. 202).

[4] Ps. 88.10 ff. (Heb. 11 ff.).   [5] Ps. 88.5 (Heb. 6).   [6] Ps. 139.8; cf. Amos 9.2.

another world, and the growth of a belief in a resurrection to life on earth. Both are sometimes traced to the influence of foreign thought, but it is more probable that neither was of foreign origin. For both emerged on distinctively Israelite lines. The idea of resurrection is sometimes traced to the influence of the Egyptian cult of Osiris[1] or to the influence of Persian Zoroastrianism, while the other idea is traced to Greek thought on the immortality of the soul. I find it hard to accept either of these theories. That there was Persian influence on Jewish thought is not to be gainsaid,[2] and the book of Daniel, in which the doctrine of resurrection is most clearly found, almost certainly reflects that influence, especially in its angelology.[3] It is less likely that Persian influence is to be found in the idea of resurrection, since it is so different in Daniel and in Zoroastrian sources.[4] In Daniel there is no thought of a universal resurrection, such as is found in Zoroastrianism,[5] but only of a selective resurrection, as will be seen.

Still less likely, in my view, is the suggestion that the idea of resurrection came into Israel from the Egyptian cult of Osiris.[6] Had it done so, it might have been expected to make its appearance very much earlier than it did. The cult of Osiris was related to the Babylonian Tammuz cult and to the Canaanite

---

[1] On this cf. H. Gressmann, *Tod und Auferstehung des Osiris* (A.O., xxiii, No. 3), 1923.

[2] On Persian influence cf. above, p. 80, n. 7. W. F. Albright (*From the Stone Age to Christianity*, 2nd ed., pp. 275 f.) says the value of Iranian religious influences for our understanding of Judaism and early Christianity has been greatly exaggerated, and again (p. 280) observes that Iranian conceptions exerted no effect on Judaism except where the ground was fully prepared for them.

[3] Cf. what I have written in *The Relevance of Apocalyptic*, 2nd ed., p. 40.

[4] Cf. F. Nötscher, *Altorientalischer und alttestamentlicher Auferstehungsglauben*, 1926, pp. 185 ff., esp. p. 195: 'Überzeugende positive Beweise für die Abhängigkeit des atl. Auferstehungsglaubens vom persischen lassen sich nicht beibringen.' Cf. also A. Bertholet, *A.J.Th.*, xx, 1916, pp. 25 ff., where it is recognized that while there was later Persian influence on the development of the Jewish doctrine, the Jewish belief cannot be traced to a Zoroastrian source. Cf. also Bertholet, *Daniel und die griechische Gefahr* (Religionsgeschichtliche Volksbücher, II. R., 17), 1907, pp. 53 f. For a statement of the later Jewish views on the subject cf. A. Marmorstein, *A.J.Th.*, xix, 1915, pp. 577 ff., and J.-B. Frey, *Biblica*, xiii, 1932, pp. 129 ff.

[5] On Zoroastrian ideas cf. J. D. C. Pavry, *The Zoroastrian Doctrine of a Future Life*, 1929; also J. H. Moulton, *Early Zoroastrianism*, 1913, pp. 154 ff., H. S. Nyberg, *Die Religionen des Alten Iran*, 1938, pp. 308 ff., and A. T. Nikolainen, *Die Auferstehungsglauben in der Bibel und ihrer Umwelt*, i, 1944, pp. 22 ff.

[6] Cf. F. Nötscher, op. cit., pp. 177 ff., esp. p. 185: 'Eine ägyptisch Beeinflussung des israelitischen Auferstehungsglaubens ist höchst unwahrscheinlich'. Cf. also P. Heinisch, *Theology of the Old Testament*, E. Tr. by W. Heidt, 1950, p. 267.

fertility cult.[1] Lucian connects Osiris with Adonis,[2] who is the Syrian counterpart of Tammuz.[3] It is certain that there was much influence of Canaanite ritual on Israelite ritual, despite the vigorous condemnation of so much in the Canaanite religion in the pages of the Old Testament. There were festivals and ceremonies which could be integrated into the faith of Israel and related to the essential message of her religion. But many of the practices could not be adopted, since, in the view of the prophets and of Israel's religious leaders, they were at fundamental variance with the whole spirit of her religion. The associations of the resurrection rites of the Adonis-Tammuz-Osiris cult would almost certainly bring them into the latter category.

The Osiris cult was originally a royal rite whereby the Pharaoh was assured of immortality after death, through his identification with Osiris. While the rites were later democratized and the ranks of the privileged opened to others,[4] it was as royal rites that they entered the world of Palestine and Syria. Much attention has been paid in recent years to the royal rites in the ancient Near East, and especially to the rites associated with the New Year Festival.[5] It is disputed how far they were incorporated in Israelite royal rites, and it would be out of place to discuss that question here. It is clear from the Old Testament itself that some Israelite kings followed Canaanite

---

[1] On the relations between the Osiris cult and the cults of Adonis and Tammuz cf. H. Frankfort, *Kingship and the Gods*, 1945, pp. 286 ff. Frankfort emphasizes the local variations, which are but to be expected (cf. also S. G. F. Brandon, *H.J.*, liii, 1955, pp. 330 ff.). Yet there were also important links between them. On the fertility character of the Osiris cult cf. Frankfort, op. cit., pp. 185 ff. For a translation of the text *The Descent of Ishtar*, the consort of Tammuz, by E. A. Speiser, cf. *A.N.E.T.*, 1950, pp. 106 ff. Cf. also T. H. Gaster, *Thespis*, 1950, pp. 50 f. W. F. Albright (*Archaeology and the Religion of Israel*, 3rd ed., 1953, p. 167) says the cult of Tammuz 'can scarcely have become popular in southern Palestine before the seventh century B.C.', but adds: 'There were many Canaanite gods of fertility which were related to Tammuz in character.'

[2] *De Dea Syra*, 7 (cf. C. Clemen, *Lukians Schrift über die Syrische Göttin* (A.O., xxxvii, Nos. 3–4), 1938, pp. 8 f.).

[3] Cf. W. W. von Baudissin, *Adonis und Esmun*, 1911, pp. 94 ff.

[4] Cf. J. A. Wilson, *The Burden of Egypt*, 1951, pp. 116 f. Cf. also Frankfort, op. cit., p. 197.

[5] Cf. S. Mowinckel, *Psalmenstudien*, ii, 1922, and *Zum israelitischen Neujahr und zur Deutung der Thronbesteigungspsalmen*, 1952; H. Schmidt, *Die Thronfahrt Jahves am Fest des Jahreswende im alten Israel*, 1927; *Myth and Ritual*, ed. by S. H. Hooke, 1933, and *The Labyrinth*, ed. by S. H. Hooke, 1935; I. Engnell, *Studies in Divine Kingship in the Ancient Near East*, 1943; G. Widengren, *Religion och Bibel*, ii, 1943, pp. 49 ff.. and *Sakrales Königtum im Alten Testament und im Judentum*, 1955; A. Bentzen, *Det sakrale Kongedømme*, 1945; N. H. Snaith, *The Jewish New Year Festival*, 1947.

practice too closely, and for this they are condemned. This means that the practices were familiar enough to the Israelites, and the fact that we have allusions to them in the Bible reinforces this. We find a reference to Adonis gardens in Isa. 17.10,[1] and to weeping for Tammuz in the book of Ezekiel,[2] while in Zech. 12.11 the mention of mourning for Hadad-rimmon is a reference to the same cult.[3] No exception can therefore be taken to the view that through familiarity with this cult Israel could have been familiar with the idea of resurrection.[4]

That this is not the source of the faith in a resurrection is clear from the fact that it does not appear in pre-exilic days, as it might have been expected to, and from the further fact that it is essentially different from the alleged source when it does appear.[5] In the rites the central thing was not to set before men the idea of human resurrection, but to maintain fertility in family, field and flock throughout the community.[6] The king ritually died and rose again in ceremonies in which he represented the god, and the ceremonies were designed to promote the renewal of Nature. The sacred marriage belonged to the rites,[7] and the ideas associated with them were reflected in the sacred prostitution which went on in the shrines, to which there is frequent adverse reference in the Bible. We are thus in the area of Canaanite religion which was utterly hateful to the prophets, and it is most improbable that they drew from this the thought of resurrection.

In the book of Hosea we read: 'Come and let us return unto Yahweh: for he has torn, and he will heal us; he has smitten, and he will bind us up. After two days he will revive us: on the

---

[1] So this passage is understood by most commentators. Cf. G. W. Wade, *Isaiah* (West. C.), 1911, p. 119; G. B. Gray, *Isaiah* (I.C.C.), i, 1912, pp. 302 f.; L. Dennefeld, *Les grands Prophètes* (Pirot-Clamer, La Sainte Bible), 1947, p. 77. On the other hand E. J. Kissane, *The Book of Isaiah*, i, 1941, p. 200, rejects this view.
[2] Ezek. 8.13 f.
[3] On this cf. J. W. Jack, *The Ras Shamra Tablets*, 1935, p. 19. On the subject of ritual weeping cf. F. F. Hvidberg, *Graad og Latter i det Gamle Testamente*, 1938.
[4] Cf. H. G. May, *A.J.S.L.*, xlviii, 1931–2, pp. 73 ff., where very many references to the fertility cult are found in Hosea.
[5] Cf. A. T. Nikolainen, op. cit., i, pp. 101 ff., and O. R. Sellers, *B.A.*, vii, 1945, pp. 6 ff.
[6] Cf. H. Birkeland, *Studia Theologica*, iii, 1950–1, p. 67: 'The belief in a resurrection of Nature and God has very little to do with the resurrection of man'.
[7] Cf. T. H. Gaster, *Thespis*, 1950, p. 51: 'When the King performed the ritual act of connubium (the so-called "sacred marriage"), a purely "economic" measure designed to galvanize the vitality of the topocosm, this was translated in the accompanying myth into the nuptials of a god and goddess.'

third day he will raise us up, and we shall live before him.'[1]
Here it is likely, as the commentators point out, that there is an
allusion to the fertility cult.[2] This is not surprising. A modern
writer may make allusion to ideas and practices in the modern
world which he does not share. Similarly, there are many
references to the fertility cult by writers who borrow expressions from it for their use,[3] while investing those expressions
with a meaning which they bring to them. In this particular
passage the thought is of the revival of the nation, and not of
Hadad, or of Nature, or of human survival after death.[4] The
same thought of the revival of the nation reappears in Ezekiel's
vision of the valley of dry bones.[5] When the breath of God came
upon the bones, which first came together and became clothed
with flesh, they were restored to life; but the passage itself is
careful to point out that the vision was a parable of the life of
the nation. It is indeed possible that the form of the vision
helped to give currency to the idea of individual resurrection,
but what the prophet had in mind was not the restoration to
life on earth of dead Israelites, but the recovery of the nation
from the death of the exile and its resurrection to national life
in its own land.

One of the most difficult and obscure passages in the Old
Testament is the word from the book of Job, which reads in the
Revised Version: 'But I know that my redeemer liveth, And
that he shall stand up at the last upon the earth: And after my
skin hath been thus destroyed, Yet from my flesh shall I see

---

[1] Hos. 6. 1 f.
[2] Cf. E Osty, *Amos, Osée* (Jerusalem Bible), 1952, p. 94: 'L'expression est peut-
être empruntée au culte d'Hadad, dieu qui ressuscitait trois jours après sa mort'.
Similarly, A. Weiser, *Die zwölf Kleinen Propheten* (A.T.D.), i, 1949, p. 44. Cf. also
T. H. Robinson, in *Myth and Ritual* (ed. by S. H. Hooke), 1933, p. 187. A.
Bertholet, *A.J.Th.*, xx, 1916, p. 5, notes that the death of Osiris, according to
Plutarch, fell on the seventeenth of Athyr, and his resurrection on the nineteenth. Cf. also W. W. von Baudissin, *Adonis und Esmun*, 1911, pp. 403 ff., F.
Nötscher, op. cit., pp. 138 ff., and E. Sellin, *Das Zwölfprophetenbuch* (K.A.T.),
2nd ed., 1929, pp. 71 ff. S. N. Kramer (*B.A.S.O.R.*, No. 77, October 1940,
pp. 18 ff.) gives an account of Ishtar's descent to the Nether World, where she
spent three days before her resurrection (for a translation of the text by Kramer,
cf. *A.N.E.T.*, 1950, pp. 52 ff.), but F. Nötscher (*Biblica*, xxxv, 1954, pp. 313 ff.)
denies that there is any connexion between what this text deals with and
Hos. 6.2. Cf. also B. M. Metzger, *H.T.R.*, xlviii, 1955, p. 18 n.
[3] Cf. H. G. May, *A.J.S.L.*, xlviii, 1931–2, pp. 73 ff., where many references to the
fertility cult are found in Hosea.
[4] Cf. H. Birkeland, loc. cit., p. 74: 'The whole context shows that a *real resurrection*
is out of the question.'
[5] Ezek. 37.1 ff.

God: Whom I shall see for myself, And mine eyes shall behold, and not another.'[1] On this passage N. H. Snaith says that it 'can be made to refer to life after death only by a most liberal latitude in translation, a strong attachment to the Latin version, and reminiscences of Handel's Messiah. The Hebrew text is difficult, but it is unlikely that the vindicator is God, and Job almost certainly means that he will be vindicated before he is dead.'[2] While I agree that the crucial words are ambiguous, I think it possible that the author of Job is here putting into the mouth of his hero the bold suggestion that he will be raised to witness his vindication after death. I say I think this is possible, because I recognize that it is not certain. In the interpretation of so obscure a passage none can fairly claim that the words *must* have the meaning he wishes to put on them. Some editors emend the text to remove any possible reference to resurrection;[3] others emend clearer references to resurrection into the text.[4] Neither course is to be commended, and whatever view is taken of the passage, it should be taken with hesitation and reserve. Elsewhere in the book the author reflects the ordinary views of his time, and some of his observations have already been cited. I think it is probable that here he ventured beyond those views, but in a daring suggestion rather than in a formulated faith. The ambiguity of his words should be recognized; but this means they should neither be brushed aside nor overpressed. There is no hint here of more than a momentary consciousness of his vindication by the God in whom he trusted, in spite of all his complaint against him.[5] He seems to me to be reaching out after something more satisfying than the common view, but not yet to have grasped it securely.[6]

A clearer faith in the resurrection is commonly found in the

[1] Job 19.25 ff.
[2] Cf. *The Distinctive Ideas of the Old Testament*, p. 90 n. For the history of the interpretation of this passage cf. J. Speer, *Z.A.W.*, xxv, 1905, pp. 47 ff.
[3] So C. J. Ball, *The Book of Job*, 1922, pp. 276 ff.
[4] Cf. P. (E.) Dhorme, *Job* (E. Bib.), 1926, pp. 256 ff., where an explicit reference to Job's resurrection is emended into the text. C. Larcher (*Job* (Jerusalem Bible), 1950, p. 96), comments that this pushes the smoothing of the text too far.
[5] Cf. A. S. Peake, *Job* (Cent.B.), p. 192: 'The hope of immortality is not expressed here, but only of a momentary vision of God, assuring him of vindication.'
[6] Cf. the note on these verses in A. B. Davidson, *Job* (Camb. B.), 1903 ed., pp. 291 ff. Davidson finds here the principle, which, 'grasped with convulsive earnestness in the prospect of death, became the Hebrew doctrine of Immortality' (p. 293). Sutcliffe (op. cit., pp. 131 ff.), on the other hand, finds no hint of an afterlife in this passage. Cf. J. Lindblom, *Studia Theologica*, ii, 1940, pp. 65 ff.

late section of the book of Isaiah,[1] containing chapters 24–27, frequently referred to as the Isaiah Apocalypse,[2] where we find the verse: 'Thy dead shall live; their[3] corpses shall arise. Awake and sing, ye who dwell in the dust; for thy dew is as the dew of light,[4] and the earth shall cast forth the shades.'[5] Taken by themselves these words seem clearly to speak of the resurrection of the righteous dead to life on earth, and many distinguished scholars so interpret them.[6] On the other hand there are others who find nothing that goes beyond the thought of national resurrection, and who link the message of the passage with that of Ezekiel's vision of the valley of dry bones.[7] In both the apparent individuality belongs to the form of the vision rather than to that which is indicated. Against this view it may be said that in the previous chapter we read 'He hath swallowed up death for ever'.[8] Taken out of their context these words suggest the conditions of the Golden Age, which we shall consider in the next lecture. In their context, however, they may

[1] R. H. Pfeiffer (*Introduction to the Old Testament*, 1941, pp. 441 f.) assigns this section to the third century B.C., and I have accepted the view that it is not earlier than the time of Alexander (*The Growth of the Old Testament*, 1950, p. 93). Some have placed it later than this, in the second century B.C., but in view of the finding of the Dead Sea scroll of Isaiah at Qumran (called DSIa or 1QIs^a), it is improbable that this date will survive. For that MS contains these chapters and is probably of the second century B.C., and almost certainly not later than the first century B.C. J. Lindblom (*Die Jesaja-Apokalypse*, 1935, p. 84) would assign Isa. 24–27 to *circa* 485 B.C.

[2] W. Rudolph (*Jesaja 24–27*, B.W.A.N.T., iv, 10), 1933, p. 59), while recognizing apocalyptic motifs in these chapters, observes that they can only be called an apocalypse with reserve. S. B. Frost (*Old Testament Apocalyptic*, 1952, pp. 143 ff.) calls these chapters Pseudo-Isaiah, and maintains that whereas Deutero-Isaiah is an anonymous section which was added to the book of Isaiah, these chapters were written by one who deliberately posed as Isaiah. Of this there is no real evidence.

[3] The Hebrew reads 'my corpses', but most editors follow the Syriac and the Targum in reading 'their corpses'.

[4] R.V. has 'the dew of herbs'. The word '*ôrôth* has the meaning 'herbs' in II Kings 4.39, but it is more naturally taken to mean 'light', and so most editors understand it. The 'dew of light' is then the life-giving dew from the realm of light in which God dwells.

[5] Isa. 26.19. G. B. Gray (*Isaiah* (I.C.C.), i, p. 447) renders the last clause: 'The earth shall give birth to the shades.'

[6] Cf. G. B. Gray, ibid., p. 446; G. H. Box, *The Book of Isaiah*, 1916, p. 118; W. Rudolph, op. cit., p. 48; J. Lindblom, op. cit., p. 48; L. Dennefeld, *Les grands Prophètes*, p. 103; J. Steinmann, *Le Prophète Isaïe* (Lectio Divina, 5), 1950, p. 356; E. S. Mulder, *Die Teologie van die Jesaja-Apokalipse*, 1954, p. 106. I. G. Matthews (*The Religious Pilgrimage of Israel*, 1947, p. 229) says this verse 'glories in the confidence of the physical resurrection and the individual immortality of Israelites.'

[7] Cf. E. F. Sutcliffe, op. cit., pp. 228 ff.; also G. W. Wade, op. cit., pp. 170 f.; A. van der Flier, *Jesaja* (T.U.) i, 1923, pp. 137 f.; E. J. Kissane, *The Book of Isaiah*, i, 1941, p. 298.

[8] Isa. 25.8.

with more probability be understood to be a promise that the nation will not again find itself in its present low estate.[1] Ezekiel could think of the exile as the death of the nation, and this author could similarly treat the national misfortunes. Between these two views of this passage, each held by scholars of eminence, it is impossible to decide with certainty. My own view is that there is here no thought of individual resurrection, though the form of the passage may have played some part in preparing men for such an idea. It should be noted that even if there is the thought of individual resurrection, it is not the thought of the Day of Judgement, but only of the resurrection of the righteous.

We come then to the only passage in the Old Testament where we have a clear and undisputed reference to the resurrection of the dead. This is found in the book of Daniel in the words 'Many of those who sleep in the dust of the earth shall awake, some to everlasting life, and some to shame and everlasting contempt.'[2] I have already said that I do not trace this passage to Persian influence.[3] I think the author was driven by the dynamic of his own faith to this as the corollary of that faith.[4] He was writing in the period of the Maccabaean revolt, and he knew of many who had given their lives as the price of their loyalty to their faith. He had encouraged men to resistance by the stories in the first part of the book, stories of men whose loyalty had brought deliverance. The three youths were delivered from the fire and Daniel from the mouth of the lions. The author was profoundly convinced that God could deliver if he would; and yet many of his contemporaries were not delivered, but suffered death. The author was also convinced that the day of deliverance for the saints as a whole was nigh at hand. The kingdom of righteousness was about to be established, and the dominion exercised through the saints of the Most High. If the stories of deliverance with which he had inspired and encouraged men were not matched in their experience, it must be because God designed some more wonderful vindication, and they who had given their lives in their loyalty would not be excluded from

---

[1] E. F. Sutcliffe (op. cit., pp. 125 ff.) differently understands this verse, but denies that its thought is of individual resurrection.
[2] Dan. 12.2.   [3] Cf. H. Birkeland, loc. cit., pp. 75 f.
[4] Cf. *The Rediscovery of the Old Testament*, pp. 160 f. (American edition, pp. 227 f.)

the glories they deserved to share. If God had not delivered them from death he would restore them from the grave to share the blessings of the kingdom.[1] On the other hand there were some of the enemies of the saints who had found in death too easy a fate, and who would be raised to receive the punishment they so richly deserved. These were probably the Jewish traitors who had helped the enemy against the saints. It is to be observed that the resurrection here is only of some of those who sleep in the dust of the earth. It is only the notably good and the notably bad who are to be raised to reap the reward of their deeds. Moreover, the background of the thought is the normal view of Sheol, where good and bad are congregated together in a common state. The whole conception is so different from that of Zoroastrianism that I find it more satisfactory to find its origin in the writer's faith than in this foreign source.

This means that the verse is not to be interpreted as reflecting any general view held in the author's day. Still less is it to be understood as though it were identical with the Christian view of an afterlife in another world. It has been said that in the New Testament we find variety of thought, and amongst that variety the thought of eternal bliss beyond this world in heaven is probably that which has secured deepest hold on Christian people. It is in heaven and hell that they have located the rewards and punishments of men. Here, on the contrary, in this passage from Daniel, what is in mind is physical life in this world, side by side with those who had not passed through death, as we have found in certain passages also in the New Testament. That this Daniel passage played a considerable part in the development of thought is not to be gainsaid. It did not represent the common view of the author's day, but it influenced later thought. In the apocalyptic books that were composed between the Maccabaean age and New Testament times the thought of resurrection was developed in various ways, and it came to be an article of Pharisaic belief. The Sadducees, on the other hand, rejected it as a recent fancy, without serious biblical authority.[2] That it has no secure authority in the Old Testament, apart from this one passage, is clear from what has

[1] Cf. II Mac. 7.9, 14, 23, 36.
[2] Cf. Acts 23.8. Cf. also Josephus, *Antiquities*, XVIII, i. 4 (xviii.16), *Wars*, II, viii.14 (ii.164 f.). The statements of Josephus would seem to imply that the Sadducees denied any continued existence even in Sheol.

been said, and there are few Christians who accept the view of
this passage as authoritative. Their view of the resurrection is far
more closely akin to the Zoroastrian view than is the thought here.

Before we leave the question of resurrection, however, we
must look at some other Old Testament passages which are
sometimes thought to reflect such a thought. In the Song of
Hannah we find the words: 'The Lord kills, and brings to life:
He brings down to the grave, and brings up.'[1] Does this mean
that God restores the dead to life? The Oxford Hebrew Lexicon
finds this meaning,[2] while A. R. S. Kennedy says it is difficult
to avoid the conclusion that the second line declares the poet's
belief in a resurrection from the dead.[3] Of this I am very
doubtful. The following verse says that God 'makes poor, and
makes rich; He brings low, he also raises up.'[4] It is improbable
that this means that he makes a man poor and then makes him
rich, but rather that he makes one man poor and another rich,
one man humble and another exalted. It is therefore possible
that in the verse under discussion the meaning is that God
brings one man to death and another to birth, rather than that
he first kills a man and then brings him back to life. The issues
of life and death are in his hand. In the second half of the verse
the meaning would then be that he brings one man down to
Sheol and another up into life. Even if we wish to insist that each
half of the verse refers to a single person, however, there is no
need to find here any idea of resurrection from the dead.
Kennedy, who finds such an idea, then ascribes the song to a
post-exilic date to bring it into the age in which the Isaiah
Apocalypse and the book of Daniel were composed.[5] I am not
persuaded that it is anything like so late. In the Song of Moses,
which is held by some to be pre-exilic[6] and by others exilic,[7]

---

[1] I Sam. 2.6.   [2] Cf. *B.D.B.*, p. 311 b.
[3] Cf. *Samuel* (Cent. B.), p. 44.   [4] I Sam. 2.7.   [5]Loc. cit.
[6] G. A. Smith (*Deuteronomy* (Camb. B.), 1918, p. 343) holds it to be a pre-exilic poem
which received additions in the exilic age. Cf. S. R. Driver, *Deuteronomy* (I.C.C.),
2nd ed., 1896, p. 347 (*circa* 630 B.C.), and C. Steuernagel, *Das Deuteronomium*
(H.K.), 1898, pp. 114 (shortly before the exile). Cf. H. Gunkel, in *R.G.G.*, iv,
1913, cols. 534 f.
[7] H. Wheeler Robinson (*Deuteronomy and Joshua* (Cent. B.), p. 219) ascribes it to
the latter part of the Exile. So also T. André, in *La Bible du Centenaire*, i, 1941, p.
281 b, and A. Lods, *Histoire de la littérature hébraïque et juive*, 1950, p. 481. Cf. also
K. Budde, *Das Lied Moses*, 1920, G. F. Moore (*E.B.*, i, 1899, col. 1089) thinks it is
from the exilic or post-exilic age. R. H. Pfeiffer (*Introduction to the Old Testament*,
1941, p. 280) ascribes it to the first half of the fifth century B.C., in agreement with
E. Sellin (*Z.A.W.*, xliii (N.F. ii), 1925, p. 171).

we read 'I kill and I bring to life.'[1] Here we have verbal similarity with the passage in the Song of Hannah, but it is very
improbable that the thought is of resurrection.

In discussing the passage in the Song of Hannah, A. F.
Kirkpatrick says 'Death and Sheol are figuratively used for the
depths of adversity and peril; life for deliverance and prosperity.'[2] Similarly A. R. Johnson says: 'Just as death in the
strict sense of the term is for the Israelite the weakest form of
life, so any weakness in life is a form of death.'[3] This gives the
clue to the understanding of the passage from the Song of
Moses, where the passage reads 'I kill, and I bring to life; I
have wounded, and I heal'. What is in mind is probably delivery from mortal peril. Similarly, when the psalmist says
'Thou hast rescued my soul from Sheol',[4] he does not mean that
he has been raised from the dead, but saved from death. In
accordance with this, many commentators understand the
passage in the Song of Hannah to mean that it is God who
brings a man into dire straits and who rescues him from his
danger and misfortune. There is therefore little reason to read a
doctrine of resurrection into this verse, or, indeed, to find it
anywhere in the Old Testament, save in the form of Job's
assurance of a momentary resurrection to witness his vindication, and the verse in the book of Daniel, which has reference
to the contemporary situation of the author.

The other line of development in Old Testament thought is
much richer and profounder. It points to the hope of bliss in
the presence of God in another world. It should be observed at
the outset that it is not primarily a belief in the immortality of
the soul, as in Greek thought. Plato puts into the mouth of
Socrates in the *Phaedo* the words 'After I drink the poison I shall
no longer be with you, but shall go away to the joys of the
blessed you know of.'[5] Here the thought seems to be that the
soul is the enduring element of man's being, and that he can
cast aside the body and mount on the wings of the spirit. In

---

[1] Deut. 32.39.   [2] Cf. *I Samuel* (Camb. B.), 1903 ed., p. 54.
[3] *The Vitality of the Individual in the Thought of Ancient Israel*, 1949, p. 94. Cf. also
p. 107: 'In short, the normal Israelite view . . . is that to be in sickness of body
or weakness of circumstance is to experience the disintegrating power of death.'
[4] Ps. 86.13.
[5] E. Tr. by H. N. Fowler, in *Plato* (Loeb edition), i, 1917, p. 395. On the reliability
of the ascription of such views to Socrates cf. E. Ehnmark, *Eranos*, xliv (*Eranos
Rudbergianus*), 1946, pp. 105 ff.

biblical thought the idea of immortal bliss is based on the conception of God. It is interesting to note that it is in some passages in the psalms that we find the beginnings of this thought. Their interpretation is not agreed, and we must beware of reading into them ideas which we bring to them.

In Ps. 49 the psalmist says 'They are appointed as a flock for Sheol; Death shall be their shepherd . . . But God will ransom my soul from the power of Sheol: For he will receive me.'[1] We cannot suppose that here Sheol stands for illness or misfortune. In relation to the wicked it is clear that Sheol means the abode of the shades beyond the grave; in relation to the righteous Sheol must therefore have the same meaning, and the sense be that instead of his going to Sheol, God will receive him. The general thought of the psalm is of the hollowness of the prosperity of the wicked. Nothing that he has will be his beyond the grave, and it is foolish to envy him the fleeting fortune that is his. If we were to read into the words already quoted the thought that the righteous will be delivered from his misfortune in this life, we should make the psalmist offer the righteous a very empty hope. If the wicked has but to relinquish his good fortune at death, and the righteous is merely promised that he will have some good fortune before he dies, he is still worse off than the wicked. He too must, on this view, relinquish his good fortune at death, and he is worse off than the wicked, who is spared ill fortune. What the psalmist is saying is that the inequalities of this life will be rectified in the next.[2] The wicked may have good fortune here, but the miseries of Sheol are all that he can look forward to; whereas the righteous may have suffering here, but hereafter he will have bliss, for God will take him to himself. C. F. Burney says 'The more I examine this psalm the more does the conviction force itself upon me that the writer has in view something more than the mere temporary recompense of the righteous during this earthly life.'[3] With this view I find myself in the fullest agreement.

[1] Ps. 49.14 f.

[2] E. F. Sutcliffe (op. cit., p. 102) thinks the author of this psalm half discerned the truth of a richer afterlife.

[3] *Israel's Hope of Immortality*, p. 41. Cf. C. A. Briggs, *Psalms* (I.C.C.), i, p. 411, where it is said that this verse 'implies the assumption of the righteous dead by God to Himself', though the verse is held to be a late gloss. Cf. also R. H. Charles, *A Critical History of the Doctrine of a Future Life*, 2nd ed., 1913, pp. 74 ff.; E. Podechard, *Le Psautier: Traduction . . . et explication . . .*, i, 1949, pp. 220 f.

Again in Ps. 73 we find a familiar passage, which is related to this in thought, though less clear in expression.[1] The general thought of the psalm is clear. The psalmist begins by recording his envy of the lot of the wicked as contrasted with his own. He is tempted to conclude that virtue is unrewarded, but checks himself with the realization that he would be a public menace if he uttered such a word. He then turns to the thought that the prosperity of the wicked is fleeting, and that judgement will fall on him with swift destruction and all his good fortune become as insubstantial as a dream, when it is past. Yet this does not satisfy him. He therefore ponders his problem further, and asks himself what he has that the wicked has not. He has his misfortune. True, but he also has God. Therefore his lot is superior to that of the wicked, not alone in prospect, but even when he is in his distress and the wicked is in his prosperity. He enjoys that fellowship with God, which we have seen to be the basis of man's truest well-being. 'Nevertheless I am continually with thee,' he cries; 'Thou dost hold my right hand. Thou dost guide me with thy counsel, and afterward wilt receive me to honour.'[2] If the translation of the last line were secure it would be simpler to discuss this passage. In fact, both translation and interpretation are uncertain.[3] Father Sutcliffe believes that the psalmist was thinking only of this life. He says 'The conclusion . . . is that the Psalmist is manifesting his confidence that God would, in this life vindicate his justice on the wicked and by some bestowal of honour on his servant show that virtue is what he desires and accepts.'[4] It seems to me that if this is his thought

---

[1] H. Ringgren (*V.T.*, iii, 1953, pp. 265 ff.) holds that the style and form of this psalm derive from the myth of the New Year Festival, though without claiming that this is a New Year psalm.

[2] Ps. 73.23 f.

[3] H. Gunkel (*Die Psalmen* (H.K.), 1926, p. 319) emended the last line vigorously, to yield the sense: 'And in the way thou strengthenest my liver.' H. Graetz, followed by many scholars, emended (*Kritischer Kommentar zu den Psalmen*, ii, 1883, p. 440) to yield: 'And thou takest me by the hand after thee.' G. Beer (*Z.A.W.*, xxi, 1901, pp. 77 f.) emended to secure the meaning: 'And thou instructest me in the way of glory.' H. Herkenne (*Das Buch der Psalmen* (H.S.A.T.), 1936, p. 250) excises the words rendered 'thou wilt receive me', and then emends verse 24 to yield the sense: 'With thy counsel thou leadest me in the way, Thou glory and strength of my heart.' These emendations are all without authority, and there is no reason to prefer any of them to the Massoretic text.

[4] Op. cit., p. 107. P. Boylan, on the other hand, finds a clear intimation of an afterlife in the presence of God (cf. *The Psalms*, ii, 1931, p. 8). Cf. also C. Lattey, *The Psalter in the Westminster Version*, 1945, p. 137, where it is said that there is here a distinct, if rather vague, reference to the next life.

he has an odd way of expressing it. He speaks of God receiving him, rather than of his bestowing some material boon upon him. He first declares that he enjoys God's fellowship here and now, and if God is to receive him, it must be to future fellowship. If that is still in this life, nothing is added to the thought; but if it is beyond the grave then the words contribute something to the thought. It therefore seems to me likely that the meaning is that both before death and after death he has a secure treasure in the fellowship of God. The God who delights to enrich him with the experience of himself now will grant him fuller fellowship hereafter.[1]

It is perhaps not without significance that in both of these psalms God is said to 'receive' the righteous. Many writers[2] have noted that the same word is used of Enoch, of whom we read that he walked with God and was not, 'for God took him'.[3] The word is a common one in Hebrew, and could not by itself require the thought of the afterlife. It is used in Ps. 18.16 (Heb. 17) where there is certainly no such thought. Nevertheless, there is so close a link of thought between these two passages in the psalms and the story of Enoch that the choice of word may be significant. Enoch was one who knew the fellowship with God in this life to such a degree that he was spared the experience of death, but was lifted into enduring fellowship. The story of Enoch is commonly assigned to a late strand of the Pentateuch; but it was certainly not invented by

[1] N. H. Snaith (*The Distinctive Ideas of the Old Testament*, p. 89) says 'the argument is valid only in the English version. The Hebrew reads "the heavens". He is speaking geographically. Further, *Kabod* (glory) means honour and prosperity in the things of this life; it means heavenly bliss only with the English Evangelicals of a former generation. The "after" means after these temporary distresses.' In contrast to this Oesterley and Robinson (*Hebrew Religion*, 2nd ed., 1937, p. 364) say: 'As to the belief concerning the future life, the passage witnesses to the conviction that it is a glorious life, for in the Hereafter God is man's portion for ever'. It is interesting, too, to note that the Jesuit, Father C. Lattey, adopted the rendering and the interpretation which Snaith would confine to the English Evangelicals of a former generation (cf. preceding note). C. A. Briggs (op. cit., ii, 1909, p. 147) comments that 'the psalmist finds the solution of the inconsistencies of this life in the final reward of the righteous after death'.

[2] Cf. F. Delitzsch, *Biblical Commentary on the Psalms*, E. Tr. by D. Eaton, ii, 1888, pp. 137, 368; T. K. Cheyne, *The Origin of the Psalter*, 1891, p. 149; R. Kittel, *Die Psalmen* (K.A.T.), 1929, pp. 182, 348; G. R. Berry, *The Book of Psalms*, 1934, p. 144 b; F. Zorell, *Psalterium ex hebraeo latinum*, 2nd ed., 1939, p. 121; E. Podechard, op. cit., i, 1949, p. 221; Pannier-Renard, *Les Psaumes* (Pirot-Clamer, La Sainte Bible), 1950, p. 291 a; O. Schilling, *Der Jenseitsgedanke im Alten Testament*, 1951, pp. 26 f.

[3] Gen. 5.24.

the late writer. It is an ancient story, testifying to the thought of continuing fellowship with God after death, and without any suggestion of resurrection to life on earth. In Ps. 73 we have the same thought of satisfying fellowship with God in this life, followed by God's receiving the psalmist. In Ps. 49 the receiving saves the psalmist from going to Sheol, as the receiving of Enoch saved the patriarch. Sheol was not the last word of the Old Testament on what followed death. For God is the Lord of all things, and even Sheol is under his hand. From its insatiable maw he is able to save for himself those whom he will.

In the light of these two passages we may look at a third from the Psalter. In Ps. 16 the writer says 'Thou wilt not abandon my soul to Sheol; Neither wilt thou let thy devotee see the Pit.'[1] Here the general thought of this psalm is not very different from that of the two at which we have looked. A modern Jewish commentator believes that it is dependent on Ps. 73.[2] The psalmist declares that he has no good beyond God, and that God is his portion and his strength. So far he is clearly thinking of this life, as is the author of Ps. 73 when he says 'Nevertheless I am continually with thee.' There is no suggestion here, however, that he is in any danger or distress. Hence when he says 'Thou wilt not abandon my soul to Sheol',[3] there is no reason to suppose that he is thinking of deliverance from misfortunes, or recovery from sickness. He is cherishing the hope that in this life and beyond he may find in God his portion still, and so may be delivered from Sheol. He continues 'Thou wilt show me the path of life; In thy presence there is fullness of joy; In thy right hand there are pleasures for evermore.'[4]

---

[1] Ps. 16.10. The final word is rendered 'corruption' in R.V., and this is defended by E. F. Sutcliffe (op. cit., pp. 76 ff.), and J. Calès (*Le Livre des Psaumes*, i, 1936, p. 199. *B.D.B.* allows only the meaning 'the pit' for it (p. 1001 b). It may be agreed with Sutcliffe that the word could be derived from the root *shāhath*, which is used of corrupt, or immoral, behaviour, and more widely of spoiling or destroying things. It is not used of the corruption of the body in decomposition, and though it is once used in poetry parallel to the worm of corruption (Job 17.14), the meaning 'the pit' would yield a good parallel there. It is very improbable that the meaning 'Thou wilt not allow me to experience decomposition' would be expressed by saying 'Thou wilt not allow me to witness destruction'. Hence the meaning 'the pit' is to be preferred with most editors.

[2] Cf. M. Buttenwieser, *The Psalms*, 1938, p. 511.

[3] Briggs (op. cit., i, pp. 121 f.) holds that the meaning is that God will not abandon him in Sheol, but will go with him and remain with him there, and will save him from seeing the dungeon of Sheol, where only the wicked go.

[4] Ps. 16.11. F. Schwally (*Das Leben nach dem Tode*, 1892, p. 123) holds that the speaker in these verses is not an individual, but the personified community.

In all these three passages from the Psalter, therefore, I find an incipient faith that God, who is the source of man's well-being here, will continue to be the source of the well-being of his own in the hereafter. Writing of the first two of these psalms, 49 and 73, W. E. Barnes, says 'It should be observed further that in both Psalms it is an individual hope; the two Psalmists confess the hope as a personal testimony to a prospect which doubtless they wish "the Righteous" to share with them. But for them the Future Life is a hope, not a doctrine, a hope struggling to express itself in a *milieu* in which almost all men felt that Death was the end of all for the individual life.'[1]

This may seem a meagre gleaning from the Old Testament; yet it is not without value. There is no uniform or sure faith in an afterlife that is meaningful, but there are these reachings out after such a faith.[2] What is of most importance, in these glimpses we do not have the thought that man is too great to die, or that life is too rich to come to a final end in the grave. We have the thought of life with God, and deriving from his fellowship. There is here something more satisfying than philosophy can offer, and something more deeply religious in inspiration and character. It is God who offers life that is worthy to be called life, both here and in the beyond, and he offers life because he offers himself. It is because the abiding God is the source of that life that the life itself is abiding. Such a thought is closely akin to what we find in some passages in the New Testament. Jesus

---

[1] *The Psalms* (West. C.), ii, 1931, p. 348; cf. T. K. Cheyne, *The Origin of the Psalter*, pp. 380 ff., esp. p. 409, where, after studying these passages, he says: 'I have endeavoured to show critically that among the religious ideas of the Psalter are those of immortality and resurrection.' Cf. also R. Kittel, *Die Psalmen* (K.A.T.), 1929, pp. 182, 248.

[2] A. F. Kirkpatrick (*Psalms* (Camb. B.), 1906 ed., *in locis*) finds no thought of an afterlife in any of the three passages from the Psalms examined above, and O. J. Baab similarly understands them (*The Theology of the Old Testament*, p. 218). So also H. Gunkel (*What Remains of the Old Testament*, E. Tr., p. 105) says 'the idea of life after death appears nowhere in the Psalter'. Cf. also Ch. Barth, *Die Errettung vom Tode*, 1947, pp. 158 ff., B. D. Eerdmans, *The Hebrew Book of Psalms* (O.T.S., iv), 1947, pp. 266, 350, and S. H. Blank, in *To Do and to Teach* (Pyatt Memorial Volume), 1953, pp. 1 ff., where a similar view is taken of Ps. 49 and 73, or of the latter alone. G. R. Berry (op. cit., *in locis*) understands the passages in Ps. 49 and 73 of the afterlife, but not that in Ps. 16, while S. R. Driver (*The Expositor*, 7th series, x, 1910, pp. 35 f.) finds the thought of the afterlife in all of these passages; so also A. T. Nikolainen (op. cit., i, pp. 122 f., 124, 125). That scholars are so divided in their understanding sufficiently indicates that no clear doctrine is here enunciated, and it is unwise to press the interpretation on either side. That is why I speak of a glimpse, rather than of a firm faith. Cf. G. Quell, *Die Auffassung des Todes in Israel*, 1925, p. 40.

said 'I have come that they may have life, and may have it abundantly';[1] and again he claimed that he himself is the life.[2] It is therefore by giving himself that he gives life, and the life endures because its source endures. 'Whoever drinks of the water that I shall give him will never thirst; but the water that I give him shall become in him a well of water springing up into eternal life.'[3] In giving himself he gives God, since 'I and my Father are one'.[4] 'He who eats my flesh and drinks my blood abides in me, and I in him. As the living Father sent me, and I live because of the Father; so he who eats me will live because of me.'[5] The life that is mediated through Christ is the life of God, and in both Testaments God is the only source of man's true life, whether here or hereafter. While there are only a few passages in the Old Testament which carry that thought to the hereafter, it is important to observe that they are in harmony with the fundamental principles set forth in the Bible in relation to this life, and are but an extension of those principles.

[1] John 10.10.   [2] John 14.6.   [3] John 4.14.   [4] John 10.29.   [5] John 6.54.

VII

THE DAY OF THE LORD

THROUGHOUT the Old Testament there is a forward look. By this more is meant than the prophetic announcement of the issue of men's deeds and of the policies of the state in the ills that were so commonly foretold. Israel believed that while there was a brief period of innocence and bliss at the opening of history, the real climax and crown of history lay in the future. She had a firm assurance that 'the best is yet to be', though that assurance, like every aspect of her faith, was rooted and grounded in God and not the mere expression of human optimism. It is increasingly recognized that this element was found in her thought from an early age,[1] and there is less disposition today than there once was to assign every passage which expresses this hope to a late period. Various terms are associated with this hope, and at some only of these, and the passages in which they are found, can we look here.

It is clear that in the popular hopes of the time of Amos the 'Day of Yahweh' was such a term. Men believed that this was the day on which God would arise to scatter all his foes and save Israel in a signal way.[2] But Amos turned the phrase into the

---

[1] Cf. J. M. P. Smith, *A.J.Th.*, v, 1901, p. 533: 'The development of the idea of the Day of Yahweh in Israelitish history was marked, not so much by the addition from time to time of new features as by the expansion and deepening of elements already present, at least in germ, at the time of the origin of the prophetic conception'.

[2] This represents the common view of the interpretation of the passage in Amos. Cf. A. B. Davidson, in *D.B.*, i, 1898, pp. 735 ff., H. Gressmann, *Der Ursprung der israelitisch-jüdischen Eschatologie*, 1905, pp. 141 ff., and *Der Messias*, 1929, pp. 74 ff., R. H. Charles, *Critical History of the Doctrine of a Future Life*, 2nd ed., 1913, pp. 86 ff., Driver and Lanchester, *Joel and Amos* (Camb. B.), 1915, pp. 188 f., Oesterley and Robinson, *Hebrew Religion*, 2nd ed., pp. 227 f. Davidson and Gressmann argued that the term had an eschatological content, but this is denied by R. S. Cripps, *The Book of Amos*, 1929, pp. 59 ff. S. Mowinckel (*Psalmenstudien*, ii, 1922, pp. 45 ff.) linked the term 'Day of Yahweh' with the annual New Year Festival. His view was contested by K. Cramer, *Amos* (B.W.A.N.T., iii, 15), 1930, pp. 136 ff., where it is maintained that the term was not of popular creation, but was fundamentally a prophetic term. A. Neher (*Amos: Contribution à l'étude du prophétisme*, 1950, pp. 114 ff.) follows Cramer, though he allows that

symbol of the coming judgement on Israel. 'Woe to you who desire the day of Yahweh! What is the day of Yahweh to you? It is darkness and not light. As if a man should flee from a lion, and a bear should meet him; or should enter the house and lean his hand on the wall, and a serpent should bite him.'[1] Zephaniah thought of it as a day of more general judgement. 'The great day of Yahweh is near, it is near and coming swiftly . . . That day is a day of wrath, a day of trouble and distress, a day of ruin and desolation, a day of darkness and gloom, a day of cloud and thundercloud, a day of trumpet and alarm, against the fortified cities, and against the high battlements,'[2] and the sequel makes it clear that the desolation was to be widespread amongst all the nations of the world.

This element of judgement belongs essentially to the thought of the Day of the Lord. What Amos brought to the term was not the idea of judgement, but the idea of a moral judgement. It was not to be simply a judgement on Israel's foes, but a judgement on men whose lives were offensive to God, whether within Israel or without. The book of Joel presents this aspect of the Day of the Lord, which it too describes as 'a day of darkness and gloom, a day of cloud and thundercloud.'[3] But it makes it clear that beyond the judgement in which all that was alien to God's will should be consumed there would be a new glory and light. 'It shall come to pass afterward, that I will pour out my spirit upon all flesh . . . And it shall come to pass that everyone who calls on the name of Yahweh shall be delivered: for in mount Zion and in Jerusalem there shall be those who escape, as Yahweh hath said, and among the survivors those whom Yahweh calls.'[4] In the section of the book of Isaiah which is most closely akin to apocalyptic writing we find a similar idea of judgement followed by a Golden Age. 'The earth

Mowinckel may be right in thinking that behind it lay some ritual or liturgical usage. J. Halévy (*Revue Sémitique*, xi, 1903, pp. 104 f.) holds that the term was always one of judgement, and that those to whom Amos referred, who professed to desire to see the Day of Yahweh, did so mockingly. On the concept of the 'Day of Yahweh' cf. further J. M. P. Smith, *A.J.Th.*, v, 1901, pp. 505 ff., A. Weiser, *Die Prophetie des Amos* (B.Z.A.W., No. 53), 1929, pp. 213 ff., A. S. Kapelrud, *Joel Studies*, 1948, pp. 54 ff., V. Maag, *Text, Wortschatz und Begriffswelt des Buches Amos*, 1951, pp. 246 ff., and A. Gelin, *Lumière et Vie*, September 1953, pp. 39 ff.; also the monograph by L. Černý, *The Day of Yahweh and Some Relevant Problems*, 1948, where a critical survey of the modern history of the interpretation of the Day of Yahweh may be found.
[1] Amos 5.18 f.   [2] Zeph. 1.14 ff.   [3] Joel 2.2.   [4] Joel 2.28, 32 (Heb. 3.1, 5).

shall stagger like a drunken man, and shall sway to and fro like a hut[1] . . . And it shall come to pass in that day, that Yahweh will punish the host of the height on high, and the kings of the earth on the earth.'[2] Yet following the judgement we find 'and it shall be said in that day, Lo, this is our God; we have waited for him, and he will save us: this is Yahweh; we have waited for him, let us be glad and rejoice in his salvation'.[3] The same pattern is found in the book of Daniel, where the thought of a general judgement on the nations introduces the promise of the inauguration of the enduring kingdom of the saints of the Most High.[4]

While in some passages the Day of the Lord was conceived of as nigh at hand,[5] all think of it as the time of the divine breaking into history in spectacular fashion. While God was believed to be always active on the plane of history, using Nature and men to fulfil his ends, the Day of the Lord was thought of as a day of more direct and clearly manifest action. Most of the predictions of the prophets were of the issue of the conditions of their day. These passages, on the contrary, were of a future not causally linked with the present, but of the time when it should be God's pleasure to consume all that is evil and to bring in the age of bliss. In such passages we often find the expressions 'in the latter end of the days', or 'in that day', where the meaning seems to be 'on the horizons of time'.[6] For most of the prophets,

---

[1] This is the same word as is used in Isa. 1.8 for the temporary shelter erected in a cucumber field for the watchman at the time when the cucumbers were ripening.

[2] Isa. 24.20 f.   [3] Isa. 25.9.   [4] Dan. 7.10 ff.

[5] Isa. 13.6, Ezek. 30.3, Joel 1.15, 2.1, 3.14 (Heb. 4.4), Obad. 15, Zeph. 1.14 N. K. Gottwald (*Studies in the Book of Lamentations*, 1954, pp. 83 f.) notes that in Lam. 1.12, 2.1, 2.21 f., we have a unique conception of the Day of Yahweh as already past. Cf. also L. Černý, op. cit., p. 20.

[6] Cf. H. Gressmann, *Der Messias*, 1929, pp. 82 ff., where it is argued that such expressions as 'in those days', 'in that day', 'behold, the days are coming', and 'in the latter end of the days' are *termini technici*, introducing eschatological passages. This is contested, so far as the second of these expressions is concerned, by P. A. Munch, *The Expression Bajjôm Hāhū': Is it an Eschatological Terminus Technicus?* 1936, and it is argued that it is always a temporal adverb. Cf. A. S. Kapelrud, *Joel Studies*, 1948, pp. 165 ff., where it is held that both Gressmann and Munch are partly right, and that we cannot impose a single meaning on all the occurrences of the term. Cf. also W. Staerk, *Z̧.A.W.*, xi, 1891, pp. 247 ff., where it is similarly argued that for the last of the above mentioned expressions the usage is not always the same. Staerk holds that it was in the period of the Exile that this expression first took on an eschatological meaning, and he therefore relegates to a post-exilic date Isa. 2.2, Micah 4.1, Hos. 3.5, and Deut. 4.30. Against this many scholars of varying schools find Isa. 2.2=Micah 4.1 to be either from Isaiah or Micah or from an earlier prophet, and therefore to be at least as early as the eighth century B.C. (cf. above, p. 137, n.6). This would not invalidate Staerk's argument, but would push back to a much earlier date the time when this expression took on an eschatological nuance.

however much the judgement might be thought to stretch down to the near future, the glory lay afar off, whereas for the apocalyptists that too lay in the near future. Nevertheless, lines should not be drawn too sharply between prophecy and apocalyptic. There are sections which approximate to apocalyptic in prophetic books, and apocalyptic is a development from prophecy.[1] Nowhere is the glory thought to be something that should be brought about by human activities, or be the fruit of human policies. It would be the gift of God. 'For, behold, I create new heavens and a new earth: and the former things shall not be remembered, or come into mind.'[2] In that new world life should be incomparably good for men. 'And they shall build houses and inhabit them; and they shall plant vineyards, and eat their fruit.'[3] 'They shall sit every man under his vine and under his fig tree, with none to make them afraid.'[4] Even the nature of brute beasts would be changed to match the glories of that age. 'The wolf shall live with the lamb, and the leopard lie down with the kid; and the calf and the young lion shall graze[5] together; and a little child shall lead them.'[6]

It is to be observed that the pictures of the Golden Age are always of a universal character. It was tacitly recognized that there could be no Golden Age for Israel until all men shared it. This, as has been said in an earlier lecture, springs out of the Old Testament conception of the nature of man. It was also born of Israel's experience as a small nation set amidst great empires. Sometimes other nations are represented as serving Israel,[7] or Israel's king is pictured as holding universal sway,[8] but there is always the recognition that unless the blessings of the coming age are shared by all men, none can have them with security. Something more than national pride lies behind this conception, which is profound and penetrating.

---

[1] Cf. *The Relevance of Apocalyptic*, 2nd ed., pp. 22 ff.
[2] Isa. 65.17.   [3] Isa. 65.21.   [4] Micah 4.4.
[5] The Massoretic text has 'and the fatling', but most editors have long believed that a verbal form stood in the original text, basing themselves on the LXX and Vulgate texts. The Dead Sea scroll text of Isaiah (DSIa or 1QIs[a]) has a verbal form, which is probably a defectively written form from a root not elsewhere found in Hebrew, but cognate with the word for 'fatling', giving the meaning 'shall grow fat', or the like.
[6] Isa. 11.6.   [7] Cf. Isa. 60.10 ff., 61.5, Dan. 2.44, 7.27.
[8] Cf. Zech. 9.9 f., with which cf. Ps. 72.8, 10 f.; also Ps. 2.8 f., Micah 5.2, 4 (Heb. 1, 3).

In an earlier lecture it has been said that the faith that obedience to the will of God is the way of man's well-being, whether on the individual or the national scale, was one side of the truth. There is also the other side, that human sin, whether individual or collective, brings injustice and undeserved suffering, and introduces forces which counteract the simple working out of the principle that merit and lot belong together. But when all that is alien to the will of God is swept away the situation will be changed, and the natural fruit of obedience in perfect well-being will be gathered by all. That is why the Golden Age had to be universal. It was the corollary of the faith of Israel, which perceived that every man is involved in the sins of others as well as in his own, and that until sin is no more he cannot know perfect well-being. He may know the fellowship of God under present conditions, and therefore know the deepest well-being. But many sides of his life may lack the fullness which it should have. For though it has been insisted earlier that it is a distortion of the teaching of the Old Testament to say that prosperity is its conception of blessing, it did not despise prosperity, which entered as an element into the totality of its thought of blessing.

From this it follows that in biblical thought the Golden Age has a fundamentally religious basis. It is essentially the Day of the Lord, and what is of importance is that there shall not only be unity of rule, but that all shall be permeated by the spirit of God, so that all life shall reflect his will. It was never conceived in merely economic or political terms, but always in moral and spiritual terms, so that it is appropriately thought of as the Kingdom of God, whether the term is found or not.[1] It was the age when peace and justice should be universal amongst men. 'They shall beat their swords into ploughshares, and their spears into pruninghooks; nation shall not lift up sword against nation, and they shall learn war no more.'[2] 'With justice shall he judge the needy, and give decision with equity for the meek of the earth.'[3]

Two things the modern world seeks with pathetic eagerness, yet always with the fear in its heart that they may be eluding it in the moment when it feels they are within its grasp. These are

[1] Cf. H. Junker, *Trierer Theologische Zeitschrift*, lxii, 1953, pp. 65 ff.
[2] Isa. 2.4; Micah 4.3.   [3] Isa. 11.4.

economic security and enduring peace. In the oracle ascribed
to Isaiah and to Micah, both prophets of the eighth century,
we see that the same yearnings filled men's hearts in the
ancient world. In the form which the oracle has in Micah we
find the already quoted dream of economic bliss when every
man would sit securely under his own fruit trees.[1] In both
forms we have the dream of enduring peace.[2] But the prophets
of Israel did not share the modern delusion of some who fancy
that it is enough to demand that swords shall be beaten into
ploughshares and spears into pruninghooks. They realized that
man's life arises from his spirit, and that God alone can cleanse
his spirit. Hence they declared the Golden Age to be the time
when all men should go up to the house of the God of Israel,
and when men everywhere should seek to know and to do his
will. 'And many peoples shall go and say, Come, let us go up to
the mountain of Yahweh, and to the house of the God of
Jacob; that he may teach us of his ways, and that we may walk
in his paths . . . And they shall beat their swords into ploughshares, and their spears into pruninghooks.'[3] The beating of
swords into ploughshares was not thought of as a cause, but a
consequence. For the Old Testament takes seriously its own
recognition that man was created to do the will of God, and
that the full stature of his manhood can be attained only when
he does it. It also recognizes that he does not stumble into the
way of that will, but must be guided into it by submitting himself unto God. Therefore it is that the Golden Age is always the
Kingdom of God. In a passage in the book of Jeremiah, which
is commonly held to be misplaced or denied to that prophet,[4]
we read 'At that time they shall call Jerusalem the throne of
Yahweh, and all nations shall be gathered there, in the name
of Yahweh, at Jerusalem; and they shall no more walk after
the stubbornness of their evil heart.'[5] Here we find the same
essential thought that only the universal submission to God
can eliminate that which militates against well-being.

Implicit in the faith of Israel is universalism, which almost
certainly finds expression long before the time of Deutero-
Isaiah. In the earliest of the documents of the Pentateuch we
find passages which say in relation to Abraham 'in thee shall

---

[1] Micah 4.4.   [2] Isa. 2.4; Micah 4.3.   [3] Isa 2.3 f.; Micah 4.2 f.
[4] See above, p. 137, n. 7.   [5] Jer. 3.17.

all the families of the earth be blessed.'[1] Professor C. R. North
has observed that 'Something like the note of universalism is
already struck in these words.'[2] While we should not exaggerate
the element of universalism here, this judgement is probably
right. In two of the five passages[3] where this thought is found,
the Hebrew uses a reflexive verbal form, which is most naturally
rendered 'all the nations of the earth shall bless themselves', or
'shall involve blessing upon themselves'. In the other three
passages[4] the verbal form is normally passive, though it was
originally reflexive and often has reflexive significance. It is
therefore natural that most scholars should render all the
passages by the reflexive, and should find expressed here no
more than the thought that Abraham will be so richly blessed
by God that other nations shall conceive of no higher blessing
for themselves than that they might know a like blessing.[5]
Before we conclude that it is no more than the expression of
national pride, however, we should reflect that Abraham's
greatness is wholly associated with his religion. It was in
response to the call of God, and therefore to a religious impulse,
that Abraham went forth from Harran.[6] It was because he
obeyed the voice of God and yielded to the divine guidance that
he became great and that he was promised that his descendants,
who were conceived of as heirs of his faith no less than of his
well-being, would become the standard of blessing amongst
men. While there is not the thought of the universal sharing of
Abraham's faith, there is implied the thought that Abraham's
faith and that of his descendants will give to Israel a universal
significance.

It is but a short step from this to the thought of Gentiles
sharing the faith of Israel, which is the foundation of her blessing, in order that they might share the blessing. That thought
we find not alone in the already quoted passages in the prophets,

---

[1] Gen. 12.3; cf. 18.18, 22.18, 26.4, 28.14.
[2] *The Old Testament Interpretation of History*, 1946, p. 26.
[3] Gen. 22.18, 26.4. These verses are ascribed to the E document by O. Eissfeldt,
Hexateuch Synopse, pp. 36*, 46*, while Oesterley and Robinson (*Introduction to the
Books of the Old Testament*, p. 35) ascribe the former to E and the latter to J,
and others ascribe both to a Redactor (so S. R. Driver, *Genesis* (West. C.), 1904,
pp. 220, 250; W. H. Bennett, *Genesis* (Cent. B.), pp. 241, 267; J. Skinner, *Genesis*
(I.C.C.), 1910, pp. 331, 364), H. E. Ryle, *Genesis* (Camb. B.), 1921, pp. 239,
274).
[4] Gen. 12.3, 18.18, 28.14. These are all ascribed to the J document.
[5] Cf. C. G. Montefiore, *The Old Testament and After*, 1923, p. 85.   [6] Gen. 12.1.

but in a number of other passages also. Already in the pre-
exilic age we find Zephaniah saying 'For then will I give to the
peoples pure lips,[1] that they may all call upon the name of
Yahweh, to serve him with one consent. From beyond the
rivers of Ethiopia my suppliants, widely scattered,[2] shall bring
me an offering.'[3] His contemporary Jeremiah similarly pro-
phesies of the day when the Gentiles shall flock to the God of
Israel and acknowledge him. 'O Yahweh, my strength and my
fortress, and my refuge in the day of affliction, unto thee shall
the nations come from the ends of the earth, and shall say,
Only lies have our fathers inherited, even vanity and worthless
things . . . And they shall know that my name is Yahweh.'[4]
In the immediately post-exilic age we find Zechariah saying
'Many peoples and mighty[5] nations shall come to seek Yahweh
of hosts in Jerusalem, and to entreat the favour of Yahweh . . .
In those days it shall come to pass that ten men of all the
tongues of the Gentiles[6] shall lay hold of the cloak of a Jew,

---

[1] The Hebrew may be rendered literally 'I will overturn to the peoples a pure lip',
which could mean 'a pure language', as R.V. has it, since in Hebrew 'lip' may
mean 'language', just as in English we use 'tongue'. But since it is the person
rather than the language that needs to be pure before one can approach God,
it is more probable that 'lip' here stands for the personality, precisely as in Isa. 6.7.

[2] The Hebrew means, literally, 'the daughter of my scattered ones', where 'the
daughter of' is simply a personification, as 'daughter of Zion' stands for 'people
of Zion'. Some scholars think this line is corrupt, however, and prefer the conjectural emendation, which yields the sense 'From beyond the rivers of Ethiopia
to the farthest reaches of the north'; so K. Elliger, *Das Buch der zwölf Kleinen
Propheten* (A.T.D.), ii, 2nd ed., 1951, p. 74. Others think the words 'my suppliants, the daughter of my scattered ones' are a gloss; so F. Schwally, *Ƶ.A.W.*
x, 1890, p. 203, and A. van Hoonacker, *Les douze Petits Prophètes* (E. Bib.), 1908,
p. 532.

[3] Zeph. 3.10.

[4] Jer. 16.19, 21. B. Duhm (*Jeremia* (K.H.C.), p. 141) separates verse 21 from
verses 19 f. on the ground that the former is in the style of Ezekiel and H, while
F. Giesebrecht (*Jeremia* (H.K.), p. 96) regards both verse 20 and verse 21 as
glosses, and observes that the latter has analogies with Deutero-Isaiah and
Ezekiel. L. E. Binns (*Jeremiah* (West. C.), p. 137) finds the connexion of verse 21
with what precedes awkward, and notes its similarity to the style of Deutero-
Isaiah. G. A. Smith (*Jeremiah*, 3rd ed., p. 220) thinks verse 21 would be more in
place after verse 18, and with this F. Nötscher (*Jeremias* (H.S.A.T.), p. 140)
agrees. On the other hand, P. Volz (*Jeremia* (K.A.T.) 2nd ed., p. 183) treats
verses 19–21 as a unit, but as un-Jeremianic, and E. A. Leslie (*Jeremiah*, 1954,
p. 325) does the same, and attributes them to a Deuteronomic editor. G. A. Smith
(op. cit., p. 356) and J. Skinner (*Prophecy and Religion*, p. 308) treat verses 19 f.
as Jeremianic, but Skinner makes no reference to verse 21. For our present
purpose it does not matter whether verse 21 is left out of account, since the thought
of verse 19 alone suffices.

[5] Or 'numerous'.

[6] E. Sellin (*Das Zwölfprophetenbuch* (K.A.T.), 2nd ed., p. 534) changes one letter
of the text, to read 'of all tongues and nations'.

saying, We will go with you, for we have heard that God is with you.'[1] In the psalms we find this thought reflected. 'All the ends of the earth shall remember and turn to Yahweh: And all the families of the nations shall worship before him.'[2] Sometimes we find the summons to the nations to recognize God's goodness to his people Israel, to praise him for it, and to be moved by it to bring him their worship. 'Praise Yahweh, all ye nations; Laud him, all ye peoples. For great is his mercy toward us.'[3] 'Sing to Yahweh a new song; Sing to Yahweh, all the earth . . . Proclaim his salvation from day to day. Declare his glory among the nations, His marvellous acts among all the peoples . . . Give to Yahweh, ye families of the peoples, Give to Yahweh glory and strength. Give to Yahweh the glory due to his name: Bring an offering, and come into his courts.'[4] Most clearly are these elements combined in another psalm: 'The nations shall fear the name of Yahweh, And all the kings of the earth thy glory: For Yahweh hath built up Zion, And hath appeared in his glory . . . That men may declare the name of Yahweh in Zion, And his praise in Jerusalem; When the peoples are gathered together, And the Kingdoms to serve Yahweh.'[5]

What Deutero-Isaiah did was not to present the thought of universalism[6] for the first time, but to relate it to the mission of Israel. With him it was not a distant hope that one day the peoples would spontaneously flock to Zion to learn the law of God. He believed that the people of God was called to proclaim that law. With him universalism was the corollary of monotheism and the world-wide mission of Israel the corollary of her election. 'Turn into me and be saved, all the ends of the earth: for I am God, and there is no other.'[7] 'I Yahweh have called thee in righteousness, and will hold thy hand, and will keep

---

[1] Zech. 8.22 f.
[2] Ps. 22.27 (Heb. 28). The Hebrew text reads 'before thee', but the LXX, the Vulgate, the Syriac and Jerome all read as above.
[3] Ps. 117.1 f.
[4] Ps. 96.1 ff., 9 f.
[5] Ps. 102.15 f., 21 f. (Heb. 16 f., 22 f.).
[6] It should be clear that the term 'universalism' is used here in the sense that the religion of Yahwism was open for men of all nations, and not in the sense that everyone will be saved. On particularism and universalism in post-exilic Judaism cf. what I have written in *Israel's Mission to the World*, 1939, pp. 39 ff.; also J. Morgenstern, *U.J.E.*, x, 1943, pp. 353 ff., and O. Eissfeldt, *Th.L.Z.*, lxxix, 1954, cols. 283 f.
[7] Isa. 45.22.

thee, and give thee to be a covenant of the people,[1] to be a light of the Gentiles.'[2] 'Ye are my witnesses, saith Yahweh, and my servant whom I have chosen.'[3] Especially is this mission associated with the Servant in the Servant Songs. 'It is too light a thing that thou shouldest be my servant to raise up the tribes of Jacob, and to restore the preserved[4] of Israel: I will make thee the light to the Gentiles, that my salvation may reach[5] unto the end of the earth.'[6] The election of Israel, and of the Servant in whom her mission is concentrated, is for universal ends, and for the carrying of the light of the faith of Israel to the ends of the earth.

The same thought is found in Trito-Isaiah, but whereas in Deutero-Isaiah the Servant fulfils the mission in suffering and death, in Trito-Isaiah the Gentiles are represented as serving Israel and glorifying her. 'I will send those of them who escape unto the nations[7] . . . and isles afar off . . . ; and they shall declare my glory among the nations. And they shall bring all your brethren from all the nations as an offering unto Yahweh . . . to my holy mountain Jerusalem.'[8] The book of Jonah, on the contrary, rose to the full height of the thought of Deutero-Isaiah, and here we have proclaimed the self-forgetting mission of Israel even to her enemies, and the compassion of God upon the heathen who repent and turn to him.

All this implies that the faith of Israel is not for her alone, but that it may be shared by men of other nations and races, who will join themselves to the Lord and to his people. Hence we get the idea of the religious proselyte, who embraces the faith of Israel. Such a proselyte was Ruth, who declared 'Thy people shall be my people, and thy God my God.'[9] Zechariah contemplates proselytes in large numbers. 'And many Gentiles shall join themselves to Yahweh in that day, and shall be his[10]

---

[1] This phrase has been much discussed. G. Quell (in *Th.W.B.*, i, 1932, p. 34 n.) renders 'a covenant of humanity', while R. Levy (*Deutero-Isaiah*, 1925, p. 147) has 'a universal covenant', referring to the Arabic *ʿāmm*, 'general', 'universal'.
[2] Isa. 42.6.   [3] Isa. 43.10.   [4] The LXX here read 'the dispersed'.
[5] The Hebrew could here be understood as in R.V. 'that thou mayest be my salvation', or as above, with R.V. margin and R.S.V.
[6] Isa. 49.6.
[7] The Hebrew here inserts a list of nations, which is probably an expansion of the oracle, either by the author or by a later hand, and which disturbs the rhythm. Cf. L. Glahn and L. Koehler, *Der Prophet der Heimkehr*, 1934, pp. 238 f.
[8] Isa. 66.19 f.   [9] Ruth 1.16.
[10] The Hebrew text here has 'and shall be to me for a people'. The reading of the LXX is followed above.

people.'[1] H. G. Mitchell observes that this means the acceptance of the invitation of Isa. 45.22 and the unlimited extension of the Abrahamic covenant.[2] Similarly Trito-Isaiah says 'The foreigners, who join themselves to Yahweh, to serve him, and to love the name of Yahweh, to be his servants . . . I will bring them to my holy mountain, and make them joyful in my house of prayer; . . . for my house shall be called a house of prayer for all peoples.'[3]

In all this we should not forget that the Golden Age was always conceived of as the Day of the Lord. While human activity and the acceptance of her mission by Israel might do something to prepare for that day, it could not itself produce the Golden Age. That could only be God's gift to men, when men were willing to fulfil the conditions on which alone he could grant it, by submitting themselves to his will. When they were so willing, he could give them a new heart, and give them a unity which derived from the unity of his own will. All their conflicting interests and purposes could be reconciled in his all-inclusive purpose for the world, and in that purpose the ultimate well-being of all could alone be found.

All the passages in the Old Testament which present in various ways the vision of the Golden Age, or of the Day of the Lord, are commonly referred to as messianic. The term Messiah is merely the Hebrew word for Anointed, and its Greek equivalent is *Christos*, which becomes in English Christ. By the time of our Lord there was a widespread expectation of the coming of a Messiah who would fulfil all these prophecies, and the Early Church indicated, by its application of the word Christ to Jesus, that it believed that in him they found their fulfilment. It should be remembered that though in that age Messiah had become a technical term for the expected figure, that term is not used in this connexion in the Old Testament.[4] The word itself is, indeed, found; but it is applied to kings[5] and priests,[6] and even to the Persian king Cyrus.[7] It is not in the

---

[1] Zech. 2.11 (Heb. 15).
[2] Cf. *Haggai and Zechariah* (I.C.C.), 1912, p. 144.
[3] Isa. 56.6 f.
[4] In Dan. 9.25 f. A.V. renders the word *māshîaḥ* by Messiah, and so imports the technical meaning into the term. R.V. corrects this and uses simply 'anointed one', and so R.S.V.
[5] Cf. e.g., I Sam. 24.7, 11, 26.9.
[6] Cf. e.g., Lev. 4.3, 6.15, Ps. 84.10 (Heb 11). [7] Isa. 45.1.

Old Testament a technical term for the expected deliverer,[1] and it is wiser in dealing with the Old Testament to avoid, as far as possible, the use of the term. This is because the term has particular, and narrower, associations than the whole range of ideas about the Day of the Lord, which we find there. Jesus himself was very reluctant to be called the Messiah, or Christ,[2] and though he acknowledged at his trial that he was indeed the fulfilment of the hope of the Messiah,[3] he had earlier forbidden his disciples to speak of him by this name.[4]

In some of the passages which present the hope of the Old Testament we find a Davidic leader figuring as the divine representative in universal government. This is the case in two passages from the book of Isaiah which have already been referred to,[5] and which have frequently been denied to that prophet.[6] Not a few scholars are today unconvinced of the soundness of that denial.[7] For our purpose it matters little whether Isaiah or another composed them, since they are in any case an expression of the faith of Israel, as it is enshrined in the sacred collection of her literature. 'A shoot shall come forth from the stock of Jesse, and a branch from his roots shall bear fruit.'[8] Of the equity of his rule, in accordance with all that has been said about the character of the Golden Age, we are given clear word. 'He shall not judge by appearances, neither give decision according to hearsay: but with justice

---

[1] It is probable that in some of the psalms the term had associations with the later technical use, and was applied both to the reigning king and to the ideal king, who was set before him as an example.

[2] Luke 4.41; cf. Mark 1.24 f., 3.11 f.   [3] Mark 14.61 f.; Matt. 26.63 f.
[4] Mark 8.29 f.; Matt. 16.20; Luke 9.20 f.   [5] Isa 9.2 ff. (Heb. 1 ff.), 11.1 ff.
[6] So K. Marti *Jesaja* (K.H.C.), 1900, pp. 94 ff., 113 f.; G. B. Gray, *Isaiah* (I.C.C.), i, pp. 167 ff., 213 f., followed by S. B. Frost, *Old Testament Apocalyptic*, 1952, p. 68. Margaret Crook (*J.B.R.*, xvi, 1948, pp. 155 ff.) argues that both passages are pre-Isaianic, having been composed for the accession of Joash, while H. L. Ginsberg (in *Alexander Marx Jubilee Volume*, 1950, pp. 357 ff.) holds that Isa. 9.2 ff. (Heb. 1 ff.) comes from the time of Josiah.
[7] So B. Duhm, C. Cornill, G. W. Wade, G. H. Box, E. Sellin, H. Schmidt, O. Procksch, J. Fischer, E. J. Kissane, A. H. Edelkoort, L. Dennefeld and J. Steinmann (for references cf. *The Unity of the Bible*, p. 87 n.). To these may be added O. C. Whitehouse, *Isaiah* (Cent. B.), i, pp. 151 ff., 174, because of his careful reply to the arguments of Marti. Oesterley and Robinson (*Introduction to the Books of the Old Testament*, pp. 245 f.) accept Isa. 9.2 ff. (Heb. 1 ff.) as Isaianic, but not 11.1 ff., while O. Eissfeldt, *Einleitung in das Alte Testament*, 1934, pp. 357 ff., holds the former passage to be probably Isaianic and the latter probably not. A. Alt (in *Festschrift Alfred Bertholet*, 1950, pp. 29 ff.) holds the former passage to be Isaianic. It will be seen that these writers belong to different schools, and it may be added that their number might be substantially added to.
[8] Isa. 11.1.

shall he judge the needy, and give decision with equity for the meek of the earth . . . righteousness shall be the girdle of his loins, and faithfulness the girdle of his waist.'[1] Of the universal significance of his rule we are told in the closing words of the passage. 'For the earth shall be full of the knowledge of Yahweh, as the waters cover the sea.'[2] These words are found again in almost identical form in the book of Habakkuk,[3] where they are thought by many to be quoted from Isaiah. Whether they are original to the passage in Isaiah is questioned by many scholars, but if they were added before they were cited in Habakkuk the addition is very early, and if they are not original it is certain that they were added because they were felt to be appropriate. They do not specifically state that the rule of the Scion of David was to be universal, but at least they make it clear that the consequences of his rule would be universal. The other passage promises the birth of a child of the line of David. 'To us a child is born, to us a son is given; and the government shall be upon his shoulder . . . Of the increase of his government and of peace there shall be no end, upon the throne of David, and upon his kingdom, to establish it, and to uphold it with justice and righteousness from henceforth even for ever.'[4]

In the book of Micah we find a similar passage which promises a ruler of Bethlehemite ancestry whose rule shall extend to all the earth, but whose rule shall be exercised in the name of God and in his power. 'But thou, Bethlehem Ephrathah, which art the smallest among the thousands of Judah, out of thee shall one come forth unto me to be ruler in Israel; whose lineage is from of old, from everlasting . . . And he shall stand, and shall rule in the strength of Yahweh, in the majesty of the name of Yahweh his God: and they shall endure; for now shall he be great unto the ends of the earth.'[5] This passage, with its reference to Judah rather than to David—the latter being indicated only obliquely by the mention of Bethlehem—reminds us of the passage in the Blessing of Jacob in Gen. 49: 'The sceptre shall not depart from Judah, Nor the ruler's staff from between his feet, Until Shiloh come; And unto him shall the peoples yield obedience.'[6] It is not necessary

---

[1] Isa 11.3 ff. [2] Isa. 6.9. [3] Hab. 2.14. [4] Isa. 9.6 f. (Heb. 5 f.).
[5] Micah 5.2, 4 (Heb. 1, 3). [6] Gen. 49.10.

for us here to examine the much discussed and problematical phrase 'until Shiloh come', which could be rendered 'until he come to Shiloh', or, with different vowels, 'until he come whose it is'.[1] However this famous crux is treated, the passage thinks of a Judahite ruler, whose sway will extend beyond the borders of his own land, and it is not surprising that it has been brought into association with the other passages at which we are looking.[2]

Of the Davidic line of the expected leader we have evidence again in Jeremiah. 'Behold the days come, saith Yahweh, when I will raise unto David a righteous Branch, and he shall reign prudently as king, and shall execute justice and righteousness in the land.'[3] Here, however, nothing is said about the universality of his rule. This does not imply any diversity of conception, since it would be unreasonable to ask that any writer should express the whole of his thought in every utterance. The character of the rule is described in terms of righteousness, precisely as in the other oracles where universality is also mentioned. In a passage in the book of Ezekiel, where the Davidic king is depicted, we find the emphasis on the peace and security which he will bring, and on the economic bliss which will mark the age of his rule, together with a reference to a new covenant, which reminds us of Jeremiah's New Covenant,[4] though it is couched in different terms. 'I will set up one shepherd over them, and he shall feed them, even my servant David . . . And I Yahweh will be their God, and my servant David shall be prince among them . . . And I will make with them a covenant of peace . . . and they shall dwell securely in the wilderness, and sleep in the woods . . . And the trees of the field

---

[1] It may suffice to refer to J. Skinner, *Genesis* (I.C.C.), 1910, pp. 521 ff., H. E. Ryle, *Genesis* (Camb. B.), 1921 ed., pp. 430 f., O. Procksch, *Genesis* (K.A.T.), 2nd ed., 1924, pp. 276 ff., E. König, *Die messianischen Weissagungen des Alten Testaments*, 1925, pp. 97 ff., L. Dennefeld, *Le Messianisme*, 1929, pp. 26 ff., A. H. Edelkoort, *De Christus-verwachting in het Oude Testament*, 1941, pp. 82 ff., J. Lindblom, in *Congress Volume* (Supp. to *V.T.*, i), 1953, pp. 78 ff. F. Nötscher (*Z.A.W.*, xlvii (N.F. vi), 1929, pp. 323 f.) connects *shīlōh* with Accadian *šēlu*, and finds the meaning to be 'ruler'.

[2] Ryle (op. cit., p. 431) thinks 'the Messianic hope is here indicated in its earliest and simplest form, although its primary application may be to the dynasty of David.' Cf. S. R. Driver (*Genesis* (West C.), 1904, p. 386): 'The clause, viewed in relation to its context, does seem to contain a Messianic thought'. A. von Gall, on the other hand, thinks the clause is a gloss, which has nothing whatever to do with the future King (cf. *Basileia tou Theou*, 1926, p. 35).

[3] Jer. 23.5.   [4] Jer. 31.31 ff.

shall yield their fruit, and the earth shall yield its produce, and they shall be secure in their land.'[1] Here we note that there is no reference to the universality of the kingdom. In Deutero-Zechariah, however, we find all the elements together. 'Rejoice greatly, O daughter of Zion; shout for joy, O daughter of Jerusalem: behold, thy king comes to thee: righteous and saving is he, lowly, and riding upon an ass . . . And he shall speak peace unto the nations: and his dominion shall be from sea to sea, and from the River to the ends of the earth.'[2] Here we have only the fact that he is Jerusalem's king to suggest that he is of the Davidic line. Universal dominion, universal peace, and universal justice are more clearly indicated as the features of this Golden Age.

This last passage is closely similar to some verses in Ps. 72, which has been traditionally interpreted as one of the 'messianic' psalms. Its theme is clearly some Israelite king, actual or ideal. 'Give the king thy justice, O God, And thy rightousness unto the king's son'.[3] His rule is described in terms so similar to those of various passages at which we have looked that it is hard not to think that it belongs to the same realm of ideas. 'He shall judge thy people with righteousness, And thy poor with justice . . . And shall crush the oppressor. They shall fear thee[4] while the sun endures, And so long as the moon, throughout all generations . . . In his days shall the righteous flourish; And peace abound, till the moon be no more. He shall have dominion from sea to sea, And from the River unto the ends of the earth . . . There shall be abundance of corn in the earth, upon the top of the mountains it shall wave[5] . . . His name shall endure for ever; his name shall be continued as long as the sun: And men shall invoke blessing through him; All nations shall call him happy.'[6] Here the phrase rendered 'shall invoke blessing' is the reflexive verb used in the passages concerning Abraham, which have been noted above. It will be seen that all of the elements of the description of the Day of the Lord are to be found here—the universality and permanence of

---

[1] Ezek. 34.23 ff.   [2] Zech. 9.9 f.   [3] Ps. 72.1.

[4] The reading of the LXX 'he shall prolong (his life)' is followed by R.S.V., and is perhaps to be preferred.

[5] This word stands with what follows according to the Massoretic accents, but rhythm favours its construction with what precedes.

[6] Ps. 62.2, 4 f., 7 f., 16 f.

peace, judgement and deliverance, economic bliss, righteousness and world-wide dominion.

It would carry us too far to examine all of the so-called
'messianic' psalms, and it must suffice to say that there is reason
to believe that while they may have been royal psalms, used in
the royal rites of the temple, they were also 'messianic'. They
held before the king the ideal king, both as his inspiration and
guide for the present, and as the hope of the future.[1] If such a
view is correct it would follow that they go back to pre-exilic
days, and they would appear to offer some confirmation for the
view that the great hope of the Day of the Lord and of the
Golden Age was no late development in Israel.

Not all of the features of the Day of the Lord are found in
every one of these pictures. This no more indicates that the
unmentioned features would be repudiated by the authors than
an artist's painting of a man's head and shoulders implies an
intention to suggest that he had no legs and feet. In the passage
duplicated in Isaiah and Micah there is no reference to the
Davidic leader, or, indeed, to any human leader. The same
thing is true of the passage in Trito-Isaiah, already referred to,
which begins 'For behold, I create new heavens and a new
earth: and the former things shall not be remembered, nor
come into mind',[2] and which ends with the promise 'They shall
not hurt or destroy on all my holy mountain, saith Yahweh,'[3]
So, too, in the familiar prophecy of the New Covenant in Jeremiah, and in the promises of Deutero-Isaiah. Jeremiah says
'This is the covenant which I will make with the house of
Israel after those days, saith Yahweh; I will put my law within
them, and in their hearts will I write it; and I will be their God,
and they shall be my people; and they shall no more teach every
man his neighbour, and every man his brother, saying, Know
Yahweh: for they shall all know me, from the least of them to
the greatest of them, saith Yahweh: for I will forgive their
iniquity, and their sin will I remember no more.'[4] Here the
thought does not go beyond Israel, but the conception is of
complete obedience to the will of God throughout the community, with the law of God inscribed on the hearts of all and

[1] Cf. A. R. Johnson, *Sacral Kingship in Ancient Israel*, 1955 (issued while the present
work was in the press).
[2] Isa. 65.17.   [3] Isa. 65.25.   [4] Jer. 31.33 ff.

therefore expressing itself in every side of their life, and we are in the same realm of ideas as in the whole group of passages we are considering. Here we are reminded of a passage in the book of Ezekiel, where also there is no reference to the Davidic leader, but where we find the promise of a new heart, leading to obedience to the will of God, and its issue in economic bliss. 'A new heart will I give you, and a new spirit will I put within you: and I will take away the stony heart out of your flesh, and give you a heart of flesh. And I will put my spirit within you, and cause you to walk according to my statutes, and ye shall keep my ordinances, and do them . . . And I will multiply the fruit of the tree, and the produce of the field, that ye shall no more suffer the reproach of famine among the nations.'[1]

Deutero-Isaiah brings the element of universality and of judgement into his picture, when he says 'Instruction shall go forth from me, and my ordinance[2] as a light of the peoples. I will swiftly bring near[3] my righteousness; my salvation is gone forth, and my arms shall judge the peoples:[4] the isles shall wait for me, and for my arms shall they hope[5] . . . For the heavens shall vanish away like smoke, and the earth shall wear out like a garment . . . But my salvation shall be for ever, and my righteousness shall not be overcome.'[6] The passage from Trito-Isaiah, which Jesus read in the synagogue at Nazareth,[7] defines 'the acceptable year of Yahweh'—by which what is elsewhere called the Day of Yahweh is meant—as 'the day of vengeance of our God'.[8] Here we see the element of judgement. Yet this is not the only element, as it would appear to be from the passage in Amos with which we started. For the prophet is sent 'to comfort all who mourn; to bring to the mourners in Zion, to give them a garland instead of ashes, the oil of joy

[1] Ezek. 36.26 f., 30.
[2] The word *mishpāṭ* here probably means 'the principles of true religion', as in Isa. 42.1, 3 (see below, p. 197, n.4). Cf. *The Biblical Doctrine of Election*, p. 117 n.
[3] This rendering follows the LXX in transferring the last word of verse 4 to the beginning of the following verse. Some editors then render: 'In a moment my righteousness (or victory) is near', while others add one letter to the word 'near' to convert it to a verb, and render as above.
[4] The meaning here is that the nation which is in the right shall be given the decisive aid of the arm of God.
[5] i.e., 'for my support they shall look'; they shall look to God for their vindication and deliverance.
[6] Isa. 51.4 ff.   [7] Luke 4.16 ff.   [8] Isa. 61.2.

instead of mourning, the garment of praise instead of the faint-
ing spirit; that they might be called trees of righteousness, the
planting of Yahweh, that he might be glorified.'[1] Fewer of the
elements of the total picture of the Day of the Lord are found
here, where the thought does not go beyond Israel, the Gentiles
only figuring as the servants of Israel in the following verses, and
where the emphasis lies in a message of comfort for harassed
people rather than on the obedience to the will of God in which
the basis of the comfort was to be found.

There is one passage which became of particular importance
in later thought because of its use of the phrase 'son of man'.
This phrase is found several times elsewhere in the Old Testament, indeed. In Ps. 8 we find 'What is man that thou rememberest him, and the son of man that thou shouldst care for him.'[2]
Here it is simply an alternative expression for 'man'. In the
book of Ezekiel, we find the prophet frequently addressed as
'son of man', where it similarly means 'man'. In Dan. 7 we
have the story of the seer's vision of the beasts arising from the
sea, and of the judgement scene in which the Ancient of Days
passed judgement on the beasts, followed by the coming with
the clouds of heaven of 'one like unto a son of man',[3] to whom an
everlasting and universal dominion was given.[4] This is quite
clearly a different conception from the Davidic leader, since
here we have not merely the absence of mention of the line of
David, but the son of man comes down from above. In the
following verses we are given the interpretation of the vision,
and here the 'son of man' is not described in individual terms
at all, but is clearly declared to be a symbol for the saints of the
Most High as invested with power.[5] The kingdoms symbolized
by the beasts arose from below, and their ignoble nature was
expressed in the form of the beasts. The enduring kingdom was
from above,[6] and its superior character was symbolized by a
human form. It is sometimes said that the saints were already
in the vision before the coming of the son of man.[7] This is true.

[1] Isa. 61.2 f.   [2] Ps. 8.4 (Heb. 5).
[3] Dan. 7.13.   [4] Dan. 7.14.   [5] Dan. 7.27.
[6] T. W. Manson (*B.J.R.L.*, xxxii, 1949–50, p. 174) maintains that the Son of Man
does not come from heaven, as is usually supposed, but goes to heaven on the
clouds, there to receive the kingdom.
[7] Cf. O. Zöckler, *Daniel* (Lange's Bibelwerk), E. Tr. by J. Strong, 1876, p. 157 b;
C. Boutflower, *In and Around the Book of Daniel*, 1923, p. 59; E. G. Kraeling, in
Oriental Studies in honour of Cursetji Erachji Pavry, 1933, p. 230.

They were there as suffering and persecuted. It is the kingdom of the saints, or *the saints as invested with power*, that is represented by the 'son of man'.[1]

The character of this kingdom is similar to the character of the rule of the Davidic leader in the passages at which we have looked. It is a universal and enduring kingdom, and since it is administered by the saints of the Most High, it is thought of as embodying his perfect will. It is therefore the kingdom of God, rather than of the saints, though the divine rule is exercised through them. 'And the kingdom and the dominion, and the greatness of the kingdoms under the whole heaven, shall be given to the people of the saints of the Most High: their[2] kingdom is an everlasting kingdom, and all dominions shall serve and obey them.'[3]

In insisting that the 'son of man' is distinct from the Davidic leader, I have no thought of removing the whole passage from association with the passages at which we have looked. It is clear that the general thought is of the Golden Age precisely as in those other passages. It may well be that the author did not contemplate a kingdom without a human leader, and most probable indeed that he did expect a leader to be raised up.[4] I would no more exclude this from his thought than I would exclude from the other pictures at which we have looked the elements which are unspecified. But whether he thought of a leader or not, it is improbable that the 'son of man' was thought of as that leader, or as identified with the Davidic leader.[5] We know that in the intertestamental period, which lies outside the range of our present thought, the Son of Man

---

[1] Cf. my *Darius the Mede*, 1935, p. 63 n.

[2] R.V. has 'his kingdom', but it is more probable that the pronoun in the Hebrew refers to 'the people', and so could be rendered in English by 'its', or better by 'their'.

[3] Dan. 7.27.

[4] Cf. *The Servant of the Lord*, p. 62: 'It is improbable that he thought of the kingdom of the saints as without any leader and head; but he was not concerned with the person of that head, but only with the thought of the kingdom which he symbolized by this figure.'

[5] A. Feuillet (*R.B.*, lx, 1953, p. 330) observes that Daniel 'ne rattache pas explicitement son Messie transcendant à la dynastie davidique et ne prononce pas une seule fois le nom de David, alors que l'occasion lui en était si souvent offerte', and suggests that this was due to the circumstances of his day. 'En ces périodes troublées, où les Juifs subissaient depuis longtemps le joug de la domination étrangère, il n'y avait aucune apparence que puisse jamais renaître de ces cendres la dynastie davidique'. I am less concerned to speculate why he does not mention the Davidic Messiah than to recognize the fact that he does not.

figured in the expectations of men,[1] and we know from the New Testament that the phrase was found on the lips of Jesus during his ministry. There are some passages where scholars have claimed that the meaning is no more than 'man', as in some of the Old Testament passages mentioned. There are some passages where Professor Manson has argued that the phrase stands for the coming kingdom, precisely as in Dan. 7.13.[2] On the other hand there are some passages where Jesus uses the term of himself. That he did not mean by this to identify himself with the Davidic Messiah, and knew that people would not so understand the term, is clear from the fact that whereas he forbade his followers to breathe a word to anyone about his being the Davidic Messiah,[3] he quite openly used this term of himself.[4] That he believed himself to be the Davidic Messiah is sure. But it would have been plain nonsense for him to suppress the use of the one term and yet to use the other, if the two terms were synonymous. That they have become synonymous for us is the result of his ministry.

For the understanding of his use of the term Son of Man we should remember that concept of corporate personality, at which we have earlier looked.[5] He could think of himself as concentrating in himself the kingdom, whose representative he was. That thought on the Son of Man had individualized this term in the intertestamental period is probable enough, and Professor Manson finds the same fluidity in its use in 1 Enoch.[6] But it represents a different line of approach to the conception of the Day of the Lord, whose fusion with the Davidic leader

[1] On the figure of the Son of Man in I Enoch cf. N. Messel, *Der Menschensohn in den Bilderreden des Henoch*, 1922; E. Sjöberg, *Der Menschensohn im äthiopischen Henochbuch*, 1946; T. W. Manson, *B.J.R.L.*, xxxii, 1949–50, pp. 171 ff.; cf. also *The Servant of the Lord*, pp. 74 ff., and the literature there cited.

[2] Cf. *The Teaching of Jesus*, 2nd ed., 1935, p. 227; *Coniectanea Neotestamentica*, xi, 1947, pp. 138 ff.; and *B.J.R.L.*, loc. cit., pp. 190 ff.

[3] Mark 8.30; Matt. 16.20; Luke 9.21.

[4] Some have denied that Jesus used this term of himself. So J. Wellhausen, *Skizzen und Vorarbeiten*, vi, 1899, pp. 187 ff.; C. S. Patton, *J.R.*, ii, 1922, pp. 501 ff.; S. J. Case, *J.B.L.*, xlvi, 1927, pp. 1 ff. It is hard, however, to suppose that the early Church invented this ascription of the term to him, since it does not appear to have been used in the early Church, and outside the Gospels it stands in the New Testament only in Acts 7.56. Cf. G. Kittel, *Deutsche Theologie*, 1936, p. 173, where it is said that the denial of the use of this term to Jesus only increases our problems.

[5] Cf. *The Biblical Doctrine of Election*, p. 157; also T. W. Manson, *B.J.R.L.*, loc. cit., p. 191.

[6] Ibid., pp. 188 f.

should not be pushed back earlier than the time of Christ. That both Davidic Messiah and Son of Man were found side by side on the lips of the circles interested in apocalyptic is not to be denied; but that they were identified is a thesis which makes nonsense of the Gospels. The one term emphasized the human agency through whom the kingdom was expected to be established; the other emphasized the divine origin of the kingdom and its establishment by the divine breaking into history in judgement and power.

Yet another figure is familiar in our thought and calls for mention. This is the figure of the Suffering Servant of Deutero-Isaiah, at which we have looked in another connexion. There is little to connect the Servant superficially with the Davidic leader, and it is not surprising that there is no solid evidence that the two were identified in pre-Christian times,[1] and definite evidence in the New Testament that the two figures were not identified until they were brought together in the thought of our Lord.[2] This does not mean that the two conceptions were wholly unrelated. I have elsewhere said that I think both derived ultimately from the royal rites, but that they developed different aspects of those rites.[3] The mission of the Servant was to set justice[4] in the earth and to give his law to men.[5] He is thus thought of as instrumental in bringing about that state of universal worship of the God of Israel which figures in the hopes at which we have looked. We find here no description of the life of that kingdom in glowing terms. Moreover, we find here

---

[1] Cf. *The Servant of the Lord*, pp. 61 ff. (=*O.T.S.*, viii, 1950, pp. 100 ff.), where I examine this question.

[2] See below, p. 200.

[3] Cf. *The Servant of the Lord*, pp. 85 ff. (*O.T.S.*, viii, pp. 133 ff.).

[4] 'Justice', or 'judgement' probably here stands for 'true religion', whose universal acceptance would bring life into accord with the will of God, and therefore mean universal justice and righteousness. Cf. K. Marti, *Jesaja* (K.H.C.), 1900, p. 286, and R. Levy, *Deutero-Isaiah*, 1925, p. 144. N. H. Snaith (*Studies in Old Testament Prophecy*, ed. by H. H. Rowley, 1950, pp. 193 f.) thinks the thought is of the divine execution of justice upon the Gentiles, for which they wait with dread. G. Östborn (*Torā in the Old Testament*, 1945, pp. 57 f.) finds instead royal traits in the Servant here, and thinks of kingly law, and the royal execution of justice. J. Begrich (*Studien zu Deutero-Isaiah*, 1938, pp. 161 ff.) thinks the meaning is that God's pardon of Israel will be announced to the world by a judicial decision, and brings the figures of the breaking of the reed and the extinguishing of the smoking flax into association with this. He says there was a custom by which sentences were pronounced in the street, when a staff was broken and the lamp of the person condemned was extinguished. This is more ingenious than convincing, though it is accepted by U. Simon, *A Theology of Salvation*, 1953, p. 83.

[5] Isa. 42.4.

that the mission of the Servant involves him in dire suffering, and that the suffering is the organ whereby he fulfils his mission. 'I gave my back to the scourgers, and my cheeks to them that plucked out the hair: I hid not my face from shame and spitting.'[1] 'He was despised, and forsaken of men; a man of pains, and familiar with suffering . . . But he bore our sufferings, and endured our pains: yet we did esteem him stricken, smitten of God, and afflicted. But he was pierced through our transgressions, he was crushed through our iniquities: the correction for our welfare fell upon him; and with his stripes we are healed.'[2] All this is very different from the way in which the Davidic leader is depicted. The death of the Servant is said to be a sin offering[3] for those whose hearts are so moved by his sufferings that they humbly confess their sin and acknowledge that his death should be theirs.[4] They therefore bring to the offering the spirit which we have seen to be essential to the validation of sacrifice. They then become aware that he has borne their iniquities and that through him they are justified. Nothing like this is said of the Davidic leader, and it cannot be regarded as one of the unmentioned features of the Scion of David in the other pictures. Here it is so fundamental that the mission of the Servant is to be achieved through suffering, and there so essential that it is to be achieved through dominion.

It has been said that the Servant is probably to be interpreted as both collective and individual. The suffering saints in Daniel appear to be identified with the Servant. For Dan. 12.3 is probably marked by references to the fourth Servant Song. 'They who are wise shall shine as the brightness of the firmament, and they who turn many to righteousness as the stars for ever and ever.' Here 'they who are wise' may be an allusion to 'Behold, my servant shall deal wisely';[5] and 'they who turn many to righteousness' an allusion to 'my righteous servant shall justify many'.[6] Moreover, there is one passage in Deutero-Zechariah, which speaks of an individual who is

---

[1] Isa. 50.6.   [2] Isa. 53.3 ff.   [3] Isa. 53.10.   [4] Isa. 53.6.
[5] Isa. 52.13. R.S.V. here renders by 'shall prosper'. While this is a possible rendering, since wisdom commonly leads to success, this rendering conceals the link with Dan. 12.3, where the participle of the same verb is used.
[6] Isa. 53.11. On the difficulties of this text cf. *The Unity of the Bible*, p. 56 n. They do not affect our present use of it, since there is no reason to question the reading 'My servant shall make many righteous', where the terms are similar to those in Dan. 12.3, which could equally be rendered 'they who make many righteous'.

pierced and slain, and whose death is associated with the inauguration of the kingdom of God. 'And I will pour out upon
the house of David, and upon the inhabitants of Jerusalem, the
spirit of pity and of intercession; and they shall look on him
whom they have pierced'.[1] Here the Massoretic text reads
'upon me', but most editors favour the reading 'upon him',
which is represented in some manuscripts, and which is
followed in the New Testament quotation of the passage in
John 19.37. Following this death we read 'In that day a fountain shall be opened for the house of David and for the inhabitants of Jerusalem, to cleanse them from sin and uncleanness,'[2]
while soon after we read of the assembling of the nations against
Jerusalem,[3] until the Lord shall arise against them and in-
augurate his kingdom.[4] 'And Yahweh shall be king over all the
earth.'[5] Professor Dennefeld thought this passage about the
pierced one is another form of the prophecy of the Suffering
Servant of Isa. 53.[6] It would certainly appear to be moving in
the same realm of ideas, though it lacks many of the elements of
that great passage. Like Isa. 53, it offers evidence of the thought
of the death of a sufferer as associated with the coming of the
Day of the Lord; but it offers none to identify that sufferer with
the Davidic leader.

All of these approaches to the thought of the Day of the Lord
belong together in that they are associated with the establishment of the coming kingdom. The Davidic leader, the Son of
Man, the Suffering Servant, all in different ways are linked with
the coming of the day when men's hearts shall be changed and
brought into harmony with God's will, and universal peace and
righteousness come amongst men. Similarly with the other
passages, where none of these figures are found, we have the
thought of the kingdom of God. It is therefore in no way surprising that all of these passages were cherished by the people
who embraced the hope of the coming of that kingdom. The
community from which the non-biblical texts amongst the
Qumran Scrolls originated was clearly deeply interested in
such passages. Here, as in other intertestamental works, the
Messiah figures as a technical term for the expected deliverer.
Moreover, it is not surprising that the community whose

[1] Zech. 12.10. [2] Zech. 13.1. [3] Zech. 14.1.
[4] Zech. 14.3 ff. [5] Zech. 14.9. [6] Cf. *Le Messianisme*, 1929, p. 153.

revered leader, the Teacher of Righteousness, appears to have been martyred[1] should have turned to Isa. 53 and thought of the Suffering Servant. Similarly it is not surprising that Messiah and Son of Man should be found side by side in 1 Enoch. There is no reason to suppose that these figures were identified in thought already, however. It has been said that the New Testament offers evidence that Messiah and Son of Man had not been identified in popular thought before the ministry of Jesus. The New Testament offers similar evidence that the Suffering Servant and the Messiah had not been identified. For even after the followers of Jesus were convinced that he was the Messiah, they were completely nonplussed by the suggestion that he must suffer.[2] Clearly this was a novel and unthinkable idea to them.

Nevertheless, just because all of these figures were linked together by their association with the coming kingdom, their fusion in the mind of Christ was not something wholly arbitrary and unprepared for. In gathering them all into himself he modified each by the others, and while it is the faith of the Church that he is the fulfilment of all these hopes, there are many details which he has not fulfilled. For the fulfilment of many of those details the Church looks to the Second Coming.[3] To the Church, which stands between the Advent and the Second Advent, there is a long time process between the one and the other, but to prophets who saw the future afar off the depth in time was lost, as depth in space is lost to the eye of one who looks at the stars, and the First Advent and the Second Advent are therefore fused in prophecy.

In the opening lecture I said that in Christ the vision of the

---

[1] Cf. A. Dupont-Sommer, *V.T.*, i, 1951, pp. 200 ff. This is disputed by some, however.

[2] Cf. Mark 8.31 ff., 9.30 f.; Matt. 16.21 ff.; Luke 9.44 f., 18.32 ff., 24.24 ff.

[3] Many Christians have lost all real belief in the Second Advent, and have eliminated it from the teaching of Jesus. So, e.g., T. F. Glasson, *The Second Advent*, 1945. This tendency is partly due to the follies to which the expectation of the Second Advent has led those who have believed they could calculate from the Bible precisely when it would take place and what form it would take, despite the express warning of the New Testament itself (cf. Mark 13.21, 32 f.; Matt. 24.23 f., 36; Luke 21.5). I have more than once expressed my dissent from this reaction, though I equally reject the claim to be able to define the place, time and manner of the Second Advent. Cf. *The Relevance of Apocalyptic*, 2nd ed., pp. 148 ff., and *The Unity of the Bible*, pp. 110 f. I share the view of O. Cullmann (*Le Retour du Christ, espérance de l'Église naissante*, 1943, pp. 12 f., E. Tr. by S. Godman in *The Early Church*, 1955, p. 141 f.), that the rejection of this hope is a mutilation of the message of the New Testament.

Suffering Servant was realized. The vision of a world in enduring peace, bound together in a common rule marked by perfect justice and full accord with the will of God, with all its life resting on a universal resort to his house and submission to his law, is one which is yet far from realized. Yet here the Old Testament has enduring importance for men. The desire for peace and well-being has not lost its fascination for men; but they pay less heed to the foundations of the kingdom as set forth in the Bible. The New Testament says 'Seek first his kingdom and his righteousness; and all these things shall be yours also',[1] where the 'these things' are the supply of physical needs. The same message is declared insistently in all the passages in the Old Testament which look forward to the Day of the Lord and the establishment of his kingdom. And all is based on the unwavering faith of Israel, that man was created in the image of God, for his fellowship and obedience, and that only as he fulfils the purpose of his being can his true well-being be found, and that because he is both an individual and a member of society, his well-being is bound up with that of society, so that only in the universal well-being can his complete and secure well-being be found. In the higher reaches of Old Testament thought this produced a deep concern for the well-being of others, not alone for selfish reasons, but through the sharing of the divine thought and the sense of a divinely given mission to the world. To all who inherit the Old Testament, whether Jews or Christians, it comes with its summons to share that deep concern. The early Church felt it, and the modern Church has felt it. Yet how partially! And how little does the world, with all its anxiety for itself and its future, heed the great message of this book, that if it would but forget itself in its desire to seek God and to understand and do his will it would best serve itself. In losing itself to him, it would find itself in him.

[1] Matt. 6.33.

INDEXES

(a) SUBJECTS

(*b*) AUTHORS

(c) TEXTS